From Jim Parker, President

In 2016 Digitell celebrates its 30th year in business. This is an exciting accomplishment for myself and our entire team. This achievement could not have happened if it were not for the people that have motivated me throughout my career. One of those individuals is Jim Cathcart, the author of this book.

For those of you who do not know Jim, he is beyond human, in every essence of his being. He has spent his entire career motivating people to be better. He continues to give his time and talents to thousands around the globe and I can honestly tell you that each and every individual that he touches leaves a better person. That is why I have decided to share this book with you.

Jim has been a professional speaker for over 40 years and is a true friend. Jim and his wife Paula open their home to their many friends, colleagues and even strangers, entertaining them with delicious food, song and conversation. Jim is an avid guitar player and singer and he shares his love of the world with everyone he meets. He truly has been a mentor and inspiration to me and to everyone he comes in contact with.

When Jim released this new book, it was with no hesitation that I wanted to share his thoughts with all of you. Over the past 30 years, everyone at Digitell has strived to provide the finest possible service to help associations educate and engage their members with lifelong learning. Over these years, it is yo..., the association executive, that have given us this opportunity.

The work of association executives is not easy and many times they are asked to do things with very little resources. I am hopeful that this book will provide you with the motivation you need to excel in your job and to keep seeking out the solutions that will create value for your members and staff.

Jim, I thank you for all that you have taught me, for the lessons I have learned and for the motivation you have provided. You truly are an amazing individual and it gives me great pride to be able to share your ideas with today's leaders throughout this great country and beyond!

May you all be blessed with health, happiness and a little more motivation!!

Sincerely,

Jim Parker

ENDORSEMENTS

Jim Cathcart is one of the most dynamic speakers and business trainers that I have ever had the opportunity to witness in the areas of leadership, sales, management and motivation. He skillfully mixes stories, examples, thought provoking questions and well-documented academic research into a tapestry of knowledge. With 40 years of experience as an award-winning speaker he is now able to skillfully help his audiences translate their learning into increased earning potential. It's amazing and something that everyone needs to witness first hand at least once."

Clay Clark
Founder of Thrive15.com
U.S. SBA Entrepreneur of the Year
Contributing Writer for Entrepreneur.com

Jim's 'strap on your running shoes and walk to the curb' idea has helped me break world records and advance my career."

Brad Barton, CSP
Masters Track & Field World Record-breaking Athlete
www.BradBartonSpeaks.com

I love this book. The tips and strategies that Jim shares are so powerful and easy to implement that people of all walks of life can use them to stay motivated to achieve their next level. Every person should have this book on their nightstand and every manager should make it a tool in their toolbox to inspire their team to stay in constant action.

Darryl Davis
www.DarrylSpeaks.com

THE SELF MOTIVATION HANDBOOK

By Jim Cathcart

Author of the international bestseller:
The Acorn Principle

Get Yourself To Do What Needs To Be Done
Even When You Don't Feel Like Doing It

Also Includes: The Self Motivation Checkup

Published by Motivational Press, Inc.
1777 Aurora Road
Melbourne, Florida, 32935
www.MotivationalPress.com

Manufactured in the United States of America.

ISBN: 978-1-62865-313-7

Contents

Other works by Jim Cathcart include:

» The Sales IQ Plus™ online assessment (Assessments24x7.com, 2015), coauthored with Jeffrey Gitomer and Tony Alessandra

» *Relationship Selling: The Eight Competencies of Top Sales Producers* (Cathcart Institute, 2015)

» *Confident Communication: Public Speaking and Leading Meetings* DVD/CD (Cathcart Institute, 2009)

» 8 eBooks in the *Relationship Selling* series:

» *Sales Presentations* (Acanthus, 2008)

» *Customer Loyalty* (Acanthus, 2007)

» *Sales Readiness: How Preparation Leads to Opportunity* (Acanthus, 2006)

» *Getting the Sale: Confirming the Commitment to Buy* (Acanthus, 2008)

» *Finding the Buyers* (Acanthus, 2007)

» *Connecting with Your Customer* (Acanthus, 2007)

» *Sales Psychology: Understanding the Mind of the Buyer* (Acanthus, 2007)

» *Introduction to Relationship Selling* (Acanthus, 2006)

» *The Eight Competencies of Relationship Selling* (Leading Authorities Press 2002)

» *The Acorn Principle* (St. Martin's Press, 1998, 1999, 2000, revised 2015)

» *Inspiring Others to Win* (Griffin, 1998)

» The Professional Speaker™ Business System & Learning Library (Professional Speaking Institute, 1997 audio and video)

» *The Sales Professional's Idea-A-Day Guide* (Dartnell, 1996)

» *The Winning Spirit* (Griffin, 1996)

» *Speaking Secrets of the Masters* (Speakers Roundtable, 1995)

» *The Acorn Principle* (Cathcart Institute, 1995 Audio Album)

» *Rethinking Yourself* (Cathcart Institute, 1993, Video)

» *Be Your Own Sales Manager* (Simon & Schuster/Fireside Books, 1990)

» *Relationship Selling* (Perigee/Putnam, 1990)

» *Insights into Excellence* (Executive Books, 1988-90)

» *Selling by Objectives* (Prentice Hall, 1988)

» *Win Through Relationships* (Nightingale-Conant, 1988, video)

» *Think Service* (Universal Video, 1987)

» *Meeting with Success* (Nightingale-Conant, 1987, audio album)

» *Helping People Grow* (Levitz-Sommer Video, 1986, video)

» *Superstar Selling* (Nightingale-Conant, 1986, audio album)

» *The Business of Selling* (Prentice Hall, 1985)

» *Relationship Strategies* (Nightingale-Conant, 1984, audio album)

» *Communication Dynamics* (US Jaycees, 1976)

Foreword by Allan Pease

Co-author of *Why Men Don't Listen and Women Can't Read Maps*

They say that nothing happens until somebody sells something—but I believe nothing happens until someone motivates him or herself to do what needs to be done. As Jim Cathcart says, "whether you feel like it or not." I've known Jim for three decades, and I've seen him dream big dreams and systematically check them off his bucket list with amazing regularity. As you read Jim's book, you'll be guided by a person who practices what he preaches. He is a genuine, self-made success.

Jim and I learned from the greats who came before us, and we've both gone on to achieve things that we never imagined would be possible for us. This is proven wisdom passed down from great minds through ordinary people like us who used these ideas to transform our lives and our businesses. You can do this, too. In this book there are hundreds of specific ideas that will help you break away from a bad attitude, or overcome the inertia of doing nothing or the fear of moving forward before you have all the confidence you feel you need.

Everyone suffers occasionally from fear, self-doubt, confusion, depressing thoughts, or negative feelings. The big achievers, the happiest people in the world, the ones who have a sense of meaning in their lives, are the ones who have learned to overcome these limiting emotions.

Small differences in your mindset can break major logjams when it comes to self motivation. For example: When Jim Cathcart was 26 years old, he was overweight, out of shape, a two-pack-a-day smoker, working in a dead-end government job for $525 a month, married with a new son, not expecting to matter much to the world. Then, after being inspired by a message on the radio, he slowly transformed his mindset and then his life and has become one of the most award-winning and successful motivational speakers in the world. With no college degree, no money in the bank, no powerful connections with successful people, and no team of encouragers who believed in him, he has now authored 17 books, delivered over 3,000 speeches and seminars for millions of dollars in total fees, traveled the world multiple times, and received the highest awards in the world of professional speaking.

The principles and wisdom Jim shares in this book can transform your life in the ways that you desire. You'll read about people who did this in various fields, including music, auto services, software, sales, leadership, and even parenting. The field you're in doesn't matter; you can stay in that field or select a new one. Either way, the processes revealed here will work for you.

Right now you may feel limited by your obligations, existing relationships, physical challenges, or financial difficulties—but you can transform your life into a life of abundance and meaning with what you will read here.

It does not depend on your circumstances, country, race, creed, or intellect. It doesn't require that you have willpower. It simply requires that you apply the simple ideas presented here to make your life amazing!

I trust Jim's approach to success and his guidance. You can, too. This is a great read!

Allan Pease

Prologue by Dr. Tony Alessandra

A Special Note from Dr. Tony Alessandra

If anyone can write a book on self motivation, it is Jim Cathcart. He is often at the top 1 percent of the top 1 percent. Here is why I can say this: Since 1977, he has been a full time professional speaker and author. There are approximately 10,000 professional speakers in the United States; 4,000 of them belong to the National Speakers Association (NSA). Of the 10,000 professional speakers, the top 1 percent would be 100 people, and the top 1 percent of those would be one person. That is a pretty narrow target. He is not there always, but let's see how often he has gotten to that status over his career.

When Jim started working as a speaker and trainer, he was earning just $18,000 a year by teaching other people's courses, and nobody had heard of him.

Today, Jim is in the Professional Speakers Hall of Fame (among 232 others) and the Sales & Marketing Hall of Fame (with fewer than 30 others), and has been president of the National Speakers Association (one of 44). He served on the board of the Global Speakers Federation, received the Cavett Award (one of 38) and the Golden Gavel Award from Toastmasters International (one of 57), was honored with the Lifetime

Achievement Award and Legends of the Speaking Profession Award, and earned the Certified Speaking Professional (CSP) designation.

His TEDx video on YouTube has been viewed over 600,000 times, which places it as the 168th most-viewed out of the 68,000 TEDx videos at the time of this writing.

Jim has shared the stage with speaker luminaries such as Dr. Norman Vincent Peale, W. Clement Stone, Og Mandino, Zig Ziglar, Art Linkletter, Jack Canfield, Mark Victor Hansen, Les Brown, John Gray, Dr. Kenneth McFarland, Charlie "Tremendous" Jones, and Earl Nightingale. He has collaborated on a book with Spencer Johnson, walked barefoot on hot coals with Tony Robbins, and completed a "Ropes (Adventure) Course" twice with Larry Wilson. He has been hired as a speaker by Denis Waitley, Ken Blanchard, Stephen Covey, Brian Tracy, Jay Abraham, Dr. Nido Qubein, and Tom Hopkins to speak at their events.

Jim currently serves on the dean's advisory council to the School of Management of California Lutheran University and has served in a similar capacity at the University of Akron, Fisher School of Professional Selling, High Point University, and Pepperdine University's Graziadio School of Business and Management.

He has delivered more than 3,000 paid presentations all around the world and in all 50 of the United States. He has written and published 17 books so far with major publishers and was a member of the exclusive Speakers Roundtable of 20 top professionals for three decades. So, of 10,000 professional speakers, where would Jim's credentials place him? I think it is fair to say that he has reached the top 1 percent of the top 1 percent more than once. By the way, as Jim's close friend and frequent collaborator, I can attest that he never asked anyone to nominate him for any of these awards, nor did he lobby or campaign to receive them. They were the natural by-products of him becoming the person who would achieve the goals he had set. He did not become a "success machine" whose life went to pieces while he was working. Moreover, these professional accomplishments were achieved while sustaining a loving relationship with his wife and a powerful bond with his son, maintaining his fitness, and growing his professional skills.

Tony Alessandra, PhD, CPAE, CSP

www.Alessandra.com

Introduction

Just Put on Your Running Shoes

This book is your tool for life change. It's about your success in business and in life. It can be focused on business, relationships, wealth, or health. Most of all, this is your tool to bring about a rebirth of the person you'd really like to be.

Have you ever tried to tackle something important in your life but just couldn't make it "stick"? It could have been stopping a bad habit, creating a new habit, or overcoming fear. For me, at first, it was my weight. Looking at me today at 5' 9" and 150 lbs, you may think I was born thin and stayed thin, but that was not the case.

For most of my youth I was overweight, usually about 20 pounds above the recommended weight for my height, and sometimes heavier. I always thought of myself as being fat—not obese, but fat nonetheless. Every year I would go on a diet, beginning when I was in elementary school. I'd lose about 20 pounds and then go back to my old eating routines.

In the mid-1970s I got involved in the field of personal development ("applied behavioral science") and started setting goals, reading motivational books, attending seminars, listening to inspiring messages on records and tapes, and going to meetings with other success-seekers. My professional life was changing dramatically, yet I was still overweight.

One day in 1975, I decided it was time to become fit and slender permanently, to change my "settings," so to speak. My friend John Buck was an occasional jogger, and that seemed like something I could do. So I elected to become a jogger too. The problem was my fitness, or my lack thereof. When I jogged, it hurt. My lungs burned, my legs ached, and my feet hurt. But I was determined to change myself.

It was really hard to get myself to jog often enough to do me much good. I had never been an athlete and didn't think of myself as someone who would do well at running. Others had told me it was bad for my knees or not the right exercise. However, I noticed that most of those people weren't physically fit. Despite their cautions, I decided that running was right for me.

I needed an action that I knew I could get myself to do, so I set a minimum commitment: Even if I could not make myself run every day, at least I could make myself *available* for a run. I grabbed a piece of paper, picked up my pen, and wrote, *"I will put on my jogging shoes and walk outside to the curb every day, no matter what else is going on."* I knew that by getting those shoes on my feet and getting my lazy self outside to the curb, my chances of going for a vigorous walk or a jog would increase a hundredfold. I committed to doing this even when it was bitter cold, windy, dark, or swelteringly hot outside. It was a silly goal by most standards; after all, what good would walking to the curb do me?

The reality is that by showing up, dressed in the right shoes, and getting myself outside, I removed most of my resistance to running. I broke the inertia of inactivity and defeated my lazy negative self-talk that was saying it wouldn't matter anyway.

It worked! By making the commitment to an easy goal, something

I knew I could achieve, the rest of the activities would usually follow. Although the main goal of losing weight was important, my focus was on the initial activity. Some days I'd only run for a block, other times I'd walk fast for almost a mile—just one more tree or street sign farther—until I ultimately created a new habit and became a jogger! Combined with my new, permanent dietary changes, I removed 52 pounds of excess weight and got into excellent shape for the first time in my life... at age 30.

Today I'm more than twice that old, and yet I haven't gone back to my fat ways over all these years. The key to this new habit was my ABSOLUTE commitment to put on my jogging shoes and walk to the curb each day—no matter what! You can't achieve the main goals in your life if you don't take action on that first step.

Once my wife and I were late for a formal dinner. I was wearing a tuxedo and was in our car in the driveway when I suddenly realized that I hadn't done my daily run. So I put the transmission into Park and headed back into the house, despite her reminder of our date. Then I put on the running shoes and dashed to the curb, like tagging a base, then quickly returned to the house, changed back into my dress shoes, and got into the car to go to our dinner. Dumb? Maybe, but it was important to me not to break my chain of consecutive days of discipline. If it was raining, I'd dash to the curb and back; in the snow or wind, I'd do it every day. Nothing kept me from doing my silly little ritual. Or was it silly? You see, on most days, I'd go for a jog. The commitment to the first few steps made it easier to motivate myself to exercise.

They say that 90 percent of success is just showing up, ready to do your part. I agree with that. If you aren't in the game, there's no way you can win.

So what is it that you want to do? How would you like to change your life? (Pause and think about that.) What do you need to "show up" for? How could you just take the first step and get yourself going?

A simple action, like making the commitment to "put on your running shoes and walk to the curb," could be just what is needed to nudge you into a new way of life. What could be your minimum daily action that you will always do in order to become the person you want to be?

How would the person you'd like to be do the things you are about to do? How would that person use this book—not just as literature, but also as a tool to transform your life?

I've crafted this book to give you multiple tools:

1. Stories and examples from real life. Illustrations of what I and others have done that perhaps you too could do. These mental images will stick with you long after you've read this book. Be sure to highlight the ones that connect with you, and make a plan to begin them.

2. Written exercises that are designed to help you internalize what's most important to you. Note: This is the turning point for most people. If you don't do the exercises, then it's unlikely anything will change for you. Once you complete these simple procedures, you will find amazing new power to do what you want to do. More knowledge won't change your life. More right actions are the catalyst you need.

3. Over 300 tips, techniques, and strategies that will most certainly help you to grow and evolve into the person you know you can be. Many of these are simple, one-minute messages to inspire or educate you. By reading just one or two of them each day, you can jot a quick action note and, over time, profoundly improve your life.

4. Video links placed throughout this book that will take you to dozens of my short video lessons on Thrive15.com; each of these is a two-minute lesson sample. You can access the full series of messages for free by using the word "acorn" to get a 30-day free pass to Thrive15.com and its 1,000+ video lessons.

(In the eBook edition these are active links.)

5. The Ten Vital Qualities of Self Made Millionaires that I discovered while interviewing more than 100 self-made millionaires, celebrities, and leaders.

6. My personal story. I will show you how my own life has evolved as I discovered and applied these principles: "By their works you shall know them."

7. A Self Motivation Checkup that will show you which parts of your life need your attention next, and whether you need more "knowing" or more "doing" now.

Here are my final suggestions to make sure you get the most out of this book: Please do the written exercises, and actually write your responses both in this book and in a separate journal or notepad. Date each entry for later reference. As you read the hundreds of ideas, one per day or many at a time, jot a note after each one as to how you can use that concept to advance your own life. By the time you've finished reading and writing in this book, you will have created a handbook with which you can truly transform your life. Then keep it handy as a daily resource and a visual reminder to take that first step.

Just flip it open each day to a random page and follow the inspiring suggestions you discover there.

Thank you for making this commitment to yourself. The world will be better because of your contributions. We need you.

In the Spirit of Growth,

Jim Cathcart

SECTION ONE

WHAT DO YOU WANT?

The world is constantly asking you this question, whether you are sitting on Santa's knee, standing at the coffee shop counter, knocking on someone's door, calling someone on the phone, wishing on a star, throwing a coin in a wishing well, or even answering a genie from a lamp. They all want to know the same thing: What do you want?

By the way, the entire universe has that same question for you. No matter where you are or what you do, if you don't know what you want, then you surely will not get it.

But you will get whatever someone else wants, by default.

Even in traffic, we watch the other cars for signs of where they want to go. If they signal or look in a certain direction or turn their wheels slightly then we assume what they will do next, and we act accordingly. That's how millions of cars can be on the roads each day with only a tiny percentage of them involved in accidents. If they don't signal their desire or intent, then we are left to wonder, "What do they want?" or "Which way will they go?" We just guess, and that's when accidents occur, both on the road and in life.

Everything starts with communicating what you want.

> "It's a mistake to assume people know what they might want. If they don't know what's possible they will ask for too little."

> *Daniel Burrus*

"All things, whatsoever ye shall ask in prayer, believing,
ye shall receive"

(Matthew 21:22 KJV)

The universe is a self-organizing system. It takes the shape that is needed around whatever force exerts influence upon it. This can be cosmic and profound or everyday simple. For example: At a family get-together, if you were to say, "I'm really in the mood for barbecue tonight," then you would potentially influence the others there. "Not me," you say. "Daddy is the one who decides where we go for dinner." But by simply expressing your desire, anyone whose mind isn't already made up will have to *consider* barbecue—and you will be much more likely to get the meal you desire. And that's without even asking for it.

As Earl Nightingale once said, "About 95 percent of people can be compared to ships without rudders. Subject to every shift of wind and tide, they're helplessly adrift."

In every situation, we have the choice to express our desire or remain silent. If we don't speak up (e.g. "vote" for something), then our interests will not necessarily be considered. We aren't talking about constantly or obnoxiously saying, "Here's what I want!" I am merely suggesting that you form a habit of letting your desires be known in some appropriate way. The more you speak up, the more often you'll get what you want. If you don't ask, you won't get!

In negotiation skills training, they tell you to always ask for more than you expect to get. For example: When buying a car, before you've settled on a final price, you could ask, "If I agree to this price, can I get the upgraded sound system?" It may be that the seller can't do that for you, but it also may be that there is enough profit in your purchase for them to give you the upgrade in order to avoid losing the sale. If you don't ask, you don't get.

Your mind works in much the same way. If you don't ask your mind to provide a solution, then it won't. For example: If you say, "I forgot" or "I just can't remember", then you are telling your mind, "It's okay, you don't need to do any more work; I've given up on this item." On the other hand, if you say, "I don't remember *yet*" or "I'm sure it will come to me," then you are asking your mind to keep working to find the answer you need. Often the answer will emerge a moment later.

Most of us try to do what we think another person wants. But it's too often a guessing game, because they haven't clearly expressed what they want. Can you recall an occasion in which you did something that wasn't valued by the other person and you said, "But I thought that's what you wanted?" Please don't be one of those people who expect others to know things even though you didn't directly tell them. If you find yourself thinking, "He (or she) should know what I want," please reprimand yourself and disrupt that way of thinking. People won't know until we tell them.

Society needs for us to get into the habit of expressing what we want. Everything can work better when we do. It is not rude unless you behave that way; it is courteous to let others know what is on your mind or in your heart. This is simply how life works. The life impulse inside of us stimulates these wants and interests, and those lead to actions.

Emerson said it well: "Desire is possibility seeking expression."

This book will ask you from start to end, "What do you want?"

What do you want in life, from your relationships, on the job, from a vendor, from a customer, coworker, or friend? What do you want to accomplish? Where do you want to go? What would you like to do? When do you want what you've requested? What kind of person do you want to be?

Here goes; let's launch into this book together. I'm your "sales clerk" in this shopping center, and, like all good sales clerks, I'm asking, "How may I help you today?" In other words: "What do you want?"

MOTIVES

A motive is something that stimulates you to take action. It is the first half of the word "motivation." It is your "why." The motive causes the action, and together they create Motivation.

In fact, Motive-Action is a good way to think about Motivation. Once you know what you want in any given situation, you will have identified your Motive. Now all that remains is getting yourself to take Action. That is where self-leadership comes in. Sometimes we need to trick ourselves into doing what needs to be done. At other times, a simple nudge will do. We will explore many ways to do this, with and without tricks.

SELF-CONFIDENCE

It takes self-confidence to succeed in life, but where does confidence come from? I was once a 9-year-old lost in Disneyland. It was 1956, and my family had traveled the legendary Route 66 highway from my home in Arkansas all the way to the pier in Santa Monica, California. Disneyland had been open for less than one year, and my uncle's family promised to take us to see it. They had been there three times already. On the fateful day, Dad, Mom, and my sister Kathy toured the park with Uncle John and Aunt Saxon. Meanwhile, cousins Bruce, Brian, and Johnny took me to explore this wonderland.

Bruce was my age, Brian was younger, and Johnny was older. The ticket into Disneyland got you onto all the rides, so we didn't need more money. We were free to roam until the appointed meeting time at Town Hall at 3 p.m. Our first stop was Tomorrowland, where kids got to drive cars in the Autopia ride. If you weren't as tall as the sign at the entry gate, then you had to have an attendant drive your car for you. I was too short, so I got a driver. Still, it was fun, and at the end, I stepped out the exit to rejoin my cousins.

But there were no cousins to be found. I called out to them, searched the area, scanned the crowd, and called out again. Then I got scared and sad, and started to cry. I didn't know that there were two exits from Autopia, and that they were at the other one looking for me. I was 9 years old and all alone in a huge place full of strangers.

As I stood there crying, something happened. It occurred to me that I was in the self-proclaimed "Happiest Place on Earth" and that I was having a meltdown. If this continued, I'd miss out on one of the best days of my entire childhood. Suddenly, I dried my tears, snapped out of my mood, and set off to explore Disneyland.

For the next five hours, I wandered Disneyland alone. I went on the Jungle Boat ride, explored Tom Sawyer's Island, sang the Ballad of Davy Crockett on stage with many other kids at the Golden Horseshoe Saloon, and more. I had a ball! When I reached Fantasyland, I saw Mom, Aunt Saxon, and Kathy, and joined them for the rest of the day. Meanwhile, Bruce, Brian, and Johnny were frantically searching the park because they had lost Cousin Jimmy and didn't want to admit it to their parents.

Where did that confidence come from, the confidence that allowed me to spend five hours alone among thousands of strangers? I believe that it came from my awareness that my opportunity was too great to pass up. My motive was to avoid missing this great experience.

When you don't have the confidence that you need in yourself, sometimes you can derive it from other places, like potentially missing a great opportunity, or feeling that your obligation or duty is greater than your fear, or remembering that others have believed in you and they must see something that you don't feel yet. In other words, "Use the Force, Luke." You might have learned a system or skill that you can put your faith in, or you might believe in the guidance of your Creator. Whatever source you turn to, there are more sources of confidence than just your own self-awareness. Think of this story the next time you feel overwhelmed or intimidated.

A SIMPLE PLANNING PROCESS

When my son was about 7 years old, I taught him a simple seven-step planning process. The purpose of this was to give him a proven process with which he could achieve his goals—a system he could place his confidence in. We wrote it out and taped it on the inside of his closet door for him to see every day, at his 7-year-old eye level. I had him memorize it like a poem: "Determine the Need; Set Priorities; Choose Goals; Plan Actions; Schedule and Budget; Watch Yourself to Improve; then Check the Results." I had him repeat it on demand over a period of many weeks, and I did my best to make it fun for him and to praise him for even partial successes.

Then I needed to give it meaning. So we selected something that he wanted ("Determine the Need"): He wanted to score a goal in a soccer game, but he wasn't a forward, so he seldom got a shot at the goal. I had him write it down: "I will score a goal in a soccer game." Then we discussed why he wanted it, what it would feel like when it happened, how he might achieve it, and when. As we did this, we "Set Priorities" for what needed to happen in order to score a goal in a game. First was to tell the other players and the coach of his goal. Second was to assure that his shooting wouldn't interfere with the existing players who were forwards, since Jim Jr. was a midfielder. Next, he needed to be sure that he assisted as often as possible in helping others score a goal. Then he practiced shooting goals from many angles and at different running speeds.

A couple of weeks later, at one of his weekend games, I called him aside during a break and said to him, "Now is the time!" He looked terrified and asked what I meant, though he knew. I said, "Now is your time to score that goal." He gulped and went back onto the field with a look of pure determination. And, in the first moments of play, he scored his first goal! Ever. It was a huge moment. Everyone—he, his Mom, the coach, the entire team, and I—was screaming and cheering his success. It happened just as he had envisioned it would.

Next we selected a bigger goal. One night, Jimmy told me that he wanted to see The Alamo, the fortress/church and site of the famous battle in San Antonio, Texas. We had recently seen *The Alamo* movie on TV with John Wayne portraying Davy Crockett, and that made it exciting to Jim Jr. I had him get his seven-step planning guide, and we went to work.

What's the need? To go to San Antonio and to tour the Alamo, soon. What matters most (priorities)? To see the site, meet the tour guides, and learn about the real story in the real place where it happened. What else? Get parental assistance—after all, he was just a kid. Then? Figure out how to pay for it and when to do it.

We went to the library and got books on San Antonio and The Alamo. We learned all that we could (this was before the Internet). Then we determined that Thanksgiving weekend would be the best time for a trip. Paula, my wife and his mom, decided to let us make this a father/son event, and she chose to visit a friend in Dallas that weekend. We looked up the airfares, schedules, hotels, and rates, and made our plans. Note that it was Jimmy who did the planning and analysis, not me. I guided him with questions. He was the one who was following the seven steps and doing the thinking and the research.

By the time we took the trip, he had the whole experience mapped out: dates, times, costs, schedules, options, and interests. It turned out to be a wonderful experience for both of us, and we came in ahead of schedule and under budget! Wow. More importantly, Jim Jr. learned a new life skill, and this confidence still serves him to this day. By the way, today he is a senior executive with the number-one hotel in Southern California*, the Four Seasons Hotel in Westlake Village (*for two years in a row, per Conde Nast Traveler). You and I can use the same process to motivate ourselves.

Many years ago, as a young leader in the Junior Chamber of Commerce, I remember being coached by a Jaycees leader, Ken Coon, who later ran for governor of Arkansas. In 1973 he taught me to follow this model, and it has served me well all these years: Awareness, Belief, Goals, Plans, Actions, and Achievement He said, First you need to learn as much as you can—gather information to expand your Awareness of the subject. Then check your Beliefs. Do you really think you can do this? If not, do what's needed to expand your Belief in your success potential. What we believe about the world and ourselves will always limit what we can and will do, unless we expand it. At this point, set your Goals, develop your Plans, and take consistent and disciplined Action to make it happen. Then you'll be able to measure your Achievement, which will expand your Awareness for the next cycle.

Now it's your turn to use this system.

What Do You Want?

THE FUTURE YOU

What kind of person do you intend to become? The clearer your description of the person you'd like to be, the more likely it is that you'll live the life you'd like to see.

My colleague Darryl Davis posed this question: What is the most important part of a jigsaw puzzle? Some say it's the corner pieces; some say the center piece. But actually, it is the picture on the box. Without a clear image of what you're trying to create, you are left with a piece-by-piece struggle to make sense out of random pieces.

Take the time to write out your answers in the following exercise. Keep a journal with dated entries of these desires, and add to it often. Take as much space as you need for each answer, even if it is several pages. You may want to photocopy the following page and make copies to work from. Notice how this picture of the "future you" evolves over the years and how it also stays the same in many ways.

Caution: Don't take this exercise lightly. This can be one of the most profound exercises you will ever complete.

I'm asking you to allow your mind and spirit to help you create a picture of the person you would truly like to be. The clearer this picture becomes, the more compelling it will be.

We all need to know what we want to do, what we want to have, and what kind of person we'd like to become.

Let's get to know the "future you."

THE FUTURE YOU

Today's Date: _____

1. What words would best describe the person you'd truly like to be?

2. What character traits would you like for others to see in you?

3. What subjects would you like to know much more about?

4. What skills would you like to acquire?

5. How would you like to be regarded by others? (Write out what you'd like them to say or think about you.)

6. In what places (and among what groups) would you like to be accepted and feel comfortable?

7. What life experiences would you like to have? (Take your time and make a big bucket list.)

8. What credentials would you like to acquire?

9. What would you like to do for the world? How would you like to make a difference?

10. How would the person you'd like to be do what you are about to do?

Once you have described the person you'd like to be, look over your personal priorities in the coming chapters to see which areas you should be placing more emphasis on today in order to make your dreams a reality. At any given time, one needs, like a tree, to be either expanding your roots (gaining more awareness and resources) or bearing fruit (behaving productively) in order to grow. When you spend too much time in one area, your needs will increase in the other areas. You will need to have a daily plan for both expanding your roots and bearing fruit.

This can be like going on a diet, but with many more applications than just what or how you eat. It's a change in how you think and live.

THE THOUGHT DIET™

Your Growth Starter

When exerting control over our weight or wellbeing, we often use a diet: a specific plan to do or not do certain things. This is designed not just to alter our intake but also to retrain our thoughts and tastes to a healthier daily menu. The same can be true for retraining your thoughts and actions in order to create a better you.

"The Thought Diet" is designed to influence your thinking through your behavior and to groom your behavior through your thinking. Using this approach, you can follow The Thought Diet to guide your growth as you develop and cultivate the habits of success. The Thought Diet is a tool for helping you become more of the person you need to be in order to achieve your goals.

If you cultivate the thoughts and habits of the person you want to be, you'll automatically start getting the things you want to get.

There are three simple rules, in this order of importance:

1. Read your Thought Diet Card once every morning and once every night

2. Reduce your contact with cynical or negative people

3. Perform an unselfish act every day without expecting gratitude

The Thought Diet Card is a simple 3x5 card (or a blank postcard) with three important parts:

1. Your current primary goal (a brief description of the goal that matters most in your life right now)

2. Traits you are developing (five of the qualities you most want to cultivate within yourself to become the person you want to be)

3. Minimum daily actions (behaviors that will break your inertia each day and get you started growing again)

Thought Diet™ Card (Side 1)

Thought Diet™ (Side 1)

My current primary goal

_____

_____

_____

_____

Five traits I am developing

1. _____

_____

2. _____

_____

3. _____

_____

4. _____

_____

5. _____

_____

Thought Diet™ Card (Side2)

Thought Diet™ (Side 2)
Minimum Daily Actions
Mind_____

_____

Body_____

_____

Spirit_____

_____

Emotions_____

_____

Friends_____

_____

Family_____

_____

Career_____

_____

Finances_____

_____

This is not a mere list of goals to achieve or steps to complete; it is a list of traits and behaviors that bring out your desired qualities. Parts one and two—the goal and the list of five traits—go on one side of your card; part three—minimum daily actions—goes on the other side. On the actions side of the card, list eight categories: mind, body, spirit, emotions, friends, family, career, and finances. Then, beside each one, write a minimum action that will help you to grow in that area. Be practical here; don't challenge yourself too much or too little.

THE FUTURE YOU FORESEE DEFINES THE PERSON YOU'LL NEED TO BE

If you know you'll be starting a new business, then you can easily determine which skills and knowledge you'll need to acquire. If you want to play violin in an orchestra, you will know what skills you'll need.

No matter what your goal, the skills and knowledge to make it happen are usually easy to identify. As you develop the traits of the future you, you will start becoming the person who would achieve the goal you have written down—then the goal will be the natural by-product of your daily actions. It's the reverse of what a lot of people do, which is to solely focus on the goal. You can go about it from either direction. If you figure out what kind of person you want to be, think about the goals that person would achieve, and then become him or her—the goals will be the automatic by-product.

The next time you find some unscheduled time, take a moment and do a quick personal priorities assessment. (You'll find this in the SelfMotivation Checkup.) See which parts of your life are getting most of your attention, and which ones you might be neglecting. Then use The Thought Diet™ to quickly plan some adjustments. These little "course corrections" will have an amazing effect on your life. Caution: Don't turn this into "work" and start to fret over it. Just stop occasionally to notice how fully you are living. Then take some small first steps to live even more fully.

WHAT NOW? JUST DO IT!

Each section of this book leads you to a new level of awareness about yourself and your current patterns. This awareness equips you to make minor changes that will have major impact. You'll learn to live more fully than ever before. Regardless of job requirements, financial pressures, or family commitments, you will discover scores of ways in which to expand your life. Do it! Don't let these life impulses die. You've been given a vehicle and an avenue. Your acorn (the seed of your potential) contains unlimited potential for abundant living. The potential within you is your *vehicle* for making this world a better place. Your choices are the avenue of self-expression. So set your goals, and start taking those actions that will stimulate your growth. If you don't act on it, all of us miss out. If you do, all of us benefit.

There is so much more living available to you. It may not even require you to do *more* than you are currently doing; just doing things *differently* might increase your results. If you are not living abundantly, then get out your Thought Diet card and start growing. Turn off the TV for a few days, unplug from social media, and call some friends or family. Call them or visit them—don't just text them. Get out of the house, talk with your neighbors, volunteer to help someone, or fix something that is broken. Above all, connect with people. Do this in whatever healthy ways will expand your life. The world isn't waiting for you to show up; you have been waiting for it. The world is fully operational already. Stop waiting, now is your time.

Live your life; don't wait for it.

SECTION TWO

68 WAYS* TO MOTIVATE YOURSELF

(*268 more are waiting for you in the third section of this book.)

WHAT DO YOU WANT?

Once you know what you want, there are many ways to get yourself to do what is necessary in order to bring it about. Whatever you want, write it down, and then follow these steps. Here are 68 proven techniques that will motivate you. (Mark or highlight the ones you'd like to work on so that you can come back to this list as needed and take action.)

1. **Make your goal or motive obvious, impossible to ignore, easy, and convenient.** Tape a reminder on your bathroom mirror, the visor or dash of your car, the screen of your computer, or on your smartphone.

2. **Make it difficult to avoid taking action.** Make promises; write your "to do" list in permanent ink. Schedule things so that others are depending on you to take action. Put the action items into your workflow so that you cannot avoid dealing with them, even if you choose to delay them.

3. **Make it fun.** Smile and look for ways to increase the fun factor. Add music, make a game of it, etc. Start acting happy and eager, and those emotions will often follow. Do it outdoors or on a playing field. Get creative.

4. **Reward yourself for taking action.** My grandson Jason was once doing his math homework and lined up small candies next to each equation, so that upon completing each problem, he could reward himself with the candy. It would have been easy to just eat them all, but he was working his self-discipline muscles too. Be careful, though—don't celebrate a big sale by spending your profits on self-indulgence. Don't reward your workout or dietary wins with a big ice cream treat that reverses the effect. Instead, buy some new workout clothes.

5. **Make a minimum commitment.** They say the first olive out of the bottle is the only one that's difficult, because the rest will

then roll out easily. The same is true in other areas. Just do the first step, and often the rest will follow. Put on your running shoes and step outdoors, and you might just go for a run. What could be your "first olive" activity?

6. **Get an accountability partner.** Tell others of your commitment. When someone is relying on you or expecting you to perform, then the pressure is on, and you'll likely try harder so as not to disappoint them. Meet someone at a specific time and place each day; set yourself up so someone else is affected if you don't do your part. Often that extra pressure will get you going.

7. **Make a Declaration of Independence!** State boldly, "Today is the day!" When I decided to quit smoking, I told all my friends. They said, "Oh, you're trying to quit." I replied, "No, I have permanently quit as of now. Now I need to figure out how to deal with the withdrawal process." Don't try; do! (Yes, I learned something from Yoda.)

8. **Review your Wants list often.** Make a daily habit of reviewing of your list of goals. Do it at the same time each day. Even if you take no other action, at least keep the goals in the top of your mind. Read it even when you know you won't do anything yet.

9. **Get the tools, information, and equipment you'll need.** If you want to fix the car, get the tools out and put them by the car. If you need to update your software, put the information where you can easily act on it. If you need to teach your kids to manage their money, get a book or app for them and decide where, when, and how long you'll meet. List the first few topics you'll discuss. Get the checkbook or savings records printed out so you can discuss them. Put the tools for step number one in your way so that you have to move them in order to do anything else.

10. **Break the inertia—act!** Don't just think about it; do something, anything. Stand up! Take five steps toward the task; say something positive about getting it started. Act now.

11. **Review the downside occasionally.** Answer aloud, "What will happen if I don't do this soon?" Remind yourself of the potential pain of not acting.

12. **Become a *Thriver* (Thrive15.com).** The online learning and edutainment resource Thrive15.com has over 1,000 short video lessons on every business or motivational topic you can imagine. For a free 30-day exploration of their resources, use the code word "Acorn." There are over 110 Jim Cathcart videos on Thrive15.com, and each is under 10 minutes long.

13. **Surround yourself with stimuli.** When Tim Seward decided to become the international sales leader of his company and win a new Chevrolet Corvette, he went to the Chevy dealer and test-drove a Corvette. Then he put Corvette posters over his bed, above his workbench, and in other places to remind him of his goal. He later won the Corvette that year! Put things around you that lift you up and focus your mind.

14. **Chart your progress on a wall chart.** See where you stand every day. You can also do this with an app. There are many tools for this, but it really helps to have a wall chart that is in your face daily. Track your results even when you're not thinking of your goal.

15. **Get rid of temptation.** If you tend to get stuck in social media, don't log in today. If your office bogs you down from making calls, don't go to the office today. If working from home tempts you to watch TV, do chores or amuse yourself otherwise, then get out of the house! Don't hang around with the folks who easily give in to temptation. Get on track early and avoid the temptation. Leave your phone and focus on the activities.

16. **Clarify your mental picture daily.** Put one more pixel into the picture that describes your goal. State your goals clearly, and put them in writing—not digits, actual ink! Something magical happens from the head to the hand. And, every day, add something to the description to make it more vivid and appealing, one more detail or photo.

17. **Avoid or diminish contact with Doubters and Pessimists.** It's not being "nice" to be an enabler: When someone with a kind heart but weak discipline tells you that it's okay not to work toward your goal, get away from them. You don't need people who help you justify being weak. You need strength, and you have that strength within you. If someone else discourages you, meet with them and ask for a change. If they can't change their support, then reduce the amount of time you spend with them. Say goodbye to friends and family who discourage and doubt you. Be courteous and firm—no more pity parties or gripe sessions for you. Just start being unavailable for the get-togethers where people-bashing and complaining are on the agenda. Reprimand your critics gently, and let them know that you want to avoid even mild discouragement, no matter how well intentioned. Say, "I know you mean well, but when you talk like that, it discourages me. Please don't do that anymore. It is hard enough to keep myself motivated without resistance from others."

18. **Make a radical break from the patterns of the past.** The old you got the old results. Only a newly vitalized you will be able to achieve your goals. Do what you need to do to start your new life. For example, if you are giving up alcohol, then pour all of it out. Don't keep some for guests; just trash it all and don't worry about being wasteful. Remain clear on your motive. If it is to stop drinking then everything else is merely a secondary consideration. Get away from other drinkers for a while; make

a clean break and start a new life. Only when you remove the supplies of the past will you be required to find new and better alternatives. When I quit smoking, I made a point of giving away all of my engraved cigarette lighters and fancy ashtrays to people I didn't know, so that they'd never be tempted to return them to me. I got out of the smoking business completely. Since I was never going to smoke again, there was no justification for keeping any of the tools of smoking around "just in case." I also destroyed almost a full carton of perfectly good cigarettes on the day I quit. What do you need to make a break from?

19. **Go to church, temple, synagogue, or mosque.** Join, attend, subscribe, or at least download resources to gain inspiration. We all need to be uplifted occasionally—whether it is through reading scriptures, going to church, attending inspiring lectures, watching TED talk videos, or reading inspiring magazines. You need it, and you'll be stronger with it in your life. You don't have to follow anyone else's beliefs, necessarily—just inspire yourself and clarify your own beliefs. There is more to life than just you and me. This is not about religion; it is about inspiration.

20. **Leave SUCCESS Magazine on your coffee table.** I have always loved SUCCESS Magazine. I knew its former owner, W. Clement Stone, and its publisher, Og Mandino. I also know the recent publisher, Darren Hardy. This magazine is filled with tips, stories, and in-depth articles

---

HOW I MOTIVATE MYSELF

My TOP 7

What motivates me?

1. Giving a smile – getting a smile
2. Knowing that I did it!
3. Feeling of accomplishment
4. Proving that I can
5. Freedom to do the next thing
6. Endorphins!
7. Feeling of more energy

Jan Payne

---

that will make your life better. Subscribe today and read every article. Naturally you can access it online as well, but the physical reminder of the printed magazine has power.

21. **Change the rules you live by: for home, work, friends, and family**. By observing your patterns for a few weeks, I could easily tell you what your "life rules," "work rules," and "family rules" are. We all have rules, even when we haven't written them down. Think about the rules you operate by, and change those that don't serve you.

22. **Get a taste of success.** Acquire some of the artifacts and experiences of the future you want—and dress accordingly. The founder of McDonald's, Ray Kroc, bought used luxury cars long before he could afford a new one. He experienced luxury in that way without paying the price of a new luxury car, and without going into debt. It's not just the car you drive, but also the way you dress and carry yourself, the neatness and organization in your life. All of these contribute to your motivation.

23. **Get used to operating at a higher level.** Sample the new lifestyle. If you can't yet afford to stay at a Four Seasons hotel, then just meet a client there for lunch or breakfast. Start tasting the luxury you'd like to afford. Don't go into debt to buy things you can't yet afford. It is a great idea to get familiar with what going first class feels like. Order a steak once in awhile. Buy one really nice piece of clothing. Start thinking and feeling like successful people, on all levels.

24. **Fix your teeth! Wash your car, comb your hair, and get ready to succeed, NOW!** My dear friend Sam once came to me and said, "My life's a mess, and yours works. Help me make a change." I said, "Okay, go get your teeth fixed. Then I'll work with you. But not until then." He didn't understand at first.

Sam's front teeth had needed repair for a long time. He put it off due to the expense and potential pain. That meant that all day, every day Sam was self-conscious about his teeth. He adjusted his smile and the way he talked in order to hide his bad teeth. It diminished him moment by moment. Once he got his teeth fixed, he jubilantly proclaimed, "Jim, you've changed my life!" Not true: *He* changed his life. So can you. Fix your teeth.

25. **Green Bag your clothes and belongings.** Clean out your files, garage, workspace, closets, and briefcase. Image consultants speak of a process known as "green bagging," wherein you go through your entire wardrobe and put anything you haven't worn in a year or more into a green bag for donation or recycling. Get rid of the faulty, out of date, low-quality, or old items that you still use. Share them with the underprivileged. And don't ever go out in public dressed in worn-out or grossly out of style clothing.

26. **Change your self-talk.** I once stayed with a colleague in Juneau, Alaska on a business trip. From the moment I arrived, I noticed his negativity. His language was filled with "I can't, they won't, it couldn't, it probably doesn't" and similar pessimistic proclamations. I tried to encourage him and even got him to put a coin in a jar each time he said, "I can't," but the jar filled up overnight, and he said, "I can't even do that!" His self-talk was keeping him small and unsuccessful. Do what you need to do to change to a positive dialogue in your words and in your mind.

27. **Forget FOMO (fear of missing out).** Do you find yourself with hundreds of unread or un-replied-to emails, stacks of papers and magazines, notices that your cell phone "storage is full," and other indicators that you're hoarding because you are afraid of missing out on something? This procrastination

is unhealthy and will limit your success. Get into the habit of letting things go. If you subscribe to magazines, just know that next month there will always be another and that there's no way you can keep up with all articles in all of them. Consume magazines; don't collect them. Scan for the information you like, and rip out the articles to read as you travel. Recycle the rest. Get off of notification lists, and unsubscribe from virtually every shopping source and club. Free your mind for growth. You can always search for updated info without subscribing.

28. **Get around winners, often.** Birds of a feather flock together. Achievers talk about big ideas and possibilities. Non-achievers talk about limitations and useless topics. Winners like talking about productive actions, and they love optimism. Losers like talking about others and unproductive things, and they love distractions. Get with the folks who are going where you want to go. Study how they talk, think, and respond to challenges.

29. **Give up.** No, don't give up on succeeding. Do give up what is holding you back. What could/should you give up? Is there a habit that's holding you down? Are there friendships that limit you? Maybe you could diminish your time with those folks for now. Are there lifestyle patterns that surely will never help you succeed? Give them up completely for now. And don't watch soap operas (daytime TV drama) or cynical situation comedies. They feed on the weaknesses and fears in people. Watch uplifting shows, instead; look for inspiring stories and success profiles. Learn from the folks who are living as you would like to, not the ones who are self-indulgent cynics.

30. **Learn from everyone.** Emerson said, "Every man I meet is in some way my superior; and in that I can learn of him" True. Even the lowliest person on the success ladder still knows some things that you and I don't know. There's another old

saying: "Nobody is completely useless. You can always serve as a bad example." Humor intended. Honor the fact that everyone has something you can learn about. Pay attention with respect.

31. **Never blame.** The problems that limit you aren't with other people—they are in your own thinking. When you blame people or circumstances for your failures, you push the responsibility for taking action away from you. You are the only one who can take the actions you need. Don't make excuses. Instead, find solutions. P.S. Other people never admire those who blame.

32. **Breathe. Stop to think.** Occasionally the noise of activity needs to stop so that you can reflect on what you're seeing or feeling and acquire a new insight. Make time to just pause and breathe. While you're there, notice the beauty of the world around you. My friend Kevin Buck says, "Without reflection, there is no true learning."

33. **Shut up and listen:** Observe, notice, and remember that it's not all about you. You need others, and vice versa. Sometimes in our zeal to succeed, we just talk all the time, thinking that our speaking will motivate others to help. Not true. Everyone is driven by his or her own motives, and if you don't understand what they care about, then they won't be interested in what you care about. When you're talking, you only know what you know now. When you're listening, you acquire knowledge from others.

34. **Do something selfless daily.** Track the giving, but never expect payback. Generosity is the most powerful of all our actions; it is love in action. When we give of our time, our attention, our skills, or our resources, we make the world a better place. Look for ways to develop the habit of doing things for others, especially others you don't know. Pay it forward, and it will return to you.

35. **Gratitude is the master emotion.** Develop a grateful heart and the habit of openly thanking others and praising them. We love to be around people who admire us. When someone praises us sincerely or points out what we do well, we revel in the attention. Be a person who does that for others. In turn, you will like and respect yourself even more.

36. **Accept your lack of power over your impulses.** Gain the tools and support that you need. In recovery programs, one of the main obstacles is getting the patient to accept their powerlessness over their problem. We are all addicted to something, whether it is a routine, a behavior pattern, a substance, or an activity. Habits need to be chosen, not just accumulated. Be very selective in what you allow yourself to give in to. Your emotions may not be directly under your control, but you can learn to control how you act when you feel strong emotions. For example: You don't have to run just because you're afraid. You don't have to strike out just because you're angry. When at first you have trouble resisting the bad action, just practice delaying action. Over time, you'll increase your control.

37. **State what you want in writing.** State it fully, and date it! If it's not written, then you may not get it. The power of a written goal is immense—not typing it, but actually handwriting it. There is a mystical element in this process that matters. So write down what you want, and by when. Also write the day's date on the page every time.

38. **Assess yourself often: Do a Success Readiness Interview.** If you want to know how ready you are for success, then you may want to "interview" yourself in writing or into a recorder. Just craft a series of questions that would reveal how ready someone is to succeed. Then answer them yourself. There are many online assessments you can use as well. For a catalog of assessments that tell you different things about yourself, send us a note at info@cathcart.com and add the word "assessments" to the subject line.

39. **Identify your state: your M.O., or Modus Operandi.** Later in this book, there is a SelfMotivation Checkup. This includes a tool to help you know your current "M.O.," your mode of operation in each part of your life. It measures Knowing and Doing—in other words, information and motivation. These two will reveal whether you're in Passenger, Critic, Competitor, or Leader Mode.

40. **Do the Priority Wheel exercise often.** The Priority Wheel, also presented in the SelfMotivation Checkup, reveals where you've been putting the emphasis in your life lately by measuring all eight major life areas: mental, physical, family, social, spiritual, career, financial, and emotional.

41. **Start now, today—not next week or January 1 or after the holidays, birthday, first of the month, etc. NOW!** If you've been thinking about, say, going on a diet, then do it now. Not an hour from now but this very minute. Draw a line; start this moment to eat differently and exercise intelligently. Don't wait to be perfectly prepared. If you want the outcome, go for it now.

42. **Create a simple planning process for achieving your goals**, or use mine. Determine the need, set priorities, choose goals, etc.

43. **Use apps to reshape your daily habits.** Find the one that fits YOU. My friend Tony is numerically motivated. Actual numbers are what reach him best. He tracks his income and outgo daily, and he's on top of his finances. For wellness, he tried many diets and fitness programs with no results. Then he discovered an app that tracked his intake of calories and burn rate daily. He

couldn't wait to see his numbers improve. It worked for him, but not for me. I am more motivated by a visualized outcome and daily weigh-ins. My wife Paula is motivated more by the influence of others, so she likes workout partners and group activities like Jazzercise®. Find out what works for you.

44. **Retrain your Ed or Edie (E.D., the "Executive Director"),** an aspect of your thinking process that reviews and makes decisions. Teach it to be even better. Let the executive function of your mind help you to make new choices, take new actions, and break old patterns. Train your brain to be your ally and to help you form new habits. Learn critical thinking and strategic thinking. (Read Gerhard Gschwandtner's new book on The High Performance Mindset.)

45. **Find some new options, and keep them handy.** For example, if you always have fast food for lunch, find some healthier alternatives, such as vegetable soup. Learn to enjoy plain water, and substitute it for sodas. Retrain your taste buds. Fill your cupboard with snack alternatives, and make it easy to prepare them. Don't allow the healthy items to be stored where you'll have to go look for them—otherwise you'll just default to the convenience of chips, burgers, pizza, or tacos. The same applies to work routines and tools. Don't hang out in the break room.

46. **Make a commitment to yourself that you WILL succeed at this goal**; details are to be worked out later. You will do whatever it takes and find a way. When you tell yourself that you will somehow, somewhere find a way to reach your goal, even if it takes longer and is more difficult than you thought, that commitment brings you strength.

47. **Jump, and the net will appear.** When I quit smoking many years ago, I had to endure three months of misery. Now, 40 years later, I'm still a nonsmoker. Commit—don't just think about it

or try. Make it happen. If you've fastened your parachute and reached jumping height, stand in the door and then JUMP!

48. **Keep your goals visible, and don't worry about critics.** None of the people who might make fun of you or criticize you will care whether you succeed or fail. They have their own lives to live. So do what is needed to keep your goals in your field of vision every day.

49. **Fill your unproductive times in productive ways.** Stuck in traffic? Listen to audio books. Going for a walk or jog? Listen to inspiring messages, podcasts, or music. Can't sleep? Think about an appealing goal you're working toward. Waiting for an appointment? Review your notes and goals. Learn more about your customers. Use waiting time creatively. Bring this handbook along, and do the Priority Wheel exercise again. Then focus on the areas of your life that haven't been getting much attention. Keep some notepaper and stamped envelopes handy so you can write a personal note or a thank you and mail it soon.

50. **Turn your car into a classroom or auditorium.** Put CDs or downloads into your system; subscribe to information or inspirational channels to bring value into your commute. Make it easy to tune in to learning. Stop listening to angry talk shows or cynical hip-hop music.

51. **Set some meetings with Thrivers like you.** Make the appointments now. Increase the amount of time you spend with fellow success seekers. Act on it, and set an appointment. Today.

52. **When you get depressed, go do something for others.** Never allow the depression to cause you to stop moving. The fuel that sadness and depression depend upon is inactivity. The longer you delay action, the stronger your depressed feelings grow. So

break the shell and take action, any action, especially generous or helpful actions toward others.

53. **Change your settings to eliminate distractions and difficulty.** Don't let the automatic features of your software or radio or smartphone get in your way. Reset your devices to help you, not to distract you. If you tend to get sucked in by social media, then change your settings to bring other information to the front of your desktop.

54. **Go to the "genius bar" and get coaching.** If something has been limiting your advancement and you don't know what to do, then find an expert. Go to the store or call the support line and get someone to coach you or fix your problem. It may already be in your contacts list. Do it now. Go to sources like Fiverr.com and see if someone can help you for a very small fee.

55. **Hire a personal coach.** All great athletes rely on coaches to help them grow. So do top entertainers. Great singers also have voice coaches. How about you? What do you need coaching on? Do a search, look for certified coaches or top experts, and get some of their expertise focused on you for a while. Even when you're at the top of your game, a coach can help you improve.

56. **Hire a kid.** Maybe there is a young person who loves to do what you need and would welcome a flexible assignment to assist you for pay. For very little money, you can give them a fascinating project that will relieve your workload and help you to advance.

57. **Acquire a skill you don't need yet.** Get ready. For what? I don't know, but I do know that the more things you prepare for, the more opportunities will be open to you. So acquire the general skills and the specific knowledge that will make you eligible for even more opportunities. Do this before you know when, where, or why you'll need it. Learn a new language, for example.

58. **Prepare for your opportunities.** The Scout motto "Be Prepared" is a great motto for us. Assemble your tools, information, and supplies. Cultivate your relationships with people who are succeeding. Give of yourself every day and pay it forward to create even more opportunities for yourself.

59. **Do the toughest items first.** As Danny Cox says, "If you've got a frog to swallow, don't look at it too long. And if you've got more than one to swallow, swallow the biggest one first." Amen. Don't let the things you dread dampen your whole day. Get them done first and out of your way emotionally.

60. **Ask for help.** If you're stuck and not sure how to handle part of your task, reach out. Seek input or assistance. Get over the hurdle and eliminate the resistance. Tell someone what is holding you back.

61. **Get rid of the de-motivators.** My friend and colleague Joel Weldon is a professional speaker who travels a great deal, just as I have over the years. He found that the hassle of carry-on or even checked luggage was a de-motivator to him. It made him dread travel. Then he discovered that he could ship his luggage ahead to his destination hotel. So he put in place a system that allows him to travel with only a briefcase, knowing that his luggage awaits him at the other end. Now he looks forward to the trip and no longer worries about getting enough overhead space or lugging things around an airport. What de-motivates you?

62. **Don't let things accumulate.** When I called my office from one of my 120 trips a year, some staffers would say, "I know you called to go over your mail and calls, but there's nothing that can't wait till you return." I'd correct them: "No! Don't let anything wait if it can be handled now. Otherwise I'll dread the workload awaiting me when I get home. I want a clean desk and happy feelings when I get back. Let's handle it now!" So when I called in from the road, they'd say, "Wait just a second, and I'll go to your desk..." Perfect!

63. **Pick a lane.** You can't work on multiple goals at the same time. Multitasking is a myth. It is merely the rapid shifting from one focus to another, and you're never at your best when you do it. So decide which big goal you're going after now. Often one bigger goal will bring several smaller goals to completion as well.

64. **Procrastination isn't a motivator**; it is a slave master. If you put things off until you can no longer avoid them, then doing them becomes stressful and urgent. That means you're not doing your best work. Do it now. Get things off your list and done.

65. **Create a motivation playlist.** Pick the music you most love, and divide it into fast and slower songs so you can listen to the music with the right pace for what you are doing. On mountain trail running, my friend listens to powerful rock music. He pushes hard, and the music keeps him going. If you're seeking inspiration, choose music with a soothing pace and inspiring words. Build one special playlist just to kick your butt and get you going. For me, there are several

> ### HOW I MOTIVATE MYSELF
>
> "I remind myself how the good things in my life have come from action I chose to take. Or as someone smarter than me wrote, "Whatever a man sows he will reap." If I don't get moving on this task then someone else's action will determine my fate. The unexpected blessings from others are what I have reaped from sowing small steps one day at a time."
>
> *Barry Banther*

old-time rock and roll tunes that do that: Beach Boys' "I Get Around," Van Morrison's "Old Time Rock & Roll," and Elvis Presley's "Blue Suede Shoes." (Yes, I realize how much that dates me.)

66. **Discover your patterns, and interrupt them.** We all have patterns of work, stress avoidance, communication, nutrition, and more. The more self-aware you become, the more you'll see how predictable you really are. Therein lies your opportunity. Interrupt the patterns that are not serving you, and replace them with new ones. Form the habits that will take you to what you want.

67. **Ask others about you.** One method of psychological assessment is what is known as a "360 degree assessment." This is where you answer a series of questions about yourself, and then have others answer the same questions about you. You can see yourself from all sides—their views as well as your own. Start by checking with people who will tell you the truth. Ask them what you do that helps and what you do that holds you back. You will be amazed at what you discover.

68. **Read what inspires you.** Keep your uplifting resources handy. My wife has the Bible on the end table and reads it each morning to start the day off right. Some people carry pocket-sized books like *As a Man Thinketh* by James Allen, or any of Simple Truths or Tremendous Life Books' mini-books. You can also post inspiring quotes or photos around you. Keep the powerful words of others present so that they can influence you.

THREE BIG QUESTIONS

If you're an acorn today, then what will you be like when you become a mighty oak? You need to foresee your desired future if you want to become the future you.

Use three separate sheets of paper to answer these questions.

WHAT DO YOU WANT YOUR FUTURE TO LOOK LIKE?

What do you want to do? To experience? To own? To become?

Question 1. Think of the entirety of your life, and, in a big brainstorm dump, list everything you can think of that you want. Write them down. If it isn't written, it won't become real. Let your dreams flow onto the paper. No limits—list everything you can think of, whether you believe it is possible or not. What are your dreams, both great and small? Just assume that whatever you want, no matter how big, somehow a way will emerge to make it happen. *Do this before addressing question 2.*

Question 2. Next, let's limit your goals to the next three years. What do you want to do, have, or be in the next 36 months? Write it down.

Question 3. Finally, let's change the limits and the urgency. What if you learned that you only had six months of life remaining? What do you want to do, have, or be in those six months? Write it down.

The value of this process lies in harvesting your dreams from three contexts: the unlimited future, the limited future, and the urgent present moment.

By the way, I was serious about getting some paper and actually *doing* this exercise. Please go get some paper and write the three questions down, one at the top each page. If you only read this book and don't act on it, then you will not become more self-motivated. Knowing is useful, but only *doing* will change your life. Nobody's looking, so what you do depends totally on you. C'mon. This is something you are doing for yourself.

Once you're done answering all three questions, look over your lists and add anything you may have left out.

AFTER YOU HAVE ANSWERED ALL THREE QUESTIONS

Next, go over each of your three lists and select the top three goals or wishes in each section. Circle or highlight them. This gives you a total of nine finalists. There may be some duplication among these nine, but whatever final few you end up with will be your main goals. Those are the ones to work on the most.

You'll probably see some similarities among them. Note which ones are Urgent and which are Important. Some are both; some are just one. Do the Urgent and Important ones first. Sometimes the Urgent aren't important at all. Let those go. The Important but not yet urgent are ones you should schedule time for soon. Don't let them become urgent before they get your attention.

Also note which items are important to others, versus important to you. If they aren't important to you, then be careful and make a good decision as to when and how to address them.

Now that you have completed this exercise, you know what matters most to you at this time. If you structure your life around those nine or fewer goals, you will increase their likelihood of occurring.

HOW TO REACH
THE TOP 1 PERCENT OF THE TOP 1 PERCENT OF YOUR FIELD

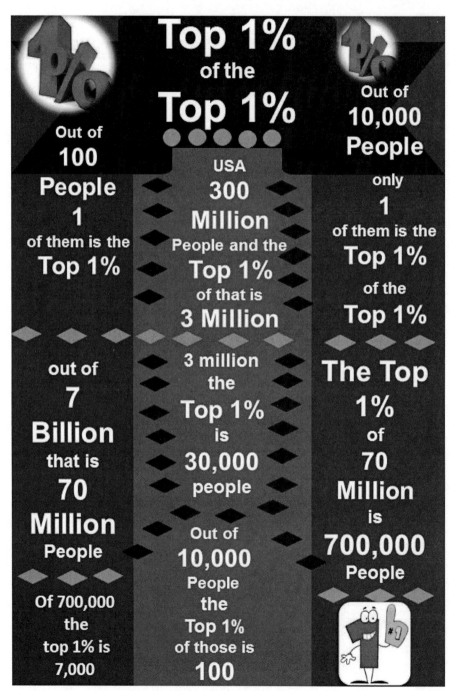

Top 1% of the **Top 1%**

Out of 100 People 1 of them is the Top 1%

out of 7 Billion that is 70 Million People

Of 700,000 the top 1% is 7,000

USA 300 Million People and the Top 1% of that is 3 Million

3 million the Top 1% is 30,000 people

Out of 10,000 People the Top 1% of those is 100

Out of 10,000 People only 1 of them is the Top 1% of the Top 1%

The Top 1% of 70 Million is 700,000 People

The top 1 percent is available to anybody, no matter your physical condition, no matter your intellectual capacity, no matter who you know, and no matter what skills you bring to the table. You can decide today which percentile you want to be in.

Out of 100 people, somebody will be the most successful. That one person equals the top percent; of 1,000 people, there will be 10 in the top 1 percent. Keep it going. In 10,000, there are 100, and in 1 million, there are 10,000 in the top 1 percent!

You will do well if you shoot for that top 10,000, but you could do so much better.

How about going for the top 1 percent of the top 1 percent? Now you're talking success! That will mean that out of 1,000,000 people, you'll be in the top 100.

The population of the USA is currently estimated at 321 million people. The top 1 percent would be 3,210,000 of those. The top one percent of the top 1 percent would be 32,100 people.

It is possible for you to count yourself among them, but let's not get ahead of ourselves.

First we have to figure out WHICH 32,100 people we're talking about.

The top 1 percent of the entire population of the USA? Or Pianists? Triathletes? Educators? Investors? Ranchers? Entertainers? The wealthiest? The best known? The most famous? The most notorious?

See what I mean? You've got to pick a category in order to make the measurement meaningful.

If you take your chosen field and apply yourself to the same 1 percent equation, see what you'd get.

I sincerely believe that **you can do that** in your own field. I've known hundreds of people who have done so. This book is designed to show you how.

So how do you do that? It's simple—not easy but simple.

First, select the field in which you want to excel. Then dedicate up to an extra hour each day studying that field and sharpening your skills. Within five years, you will have invested over 1,250 hours to learn and master your craft. This is in addition to your normal work. Doing your job day to day doesn't count toward this formula. You need to spend an extra hour of focused effort learning and practicing toward your goal of the top 1 percent of the top 1 percent. And you'll need to cultivate the 10 vital qualities of self-made millionaires that I describe in this book.

THE MUSIC BUSINESS

Let's assume that you selected the music industry as your target, and that you have zero experience in that field. First you have to "pick a lane": Determine what aspect of this business you want to focus on. It could be performance, production, publishing, marketing, distribution, artist management, recording, or writing. You could focus on orchestras, bands, solo, harmonies, synthetic, acoustic, vocals, specific instruments, arranging, conducting, playing, or sound mixing. You could be an agent or talent scout (A&R specialist), or... See what I mean?

The industry is so vast that you will need to choose a focus in order to truly advance. But even if you only focus on the broad category of music in all its myriad forms, you'd still be more specialized than most people.

LIVE PERFORMANCE OF POPULAR MUSIC

You're going for the top of the top, so select a target. Let's say it is live performance of popular music. Where do you start? Not on stage—that's an advanced point. Your starting point might need to be helping bands set up and transport their equipment, or maybe you'll work with a music store or recording studio at the entry level. You'd sweep floors and arrange inventory, or work as a sales clerk or delivery person. All the while you'd also be learning to play instruments and perform well.

In this apprentice capacity, you can learn about the different instruments and sound systems, the ways to create the right atmosphere for a good performance. You'll get to know the musicians and see the differences between them in both skill and temperament. You'd quickly start to see which attitudes and habits led to better musicianship, and which ones didn't. You'd learn to work with different venue managers and workers at the clubs and theaters. You'd see how to combine the right equipment for the venue and the musicians.

If you were truly a student of your craft, you'd also subscribe to some music industry magazines and websites, and you'd try to experience all types of music at live shows, on recordings, in videos, on podcasts, and in studios. You'd join the industry associations and attend conventions or take online courses. You'd be a sponge for any information about music.

You'd also start building relationships with people in the industry. They'd get to know you as an eager learner and a hard worker. You'd earn their respect and friendship.

Within one year, you'd not only know a lot more about the music business, but you'd also have a number of contacts in the field. That would open even more doors for you.

In a short time, you would be the go-to person for answers and help in your specialty. People would be relying on you and including you in more activities. All of that means more learning and more credentials. Your musical skills would be growing too. You'd be jamming with others, sitting in as a guest performer, doing gigs to fill in for friends, booking your own performances, and getting better all the time.

Can you see how all of this tends to compound, to build upon itself? With only one year in the business, in this way you would have advanced profoundly. By year two, you'd have new opportunities and even more depth of understanding. By the third year, people would be coming to you for answers, and by year five, you'd be a leader in your part of the industry. Shortly thereafter you'd be one of the top names in your niche. You might ultimately end up pursuing a completely different path, but these principles would apply to that field too.

A recent American Idol winner who started in poverty and only sang in church and at home drove to each audition city until she finally made it through to "Hollywood Week" and ended up at the top of the competition. She used the sheer force of her will to make it into the competition. Then she humbly accepted the coaching and feedback she got and applied herself with complete dedication. Yes, she had the raw talent, but until then, she didn't have the training, the discipline, or the experience she needed for success. She took huge risks, along with an immense work ethic and a willingness to be coached by others, and turned it into success.

You and I seldom get access to a vehicle like American Idol, but we can take the same process and create our own path:

1. Decide what you want. What's your dream?

2. Start anywhere on the path. If you have to clean bathrooms at first, then do it.

3. Humbly accept coaching from everyone. Even if you have a true gift or talent, you still need the training, discipline, and experience to go with it.

4. Stay the course whether you succeed or fail. Each failure is the beginning of the next phase.

Malcolm Gladwell wrote about "the 10,000-hour rule" and observed that the top professionals in most every field had exceeded that many hours of practice, study, and experience in their specialty. That may be true for some fields, but in others it may only take 1,250 hours. Still, there is no path to the top without tons of practice, study, and dedication.

Apply this same dedication to any field, and in a few years, you can be among the top people in it.

MY STORY

I grew up in Little Rock, Arkansas in the southern USA. My dad was a telephone repairman, and Mom was a homemaker. I had a younger sister, and my grandparents lived with us. Grandfather Cathcart was completely disabled by a stroke and occupied a hospital bed in our front bedroom for seven years. Grandmother Cathcart helped care for him.

Upon high school graduation I went to a state college that admitted 92 percent of their applicants. After two years of poor performance in college, I dropped out and took a series of jobs in various fields. I was a bartender, bill collector, bank teller, truck driver, warehouseman, day laborer, nightclub singer, donut salesman (yes, really), factory worker, and insurance agent.

Then in 1970 I got married and sold investment products for a year, unsuccessfully. After that I sold cars, worked in a grocery store, and finally accepted a job as a clerk at the Little Rock Housing Authority, the urban renewal agency. In 1972, as a government clerk with no college degree, no money in the bank, no history of achievement of any type, I was newly married with a son and physically out of shape. I was strong from warehouse work but overweight and not very fit. I had no "contacts" in any field and didn't know what I wanted to do for a living. I was earning only $525 a month, and I knew nothing about psychology or behavioral science. Then everything changed.

As I sat, bored, at my desk, awaiting an assignment from my boss who was not busy, I could hear the radio in the next room. It was playing a short radio program called "Our Changing World" by Earl Nightingale, the "dean of personal motivation." He said, "If you will spend one extra hour each day studying your chosen field, you will become a national expert in that field in five years or less."

That message hit me like an oncoming train. It did "change my world." It rearranged my belief system. I thought, "An hour a day for five years is more than 1,250 hours. If I studied any subject for that long, I'd be a leading expert." Before that day, I had never suspected that I could be extraordinary at anything. I thought that I'd be a nice person with a decent life but that I'd never really make a difference in the world. But maybe it was true—maybe by following Mr. Nightingale's formula I could become a substantial person.

What did I want to be an expert about? Well, it wasn't urban renewal, per my job at the Housing Authority.

The more I thought about it, the more I realized that I wanted to do what Earl Nightingale was doing. I wanted to help people grow. But I knew nothing about that field.

So I took him at his word and decided to spend at least an hour every day studying human development, personal motivation. I read books from the public library: *Think & Grow Rich* by Napoleon Hill, *The Power of Positive Thinking* by Dr. Norman Vincent Peale, *Success Through a Positive Mental Attitude* by W. Clement Stone, *How to Win Friends and Influence People* by Dale Carnegie.

Then I got 48 audio recordings of Earl Nightingale from Harold Gash, who sold them for Nightingale Conant Corporation. I borrowed them at first and then worked out a payment plan so that I could own them. I spent hundreds of hours fanatically listening to those tapes every day for at least three consecutive years. This was done to retrain my own thinking and belief system to allow for more success.

In the meantime, I knew that I needed to do something besides read and listen, so I joined the Junior Chamber of Commerce, the Jaycees. We formed a new chapter in my neighborhood, the Pulaski Heights Jaycees, and I became so active that I recruited 13 of our initial 20 members, and I attended 400 Jaycees meetings in the next two years! I served on committees, held chairmanships, led projects, organized teams, spoke at meetings, gave reports, attended state conventions, and read every manual that they printed—most of them more than once.

Within a couple of years I was chapter president, then state chairman, then state vice president, and was winning awards for outstanding work. All of this was work I was doing for free after my regular job. I still worked at the Housing Authority. But my volunteer work began to positively affect my job performance, and I got better at most everything I did.

My bosses recognized my growth and promoted me to staff assistant to the Board of Directors, a big promotion with a nice raise. Then they gave me another raise for good performance and elected me president of the employees association. Wow!

In a two-year period, I went from being just a clerk to being the assistant to the board, and in my volunteer work, I was selected as the state chairman in charge of individual development programs for the 280 chapters of the Arkansas Jaycees. After spending one year working to help David Hale get elected national president of the U.S. Jaycees, I left my Housing Authority job to become a full-time salesman of the Earl Nightingale training programs.

Then, a year later, the U.S. Jaycees National Headquarters invited me to apply for the position of National Leadership Training Director. This involved a move to Tulsa, Oklahoma, my wife's hometown.

I got the job and another big raise to $12,000 a year. That was twice as much as I'd been making two years earlier, and in 1975 it was a good salary. They put me in charge of training 356,000 Jaycees members each year through a team of 200 state-level training managers and soon raised me to $18,000 a year. I frequently worked into the night, since I lived right next door to the Headquarters building and occasionally worked until I fell asleep at my desk.

> **HOW I MOTIVATE MYSELF**
>
> *"When I feel like staying in bed, I take a deep breath and think about all the great stuff I get to do today (which may just be seeing 1 cool person) and remind myself the faster I get going, the sooner I can get to the fun part and how excited I am by it."*
>
> Phil Gerbyshak

Still, I loved the intensity of it all. We were winning awards for my work, and I was collaborating with the people whose books I had been reading the years before. I met and worked with Og Mandino, president of SUCCESS Magazine, and W. Clement Stone, Og's boss. I met the founder of the National Speakers Association, Cavett Robert.

Every spare moment of my life was spent in personal development. I attended college night courses, went to lectures and special appearances of the thought leaders of the day. I read voraciously, hundreds of books in just a few years. Additionally I was improving my relationship with my wife and son, growing new friendships, and getting into better physical shape. I strengthened my religious faith, stopped smoking, lost 52 pounds of fat, and started running every day. My world was transformed!

After two years at the U.S. Jaycees, I got an opportunity to work as a coach and advisor to the Massachusetts Mutual Life Insurance Company's Tulsa, Oklahoma office. They had learned of me from my night job, in which I was leading classes at Tulsa Junior College.

The general agent of Mass Mutual who hired me was Joe Willard, a wonderful mentor and friend still today. He brought me aboard to help his agents develop their sales skills, and I ended up leaving the

Jaycees and moving in with the agency in their new penthouse office complex in Tulsa. Joe paid me what the Jaycees had paid but gave me the opportunity to also do outside speaking and training for others.

I joined the newly formed National Speakers Association (NSA) in 1976 and was learning how to build a practice as a professional speaker. As my speaking business grew, Joe discontinued my $18,000 salary and traded me the use of the office in return for my services. My speaking business income grew: I earned $28,000 in 1978; $64,000 in 1979; $89,000 in 1980; $108,000 in 1981; and $130,000 in 1982. All of this was done while still working with Joe's agency whenever I was in Tulsa. By applying the self motivation principles in this book, I had grown a thriving speaking business on top of my work for Joe.

I became very active in NSA and, as a result of many hours of volunteer work, by 1980 I was elected to their national board of directors. That led to many chairmanships and other duties, all on an unpaid basis. But my career kept growing, too. I hired an assistant and formed a partnership with a college professor and speaker in California, Dr. Tony Alessandra, and the business continued to grow substantially.

By the time I moved to California in January of 1983, I was doing 123 paid speeches a year and was on the road most of the time. If you had asked me in 1974 if any of this were possible, I would have said no. It never occurred to me in Little Rock that I could be a full-time professional speaker and author.

Each new level of success opened new possibilities, and my partnership with Tony Alessandra was like jet fuel to my career. We became full partners, and within a couple of years, we had books with major New York publishers, a video series published by the University of Southern California, a thriving speaking and training business, and a staff of ten full- and part-time people. Our offices were one block from the beach in La Jolla, California, a world-class resort. We had both doubled our income and were still growing. What a life!

One day the office phone rang—it was Earl Nightingale! He had read an article that Tony and I had written, and he wanted to publish our audio album.

Remember, in 1972 I heard Earl on the radio. In 1974 I was selling Earl's training programs. In 1984 he was selling my training programs!

In 1984 and 1985, Nightingale Conant Corporation sold over $3.5 million of our training program, "Relationship Strategies for Dealing with the Differences in People." What a journey!

My successes from that point began to compound, and today I'm living a life I'd never dreamed was possible. I knew it might be good, but I had no idea how good. I've been around the world multiple times and delivered speeches to hundreds of thousands of people. One of the most fun engagements ever was in 2003, when I was the keynote speaker for Harley Davidson's 100th Anniversary dealer convention. My "interview" for that role was a three-day motorcycle ride through the Rocky Mountains. One of my most meaningful engagements was in 2010, when the USA Special Olympics invited me to be the featured speaker at their Opening Ceremony in front of 13,000 fans and 3,800 special athletes.

When I was president of NSA in 1988-89, I invited Earl Nightingale to join me onstage at our national convention—with 1,500 professional speakers in attendance in Dallas—for an interview about his life in the field of personal development. He tentatively agreed. Then in May of that year, his wife, Diana, called me with the awful news that Earl had passed away. I was stunned.

She went on to mention that she'd like to hold a memorial service for Earl at our speakers' convention. I said, "Yes, we'd be honored." Diana asked me to speak at that service, and I declined. I said, "No, this should be a time for giants of industry and world leaders who knew Earl, not for me." She corrected me. She said, "Jim, you are the product of what Earl was all about. You followed his guidance and transformed your life. That makes you the right person to speak at his memorial with me."

It was one of the greatest honors I've ever had, to be the only speaker at Earl Nightingale's memorial service besides his widow, who showed us slides plus a video clip from Denis Waitley and told stories of their life together. Earl's son David was in the audience that day. It was overwhelming to me. Even today I get chills thinking about it.

Nothing could have convinced me that this was possible until it actually happened. If you are doubtful that your future could be much bigger than you ever dreamed, take heart: All the top achievers said the same thing at one point in their own journeys.

You can do this, too! You can transform your world, your worldview, and your life by following these success principles as I did. I'm not a gifted intellect, natural athlete, born salesman, or well connected socialite. My dad was a telephone repairman, and I graduated 176th out of the 430 in my high school class. **You can do this**. Just choose your field carefully and apply the ideas in this book daily until you exceed the tipping point where your habits change and your opportunities explode and transform your life.

Choose your field; decide now to become a leading authority in that field, and then dedicate an extra hour a day to personal growth until your dreams become a reality. You belong in the top one percent of the top one percent. You are worthy of this. What do you want? You can have it. Now earn it.

Stop reading for a while, and start writing down what you want. I'll still be here for you when you get back.

NOBODY SUCCEEDS ALL ALONE

DON'T TRY TO DO IT ALL BY YOURSELF. ALIGN WITH OTHERS OF LIKE MIND.

THE POWER OF A MASTERMIND GROUP

You can assemble a team of like-minded people who, like you, are committed to self-improvement and success. Napoleon Hill called this a "MasterMind Alliance." This does not start with everyone at the top of their game; rather, it is a collaboration among success-seeking peers for their mutual success. Everyone is better than you at some things, and not as good as you in others. Start today to increase your communication with the colleagues you admire. Then consider forming a collaboration with them.

What could you accomplish if you had a powerful board of advisors all focusing their energies on helping you succeed? My own life is a reflection of the influence of an amazing group of people.

I've spent 29 wonderful years in Speakers Roundtable; I was invited to join this amazing 20-person, invitation-only MasterMind alliance in 1986. In SR, due to life changes and other issues, members come and go over time. The group never exceeds 20 members, though. Members are chosen based on their heart as much as their mind or their success, and we've had some of the greatest speakers of the past two generations as members. Meetings are always profoundly inspiring. In a typical three-day annual meeting, you'll discuss your own business or life issues and then get input from people in their 40s, 50s, 60s, and some in their 80s—people who have "been there and done" whatever it is you're dealing with, people whom others the world over are willing to spend tens of thousands of dollars to learn from.

I have been truly blessed to spend three decades in the friendship and collaboration of these giants of heart and mind.

Give some thought to your own professional path: Who could you connect with and grow together with as you advance your craft and career?

P.S. You don't ask to join Speakers Roundtable; that's not how it's done. The members of the group ask you. We recommend that you form your own group with similar rules and learn from our example. www. speakersroundtable.com

Speakers Roundtable (SR) has existed since the 1960s as an invitation-only consortium of 20 world-class professional speakers and subject experts. SR members include owners of hundred-million-dollar companies, as well as solo entrepreneurs. They are a group of bestselling authors, trainers, entertainers, a hall of fame athlete, a military hero, a university president, plus speech coaches, business experts, consultants and, without exception, self-made successes.

Each of them has built his or her business through decades of disciplined creative effort, and today they guide others worldwide to do the same.

Together these current members have authored and published 160 books, many of them international bestsellers, and delivered over 80,000 paid professional presentations (as of 2016).

ACCESS TO EVEN MORE SELF-MADE, SUCCESSFUL PEOPLE

Recently I was the chair and host of an audio magazine, *Voices of Experience*. It's for the National Speakers Association, which has over 4,000 members worldwide. Every month I would interview people who were successful entrepreneurs and self-made successes—self-made multimillionaires in most cases. I interviewed over 100 people that year and edited those down and published the monthly magazines.

In addition to the VOE, I hosted a discussion "salon" for many years at the Sherwood Country Club in Thousand Oaks, California. We called it "Sherwood Parlor." This was a series of two-hour living room discussions of important ideas among interesting people. I'd bring in amazing guests and soon learned that my attendees were often even more impressive than my guests. Guests included: the commander of the space shuttle, an astronaut, movie stars, music producers, professional entertainers, philosophers, authors, world leaders in various fields, a famous stunt man, a friend of Thomas Edison, psychologists, and more. Attendees were a mix of billionaires, scientists, inventors, ambassadors, Olympic athletes, concert musicians, university professors, world leaders, and builders of impressive institutions. We discussed profound ideas and personal stories.

On top of all of that, I guest-hosted a drive time radio show in Ventura, California for a season and did interviews with some of the biggest names in the business world. In short, I've learned from the best of the best.

TEN VITAL TRAITS OF SELF-MADE MILLIONAIRES

Here's what I've noticed. Out of over 100 half-hour interviews with celebrities, Olympic champions, survivors, Internet marketers, event promoters, mountain climbers, talk show hosts, entrepreneurs, inventors, and investors, I found a few things:

1. **None of them succeeded by accident**. Not one single person stumbled into a large level of success. They were, every single one of them, intentional.

2. **All of them were voracious students of success**. They were constantly reading, listening, observing, reflecting, researching, going to meetings, pulling people aside, and saying, "Can I ask you a couple of questions?"

3. **Every one of them intentionally changed themselves as needed**. They looked at themselves objectively. They said, "This habit is paying off. This habit is holding me back," and they changed themselves over time.

4. **None of them did it alone**. They connected with other people in smart ways that could multiply their talents, instead of trying to be strong and independent. They were looking for ways to be stronger and well connected.

5. **The most successful among them had structured their work life so that they spent most of their time doing what they were well suited to do**. They were careful to use the prime time of each day to use their major strengths, because that was going to multiply the outcome exponentially. Then they outsourced their weaker talents to other employees or to apps during their off hours.

6. **All of them were eager to share what they had learned**, and they were generous as long as the recipient of that generosity was humble and willing to work. In other words, they weren't willing to waste time on somebody who wasn't going to learn and do the work, but they were absolutely willing to invest time in people who were eager to grow and willing to do the work.

7. **The most successful people among them were also the most trustworthy and likable**. They were good people. People often have the mistaken idea that rich and powerful people are jerks who are all just greed machines—but that's absolutely the opposite of the truth. Most of the people who have done extremely well are the people you'd want raising your own kids.

8. **They assumed there was a way to succeed, no matter how big the obstacles seemed.** In other words, they were all optimists who faced reality boldly but assumed that there

were solutions somewhere and that they'd find them if they kept looking.

9. **These successful people also all kept the numbers, their success metrics**. They tracked their progress and ratios and watched the reports, and they were always aware of the "score" in what they were doing.

10. **They were all absolutely committed to succeeding in their field.** They committed, no matter how long it took or how hard it became. They would change course only after exhausting all possibilities in this effort. They decided to figure out how to make it and stayed the course to get it done.

How many of these traits currently describe you?

You may share traits with these people, but you cannot achieve their levels of success without reflecting the right kind of attitude.

Every one of these self-made millionaires seemed quite comfortable with their own limitations. They'd say, "I'm not good at X." They didn't make any bones about it. They just thought of a situation around it, like looking at a car and saying, "It doesn't fly. I guess if I want to go across the country quickly, I'll need to find a plane."

We ought to do the same thing. Just figure out what you're not particularly good at, and then get the tools or the information to do it, or outsource it to a helper.

Take the wisdom of these achievers, and apply it within your circle. A big part of being in a mastermind group is your willingness to be open and vulnerable, to tell them the truth about what you're dealing with and what you're aspiring to. Then they can give you real, meaningful feedback to help you through tough times. Even the most successful, brilliant, and enlightened will have times of fear or depression. It just won't last as long, because they don't wallow in it.

KEEP THE FLAME ALIVE!

For any career to thrive, there has to be a bigger purpose than just being successful. Money is only a motivator to the extent that there's not enough of it. Motivation beyond money tends to wane, unless you have a higher purpose, cause, or mission.

Here are two examples: One is Four Seasons Hotels, top of the world luxury hotels, and the other is Disneyland Resorts. In both cases, the leaders … Isadore Sharp founder the Four Seasons Hotels and the late Walt Disney, founder of Disneyland, after putting people in place, working out the systems, and determining all the hardware, they realized that their job had changed, and that their new job was selling the vision. Every day they were reselling people on the importance of their cause. For Disney, it was The Happiest Place on Earth; for Sharp, it was Extraordinary Experiences.

I sat next to Kenny Ortega on a plane years ago. Kenny Ortega is the guy who designed the animated musical fountains for the Bellagio Hotel in Las Vegas. He orchestrated the opening and closing ceremonies of the Winter Olympics, the one that Mitt Romney was in charge of in Salt Lake City. He was also the producer of the Michael Jackson movie *This Is It!*

I said to Kenny, "I would think that the toughest part of being the planner or orchestrator of the opening and closing ceremonies with all the thousands and thousands of people you had to influence would be keeping the flame alive inside each person." In other words, getting each person not to just look at their task but to realize how vitally important their part was to the fabric of the Olympics.

He said, "Oh, my God!" I said, "What do you mean?" He said, "Nobody notices that. That's *exactly* what the main job was." That's it.

It's also true of us as entrepreneurs. What's our main job with our team? Getting the

> ### HOW I MOTIVATE MYSELF
>
> *"Go the extra mile. It's never crowded"*
>
> *George W Foster III*

people to embrace the DNA of our organization. What's the DNA? The genetic code: the vision, the mission, the values, the goals, the standards, the level at which we've chosen to operate.

When they buy the dream in their heart, you get their behavior as part of the bargain. When all you do is acquire someone's compliance, then what you've got is the equivalent of a machine in a flesh package and that machine is only productive when you're watching it and it's turned on because at the end of the workday their work effort is turned off and they're thinking about being something else. You have to win their hearts if you want to win their mind and body. This applies to you and me as well.

HOW GOALS WORK

When you set a goal, it's not really a goal if you already know how to reach it. If you already know how to reach it, it's just a "To-Do." A goal should exceed your awareness of how to get it done so that it always inspires you to be a bit bigger, find better resources, leverage things, and look for new ways. If you're not a little afraid that you might not succeed, then you won't grow to your best.

It is important that you get this: You don't need to know how to get there. Yet. You just need to know whether you really want it.

Think of a goal as a magnet. Until the goal is crystallized and committed to, there is no magnetic pull. It's just something you've thought about. Once you commit to achieving it, then it starts drawing the questions, the resources, the challenges, and the dilemmas for you to resolve so that the answers reveal themselves.

I found that even Cavett Robert, the founder of the National Speakers Association, who gave his first paid speech at age 61, was still studying at age 89. He was still sitting in the front row at seminars and speeches and taking notes on people's techniques. The "dean of personal motivation," Earl Nightingale, was a student up until the day he drew his last breath.

Everyone I've ever truly admired has been a voracious learner. Students notice more than mere observers.

INTELLIGENCE IS THE ...

The essence of intelligence is making distinctions, and noticing details, patterns, and principles. If you decide to become more intelligent about your business or finance or interpersonal relations, the first thing you should notice is what's going on in a broader context—then zero in on the patterns. Ask, "How can I learn that? Should I use that? What does this lead to?" People need to think in terms of the domino effect, not just the domino.

As you've read, in 1976, at age 30, I weighed 200 pounds. I'm 5' 9". Today, I weigh 150 pounds. I decided in 1976 that I was tired of being fat; at the time, I smoked two packs of cigarettes a day and didn't exercise at all. I said, "I've already proven many times over the years I can diet successfully, so I don't want to go on a diet. I want to *become a slender person.*"

What was the difference between a slender person and me? Not just weight, but also lifestyle, habits, and thought patterns. I spent three to five years just reprogramming the way I thought about myself, about food, about life, about daily routines. I did this by listening to inspiring messages, repeating positive affirmations, reading books, and committing to new habit patterns until they paid off.

As a result of this, I went from being a fat smoker who didn't exercise to being a fit, 148-pound athlete who will never smoke another cigarette, cigar, or pipe for the rest of his life, period. I didn't *try* to quit smoking—I quit smoking. I gave away the ashtrays and cigarette lighters, and I told all my friends, "I'll never smoke again as long as I live."

Of course, I went through three months of physical and psychological withdrawal; that was miserable. After that, I was free. Today, I run mountain trails three days a week and work out in the gym on the other days. I ride motorcycles, and play rock and roll in nightclubs professionally; and I'm still active as a professional speaker doing presentations all around the world.

You don't need a new, trendy diet. All the diets specify the same thing: Reduce taking in things that aren't good for you. Increase the burning up the calories that you take in. You already know what to do—you need the commitment to begin. Start now on your main goal.

THE FUTURE YOU SEE DEFINES THE PERSON YOU'LL BE

Every day ask yourself, *How would the person I'd like to be do the things I'm about to do?* The Acorn Principle™ is the seed of your future successes already lives within you - so Nurture your Nature!

As you apply the Acorn Principle in your life, you, too, will live more abundantly. As you "nurture your nature," the results you seek will come to you. The person you become will attract the relationships and opportunities you desire. Possibilities will arise that you could never have predicted. Great moments will occur as if you, personally, had been singled out by God for a special blessing. When you dedicate yourself to the ongoing process of personal growth, good things will happen in ways that will amaze you.

Success is not a contest, nor is it a mountain you must struggle to climb. Success is your birthright. It is your natural state of being. Sure, you'll have to work at it. You may even have to develop some new habits. But personal growth (the natural process that creates a successful life) is not drudgery. It is fun!

Ask anyone who is living a highly productive and happy life, "What is it like to develop new abilities and bring out your best?" They'll pause, smile, and tell you, "It is great! I can't imagine living any other way!"

SECTION THREE

268 ONE-MINUTE LESSONS IN SELF MOTIVATION

Start each day with one of these messages in order to lift your thinking and remind yourself of ways to become the person who would achieve your goals.

Write an action note for yourself after reading each of these one-minute messages.

One of the best ways to motivate yourself is by behaving as the best person that you can be. The more reasons you have to respect and admire your actions, the more easily you'll get yourself to do what needs to be done.

1. Where Are You?

Sounds silly to ask, doesn't it? You are here, right where you are sitting at this moment. But what part of the package is YOU? Is your body you? Your mind? Your behavior? Your ideas? Your thoughts? What part of you is actually you?

It is my belief that YOU are the being that inhabits your body, not your body itself. You are the occupant of your mind, not your mind itself. Otherwise, why would we say "my body," "my mind," "I had a thought"? There has to be a being that is doing all these things. That being is the real you.

You are the master of your body. You can control your thoughts; you can choose your behaviors, select the habits you desire, and become more than you have ever been. Or you can abdicate that ability and just let nature take its course. I suggest that you take charge of you.

The next time you say, "I was thinking..." pause to realize that you are not your thoughts—instead, you direct them. When you say, "I'm overweight," stop yourself and restate it as, "My body is currently overweight." You can change that if you choose. People aren't fat, slim, tall, or short—their bodies are. The Person is the free spirit that lives within the body, and the Person has the freedom to choose thoughts and behaviors that make life better, whatever they are.

What actions will you take on this idea?

2. Who Should You Take Time to Thank?

The more genuine gratitude you express, the more good things come to you.

Last year I was reflecting on some of the turning points in my life, and I remembered Bill Webster, the trust officer at my hometown bank when I was in my twenties. At that time, I wanted to become a bank trust officer, so I went to see Bill.

He gave me a book on trust services and asked me to call him when I had read it. Three days later, after devouring the book, I called on him again. For a short while he became my mentor.

I called him recently and asked if he remembered me. He said, "Yes, I think I do." I told him how grateful I was for his encouragement those many years ago.

He replied that my call couldn't have come at a better time. He had recently experienced a stroke, and his physical therapist was on the way over for his first rehabilitation session. He then thanked ME for encouraging him!

Who should you take time to thank?

3. Do It Right the First Time!

Have you ever considered how much of your day is spent in double-checking, re-doing, or correcting work?

If everyone did things correctly the first time, supervision would be unnecessary. Errors and omissions insurance would be obsolete. Most lawsuits would not exist. By simply doing what we agree to do, the first time, we eliminate the need for cabinets full of legal files, extra inspections, and follow-up notes.

When we recently renovated our home, the drapes had to be re-measured and replaced, three service calls never fixed our air conditioner, and... well, you get the picture.

When something isn't done properly, it costs:

1. The time and resources to do the initial work.

2. The calls and correspondence to correct the problem.

3. The cost of undoing and redoing the job.

4. Lost productivity from other work you would have done.

5. Missed opportunities.

6. Diminished customer loyalty.

7. The pride of ownership that is missed.

Low quality is not just a bad idea; it can destroy your business. Let there be "quality workmanship" on earth, and let it begin with you and me.

What actions will you take on this idea?

4. Live Your Beliefs

Bill Patrick called me on a Wednesday and said, "You are preaching a sermon for me next Sunday."

I laughed aloud. I'm not a preacher, nor even a deacon in the church. I quickly informed Bill that he should call someone else.

But Bill insisted that I was the man for the job. He said, "Jim, you have the skills, the experience, and the beliefs to do this job well, and I need for you to do it. I have to travel to Boston, and there is nobody else to cover for me. I have outlined the service and made notes of all that you need to know; all you have to do is follow the notes and develop a sermon."

After much anxiety and prayer, a message finally occurred to me. Here is the structure of that Sunday's message:

1. Know what you believe.

2. Explore and test what you believe.

3. Live what you believe.

In every field, we need to know what we think is true, test it by study and experimentation, and finally put our full effort behind acting on that belief.

Walk your talk; live your beliefs.

What actions will you take on this idea?

5. Fanatical Dedication

Every great achievement is preceded by a period of fanatical dedication. When there is a big gap between you and your goal, the only reasonable way to bridge that gap is by being unreasonably dedicated... at first.

"Moderation" is not the key to success. One might exercise with moderation to STAY fit, but nobody BECOMES fit by exercising in moderation. Great athletes are fanatics—they show up earlier and train longer than their competitors, and they win. They learn to love the work.

When building a new business, it consumes your every thought. Every person is a prospect or resource. You become a fanatic about it, at first.

When you totally commit to a goal, you tap your full potential. Then, once you have bridged the gap, you can do your work "in moderation." To get to the top, give it all you have got—be a fanatic, at first.

What actions will you take on this idea?

6. Get Over It

To what extent is yesterday interfering with your ability to enjoy today? How much baggage are you carrying into each day? Do you carry resentment or grudges for betrayals, insults, or hurts in your past?

Well, get over it!

I don't mean to be harsh or insulting. It is just that our "baggage" sometimes keeps us from living effectively—and it really doesn't have to.

Consider how much good energy you have wasted over the years by dwelling on the past. How many times have you told the story of how you were wronged or how bad someone else was? I'd say it is time to get on with living. End the soap opera today, and just accept that it happened—then thank God that it is over so you can go on with your life.

I once heard someone say, "Don't tell other people your troubles, because half of them feel their own troubles are worse than yours, and the other half are actually glad that you are unhappy." So, get over it, and get on with living.

What actions will you take on this idea?

7. Punishment Doesn't Work

I've noticed that punishment almost never works. The intent of punishment is to prevent people from repeating a wrong—but this doesn't work.

Punishment does one thing very well; it stimulates fear and resentment. It causes the person we are punishing to look for ways to avoid us in the future. But it does not cause them to discontinue the bad behavior.

If it did, our prisons would produce good results. People would go in, serve their time, and then return as productive members of society. Instead, people go in, serve their time, reinforce their criminal mindset, learn how not to get caught, and, often, return to a life of crime.

I believe that people should be held accountable for what they do or don't do. But make the consequences fit the actions. Have them right their wrongs instead of endure punishment. If you took someone's property, restore it. If you harmed them, repair the damage. Make it right again.

We must be fair and compassionate when wrongs are done, but we must also assure that lessons are learned. People learn only when they are held accountable, not when they are punished. Of course, evil people need to be segregated from others but not to punish them, instead to keep us safe from them.

What actions will you take on this idea?

8. Pub Wisdom

In Edmonton, Alberta, I saw the following quote on the wall of the Sherlock Holmes pub:

"Life should not be lived in such a way that you arrive at the grave in perfect condition, looking your best. It should be slid into sideways with a cigar in one hand and your favorite beverage in the other, totally used up and unsuited for further activity. Fully spent and screaming, 'Wow! What a ride!'"

Isn't that a great attitude? Though I don't suggest we get totally used up, I do recommend that we live our lives fully. If there is something you have wanted to try, put it on your list and go for it. Don't just accept the ruts that others have trod before you—blaze some new pathways. As Earl Nightingale once said, "A rut is just a grave with both ends knocked out." Get outside of your routines, and live more fully.

As I've said before, the purpose of life is living, really living!

What actions will you take on this idea?

9. Saying, "Thank You" Isn't Enough

Just saying, "Thank you" is not enough. When we want to thank somebody, we should make sure that they hear our thanks—not just audibly, but also emotionally. Which is more important: that we say, "Thank you," or that the person *feels thanked*?

It is the impact of our actions that counts most, not just their intent.

Here are a few ways you can express gratitude beyond just saying the words:

1. Send a handwritten note.
2. Mention the praiseworthy action to others.
3. Give a smile and gesture of thanks.
4. Do something in return.
5. Praise the person's good qualities.
6. Show them respect.
7. Honor the person.
8. Remember their generosity over time.

The greatest advice I've ever heard on gratitude and service is this: "Give without remembering; receive without forgetting."

Only keep score of what you are happy about. Let the rest fade away. A grateful disposition is an irresistible quality to have.

What actions will you take on this idea?

10. Optimism Is the Best Attitude

What is the difference between an optimist and a pessimist? The easy answer is: An optimist looks for the possibilities, while a pessimist looks at the limitations.

But I challenge you to find a pessimist who will proudly admit it. They fear that optimism is a denial of limitations and drawbacks. So they say, "I'm not a pessimist; I'm a realist." Then they proceed to explain how your project just "can't be done."

Well, let's pull back the curtain and expose them right now. A realist is just a pessimist who won't admit it!

I say optimism is the only productive mindset. We need to see obstacles for what they are: temporary limitations. We need to understand that in spite of all the pain and discomfort, life is still worth living; for every disease we contract, we almost always recover. There are brighter times ahead—new friendships waiting, possibilities within the limitations. Your life will be much happier, you will find more solutions than problems, and others will love to be around you. Smile and be a true realist, with an optimistic outlook.

What actions will you take on this idea?

11. What If the World Disagrees with Your Plans?

No matter how hard we work or how much we prepare, sometimes our wishes don't come true—at least not in the short term. Flights get cancelled, machines break down, emails don't get through, people change their minds, and emergencies interrupt our progress.

Someone said, "Want to make God laugh? Tell him your plans!"

So what do you do when things just don't go your way? It might help to expand your perspective. Try to see the bigger picture.

If you think of a marriage or a friendship in terms of a lifetime, you don't get so upset about little daily disagreements or discourtesies. When a child is learning to walk, we do not become alarmed that they have fallen down on each attempt. We keep our perspective on the lifetime goal of learning to walk.

Let's show the same courtesy to ourselves when the world seems to disagree with our plans for today. Think of the bigger picture.

What actions will you take on this idea?

12. Give More Than You Have To: Overfill Your Space

Nothing advances until somebody does more than they have to do. Give more than you have to. What is the quickest way to get a raise?

First give your employer and your customers a raise by increasing your service to them.

In the long run, people get paid for what they contribute. There may be short-term exceptions, but overall, this is how things work. So focus on what you could do. Look for ways to add quality or a more cheerful attitude to your work.

During the Great Depression, humorist Will Rogers said, "There is no shortage of work! There are fields to plow, fences to mend, packages to deliver. There is plenty to do. You may not get paid for doing it, but you won't get paid for doing nothing either."

Watch the people who always deliver more than they have to; you will see them advance much farther than those who are awaiting a raise in pay first.

Look for a way to increase your contribution today. Do more than you have to do. You will be glad you did.

What actions will you take on this idea?

13. SPITS: Solve the Real Problem

When you encounter a problem, stop first to examine the cause. Find the source, then solve the problem.

Here is a model I use in my consulting work that you can use day to day to determine what is causing your problems. Use the acronym SPITS: Ask if it is a Situational problem, a Personal problem, an Interpersonal problem, a Technical problem, or a System problem. SPITS.

Then address the problem at its source.

In the words of the philosophers, a problem clearly identified is a problem half solved.

What actions will you take on this idea?

14. How Do You Sell an Idea or Product?

People don't buy just because they understand your offer. They buy because they feel understood by you. Too many salespeople think they make sales by merely educating the buyer as to the wonders of their product. But, in fact, people decide to buy only when they can see that the seller understands their needs and wants and is trying to address them honestly.

The old approach to sales put the emphasis on the pitch or sales presentation. Today's approach is to put the focus on the solution the sale will bring.

So the next time you are trying to sell something, start by asking questions and listening to the answers. Then show how your offer solves their problem. And when you are the buyer, notice how you feel about buying, then notice how you feel toward the seller. Chances are good that you will buy from people you trust, not just people who have an impressive sales pitch.

I teach the concept of "Relationship Selling." Both the relationship and the sale are important. Selling should be an act of friendship, not a process of manipulation.

What actions will you take on this idea?

> **HOW I MOTIVATE MYSELF**
>
> *When I feel less than motivated, I stop and tell myself, "Remember your reason why you wanted it then use that once again to keep going."*
>
> *Bob Choat*

15. Success Has to Be MADE

Success doesn't just happen; it has to be made. Consider the word MADE as a memory tool for increasing your success:

M—Mental pictures. Visualize the success you want. See it in your mind. You will see it in reality only after you first see it in your mind. Skeptics say, "I'll believe it when I see it." Optimists say, "You will see it once you believe it."

A—Affirmations. Talk in positive terms; don't allow yourself to complain. Speak as if the success were already yours. Be optimistic about your success.

D—Daily Successes. Make sure that each day has some small successes in it. Doing the little things well adds up to producing big successes later.

E—Environmental Influences. Surround yourself with support: quotes, posters, positive books, people who encourage you, etc.

You can make your success more likely by controlling what is around you. You can do it.

What actions will you take on this idea?

16. 336 Impressions

A typical golf ball has 336 impressions on it. Each one has to be near perfect for the ball to be ready to sell. How many impressions do you make in a normal workday? How many of those are near perfect?

We meet people constantly. We talk with them on the phone, email them, see them in person, and write to them. We continually make impressions. What kind of impressions have you been making lately? The more we intentionally control the impressions we make, the better the effect we have on others.

Think about how you make impressions:

1. Your personal appearance, your workspace, your home.
2. The words you use, your tone of voice, eye contact, your handshake.
3. Your typing, spelling, and handwriting.

4. The things you talk about, the places you go, and the quality of your work.

5. The people you associate with.

All of these leave impressions. Decide today to leave more positive impressions tomorrow. You will be glad you did.

What actions will you take on this idea?

17. You Are Part of a Chain

When my grandson was about to be born, I gave my daughter-in-law a little treasure chest with an acorn in it. I told her that the acorn represents the seed growing within her. It holds the potential of all future generations of our family.

The cap on the acorn represents us, the parents and grandparents who watch over it and protect it until it is ready to grow on its own.

The stem on the cap represents its connection to all the generations that have gone before it. Their contributions have added up to what this acorn is today. It carries their legacy.

I told her, "You carry within you the hopes and dreams of all these ancestors. Their future comes together in you. Both your family and ours are now joined forever in this beautiful chain of life. Thank you for honoring us with this child."

I cried, she cried, my son and wife cried, all crying tears of happiness for the future and of gratitude for the past.

You, too, are that acorn. So live fully and honor your future and your past.

What actions will you take on this idea?

18. 1000 Days of Exercise

A few years ago, I had gotten out of shape and become overweight once again. So I decided to do some exercise every day. My goal was to go an entire month without missing a day. Some days I did full workouts, and some days I just did a few sit-ups and push-ups. But every day I did something.

When 30 days passed, I went for 100, then a year—and finally, 1000 days of consecutive exercise. I got back into top shape and lost weight. On the thousandth day, the American Council on Exercise supervised and photographed my workout. My sense of accomplishment was tremendous!

It would have been so easy to quit, but I didn't want to start over.

One late night, I even did a quick set of pushups in a parking lot, dressed in a tuxedo, just to get some exercise in before driving home at almost midnight. Silly, yes, but it worked for me.

My plan was simple: Exercise some every day. My goal was reachable, and my success was sweet.

How could you use this same strategy to reach your personal goals?

What actions will you take on this idea?

19. Trust Is Power

We grew up believing that Knowledge Is Power, but that is not true.

In a world where knowledge is limited and restricted to a privileged few, yes, knowledge is power. But in a world with the Internet, with universal access to most knowledge—in that world, Trust Is Power.

We are more connected than any generation in history. We can communicate with almost anyone on earth. In such a world, the person who is most trusted by others is the one with the most potential for influence, the most power.

Of course, we need knowledge—we must be lifelong learners—but that is not our edge. Our advantage comes when we gain the trust of our coworkers, neighbors and friends.

The great anthropologist Margaret Mead once said, "Never doubt that a small group of thoughtful, committed citizens can change the world. Indeed, it is the only thing that ever has." When we trust each other, we multiply our power. You are capable of so much more when you have the trust and cooperation of others. So multiply yourself, and build and earn trust.

What actions will you take on this idea?

20. Notice More

The essence of intelligence is the ability to make distinctions. The more we notice in any situation, the more ways we see to deal with it. So, to be more intelligent on any subject, begin by noticing more about it. See it from many points of view.

In your own field, you pick up on patterns in people or things that others simply don't see. That is because you have been trained to think in a certain way. Mothers see what fathers don't. Lawyers see what salespeople don't.

On any topic you can do the same; just make it a point to notice more. Notice what you hear, smell, taste, see, and sense. Ask yourself, "Why is that so?" Explore more.

The person who notices the most has the most options, and the person with the most options usually wins. So start today to become more intelligent about something. To know more, notice more.

What actions will you take on this idea?

21. Premise Shapes Conclusion

Your premise will shape your conclusion. Whatever assumption you start with will direct and limit your outcomes.

If you believe something is impossible, you will see the limitations instead of the possibilities. If you assume that people are good, you will find good in them. If your premise is that homework is important, you will urge your kids to do their homework. But if your premise is that homework is an opportunity to develop a love of learning, then you will turn homework into an adventure!

Companies that believe customers will steal from them tend to have rigid policies and bad customer relations. Those who see service as a privilege tend to have loyal customers and very little theft.

Henry Ford, once said, "Whether you believe you can do a thing or not, you are right! "

The next time you take on a big responsibility, ask yourself, "What is my premise? What assumptions are guiding my actions?" Then make sure your premise will lead to the kind of outcome you truly want.

What actions will you take on this idea?

22. Really Living!

The purpose of life is living, really living!

Think about it: You are capable of so many things, and there is so much living for you to do. How alive are you?

There are people to meet, trees to climb, sunsets to watch, kids to encourage, movies to watch, letters to write, rides to take, compliments to give, solutions to invent, hearts to touch, systems to develop, books to read, hugs to give, ideas to share, and songs to sing.

People you know are hurting, things are malfunctioning, mistakes are being made, and important information is being overlooked or forgotten.

There is much to do! You are truly needed in this world. You can brighten someone's day, solve a problem, share a smile, and much more.

When you live fully, all of us benefit. When you don't, all of us are short changed.

Decide today to live more fully. It is what you were designed to do. You have the potential within you to make this world a better place, right here and now. Live it up!

What actions will you take on this idea?

23. Quality Time Is a Myth

For many years, people have recommended that we spend "quality time" with those we love. This is to compensate for the quantities of time spent on job commitments or other interests.

I say the intentional creation of quality time is a myth.

The quality of our experiences together isn't dictated by an agenda we follow, but rather by the quantity of time we spend together. Think of the most meaningful moments in your life. Many of them no doubt came about by surprise; they weren't orchestrated, they just happened. When your child says something that touches your heart, or when you offer a helping hand to your mom, that moment happens because you were available for it.

Learn to think of quality time as you would think of rainbows. They cannot be planned for; they can simply be discovered, and they should be savored while they exist. So make time for those you love, and be generous in your scheduling. They need you, and you need them. Just show up more often.

What actions will you take on this idea?

24. Can't Means Can't

Words have meanings, and they are not interchangeable. Each word has a specific role conveying our meaning to one another. For example, take the word "'can't." This word means "cannot." Most people use it way too casually.

How often do you say, "Can't" when you mean, "Haven't yet" or, "I'm having difficulty with" or, "Won't"?

When my son used to say, "Can't," I'd reply by saying, "So give up. Stop trying." He'd look at me in shock and say, "You really want me to give up?" I'd reply, "Yes, if you really 'can't', then your goal is impossible, so save the wasted effort and just stop. But, if you merely 'haven't yet' succeeded, then stay the course, and you might succeed. Use the word you mean, not just the easiest word to use."

Start today to notice how often you use the self-limiting "can't." Just keep a tally. As you become more aware of your word use, you will also notice more opportunities to use a better word to say what you really mean.

What actions will you take on this idea?

25. Go Talk to Strangers

Today I'm doing for a living what Mom said not to do—speaking to strangers. When I was little, she advised me not to talk to strangers when my parents weren't around. That was good advice at the time, but good advice has a lifespan, and this one has run out. Yes, it is still good for children to be cautious, but for adults, we MUST talk to strangers! The only way business will advance or most problems will get solved is if we intentionally and consistently talk to strangers.

Our goal ought to be to reduce the number of people who are strangers to us by several people a day. Salespeople must be skilled at connecting quickly with people they don't know and building trust. New neighbors, coworkers, teachers, and service people arrive in our world all of the time. Let's become very good at talking to strangers and making new friends of them every day.

What actions will you take on this idea?

26. How Important Is Acknowledgement?

Everyone yearns for recognition. We need for others to know we exist. In primitive cultures, one of the worst punishments was banishment, in which nobody was allowed to communicate with the guilty party. It was like solitary confinement without the walls!

On my first trip to New York City, many moons ago, I took a subway ride and saw miles of graffiti in and around the trains. What shocked me at first was that the graffiti wasn't profanity like on restroom walls; it was names, logos, and symbols. The "taggers" who painted it weren't being obscene—they were seeking recognition!

When you and I make eye contact with others, offer a smile, or say hello, we are validating the other person. We are giving them what all people yearn for: acknowledgement that we know they exist and that they matter. This is the quickest way to respect someone's dignity, and it is always appreciated. So look up, smile, say hello. Someone needs your acknowledgement today.

What actions will you take on this idea?

27. Forgiveness

I made a new friend last year. He is a man who counsels patients with cancer. His observation was that one of the most powerful cancer avoidance behaviors is the act of forgiveness. Simply letting go of the resentment of "wrongs" committed by others seems to remove some of the elements in our systems that support some cancers.

When we carry a grudge or harbor hard feelings, we also inhibit the healthy processes of our bodies. It is not easy to let go of hurts or betrayals, but it is in our own best interest to do so. Notice how your body and mind feel the next time you are offended by someone. Then let it go; forgive them and move on to something new. If you wait until they "repent" or apologize, then you could be waiting a very long time, and harming your own health in the process. If someone cuts you off in traffic, back away from them, pray that they don't harm anyone else, and go on with your day. The more you can forgive, the more peace you will have, and the fewer conflicts you will face. You might just live longer, too.

What actions will you take on this idea?

28. Learn to Savor Life

When I eat homemade vanilla ice cream, I have an almost spiritual enjoyment of it! I love the stuff. When I ride a motorcycle on a winding road, I am completely happy. The same is true when I'm playing my guitars and singing. But many times I have other great experiences happening around me, and I ignore them completely.

We need to remember to SAVOR life—to drink it in and enjoy every aspect of it. They say we should stop and smell the roses, and I often do. But when you smell a rose, make sure that you really savor it. Feel the soft petals, notice the colors, and drink in the smell.

Right now there are things you can savor. Notice your clothing, the seat you are sitting in, the beauty of nature, the conveniences available to you. Enjoy what you are experiencing. Have you ever watched a child as they ate their favorite food, rolled in the grass, swung on a swing, or slid down a slide? They are fully immersed in the experience. We all need to remember to do that. If you are walking, then enjoy the walk.

Take a moment and look around. Don't just do the next activity in your mind. Stay in the moment, and live your life fully. Do this well, and then move on. Savor it.

What actions will you take on this idea?

29. What Is a Citizen?

There is a difference between residing in a community and being a citizen of it. Being a resident is measured by location, being a citizen is measured by commitment!

Learn to be a good citizen in all the "communities" of your life. Neighbors who take care of their homes encourage others to do the same. Family members who do their own chores and assist others help to create more responsibility at home. Coworkers who look out for you cause you to also look out for them. Citizens who obey the laws, vote in elections, and do good works are a joy to be around.

How do we have more peace in the world? By being more committed to citizenship! Remember that wonderful lyric: "Let there be peace on earth, and let it begin with me."

When we realize that we are dependent upon each other to behave responsibly, then we are motivated to do the right thing. As more people find that their neighbors and coworkers are behaving responsibly, they too will become better citizens.

What actions will you take on this idea?

30. The Platinum Rule®

My friend and colleague Dr. Tony Alessandra says we should learn to practice the Platinum Rule®: Do unto others as they would like to be done unto! This is actually just a new way of stating the Golden Rule: Do unto others as you would have them do unto you. But Tony's Platinum Rule® puts the other person more fully into the equation by treating people the way they would like to be treated. Not all people are like you. It is like the old statement of When in Rome, do as the Romans would have you do. They don't expect you to become a Roman they just expect you to understand that they are Romans.

To practice the Platinum Rule®, you have to first pay attention to each individual so that you understand them better. Learn to listen more before you speak. Try to determine how each person would like to be treated. The more you tune in to their preferences, the less tension you'll experience, and the more quickly you will build rapport with everyone you meet.

What actions will you take on this idea?

31. Remember the Movie *City Slickers?*

A classic line from that movie happens when the character Curly, played by Jack Palance, says that life is about finding that ONE THING that matters most to you and doing only that. Well, that may be oversimplifying a bit, but still, once you know what matters most to you, you can quickly reorder your priorities.

What one thing could you work on over the next month with all of your spare time to produce a major advancement at home or at work? What would happen if you did it? What would happen if you don't?

Let's say your one thing is money. If you decided right now to designate managing and producing revenue as your only discretionary activity for an entire month, how much good could you do? In the first day you'd find ways to save money. By day three, you'd have identified new ways to earn more. At the end of one week, you'd be organized and ready to manage all your money even better. By the end of a month, you'd have met new resource people, streamlined your finances, and strengthened your monetary world.

Find your one thing now. Make finding it your only priority, and then go to work on it with all you've got.

What actions will you take on this idea?

32. Dad, I Want My Own Money!

At age 13, my son asked me for a bigger allowance that would allow him to control his own money. I agreed but stipulated that it had to work like the real world. He had to determine how much he'd need in a year, and then report to me each month what he had earned and spent. I helped him determine everything he'd need money for, then we came up with an annual budget. Beyond the budget, he'd just have to get a part-time job for extra money. He agreed.

The rub came when I required him to turn in a simple monthly record of expenditures and income to get his next allowance check. It took a while for him to accept this feature, but once he did, he was his own boss!

For several years he recorded where his money went and where it came from. He also started a savings account, and by the time he went off to college, he had saved over $3,000! It wasn't as easy as I make it sound here, but it did really work. Today he knows how to manage money. How will your kids learn to manage money? By the way, most public schools don't teach personal money management.

> **HOW I MOTIVATE MYSELF**
>
> *"At the end of life, we will never regret the things we risked doing... We will only regret the chances we never took."*
>
> *Jasun Light*

What actions will you take on this idea?

33. Things That Last and Things That Don't

When my son was learning to manage money, I had him keep a record of expenditures categorized by "Things That Last" and "Things That Don't." I intended to teach him the difference between assets and experiences. A meal, a movie, or a game is an experience. A book, a shirt, or a skateboard is an asset. Both have their places, and it really helps if we keep them in mind.

As you look over your credit card bill or checkbook record for the past several weeks, which column has the most entries: assets or experiences? If you are close to retirement age, the assets column needs to be longer. If you are financially secure, then maybe you should add more to the experiences column. Either way, it needs to be a conscious act. The more aware you are of what you are spending your money on, the more your assets and memories will last.

What actions will you take on this idea?

34. Peter Urs Bender

I once had a speech booked in Toronto, and my colleague, Peter Urs Bender, called to offer me a ride from the airport. As we drove, he gave me a list of facts about Toronto that I could weave into my speech the next day. Upon reaching the hotel, he departed with a smile and wished me well. I had invited him in, but he politely declined. What a wonderful gesture! His hospitality was straight from the heart; he gained no benefit other than being generous, and he won my lasting admiration. He is an excellent example of a generous spirit.

Too often we give generously but then spoil it by expecting gestures of gratitude. When you give, just give. The joy is in what you've done, not in what the recipient does in return. When we give, let's follow Peter's example:

1. Take the initiative—find an opportunity to serve, and act on it.

2. Give something that the user can benefit from.

3. Give without expecting anything in return.

Postscript: Many years later, I got a call from Peter while driving my car in California near my home. He sounded weak and serious, so I pulled over to talk with him. Peter was dying from cancer, and this was one of the calls he made to say goodbye. His gentle soul will be missed. I'm still stunned that he took the time to call me to say thank you for my influence in his life. He is the one who deserves my thanks.

What actions will you take on this idea?

35. Velocity

I once saw a cartoon of a snail on the back of a turtle. The snail was screaming, "Wheeeee!!"

I suppose for him it was a joy ride, but for others it was just a crawl.

People are like that; we have different energy levels. Some of us are high-velocity types with loads of energy and drive. Others are lower in velocity and prefer a slower pace. What about you?

Everyone has a predisposition toward high, moderate, or low velocity, and there are places for all of them in society. The low-velocity folks do better when working on a team, while the high-velocities prefer independent action and lots of change.

You should know your own velocity. If it is low and you become an independent sales rep, then you will burn out sooner. If it is high and you take a clerical position, you may go stir-crazy. Learn to fit your lifestyle, work habits, and goals to your natural velocity. This act is called "alignment," and it leads to a more satisfying and less stressful life.

What actions will you take on this idea?

36. Romance

Experts agree that the most romantic place in the world is... between your ears. It is the mind that creates and experiences romance—beaches, fireplaces, hot tubs, candlelit dinners, and even chocolate cannot compete with a great thought or gesture.

I once learned that my wife and I were traveling through the Dallas airport at the same time on separate trips. When I got to Dallas, I quickly went to her connecting gate and took a single rose to greet her. Trouble was, I was too late—her plane had already boarded its passengers and was about to close the door. Luckily I was able to persuade a gate agent to take the rose on board to Paula with a note from me. She was thrilled, and I was happy. I didn't even get to see her, but we had a romantic moment.

Was it the rose? No. It was the knowledge that I was thinking of her and was willing to go out of my way to show her some special attention.

Want to be more romantic? Look for a way to show the person that you care and are willing to take special steps to say so.

What actions will you take on this idea?

37. Don't Celebrate Weight Loss with Dessert

I've always been prone to becoming fat. As a youth, I tried several diets, and all of them worked—I lost weight. But I always gained it back. Since 1976, however, I have not been fat. For an entire generation, now, I've stayed within 12 pounds of my ideal weight. This is because I learned a fundamental truth: Slenderness is not the result of your diets. It is the result of your habits.

To change your weight, change your habits. To change your habits, change your thinking. Slim people think differently about food and exercise than heavy people. It is the mind that controls the weight. My niece once asked her mom for "skinny food" so she could lose weight; it didn't work.

Step one is to decide to become a slender person. Step two is to behave as slender people do, even if you are still heavy. Step three is to never stop behaving as a slender person. Your body will soon follow your mind. And, by the way, don't celebrate your weight reduction by eating ice cream. Buy new workout clothes, instead.

What actions will you take on this idea?

38. Changing People Is as Difficult as Nailing Jelly to a Tree

Have you ever tried to push a rope? Nail jelly to a tree? Carry water in your hands? Some things are just doomed before they start. But how many times have you tried to get another person to change their nature?

If someone is genetically disorganized, they will never become highly organized. They can do better, but it won't become their strength. In the same way, people who are adventurous will always explore. It is their nature to be curious and to try things "just to see what will happen." Will they ever be content to just sit still? I doubt it. But they can learn when it is appropriate to explore and when not to.

Everyone can improve—they can even change on some levels, but there are parts of us that never change. Once we learn to recognize people's nature, we can be more effective in working or living with them.

The famous Serenity Prayer says it all: "God, grant me the serenity to accept the things I cannot change, the courage to change the things I can, and the wisdom to know the difference."

What actions will you take on this idea?

39. If You Don't Stand for Something, You Will Fall for Anything

Everybody needs a belief system. Without something to believe in, we drift aimlessly from pleasure to pleasure, seeking happiness but finding only momentary good feelings. It's like eating refined sugar and expecting to get nourishment. It's not in there.

Happiness needs to be redefined. It used to mean "having a fulfilling and rewarding life", but today it often means merely good feelings. I believe that everyone seeks to be happy, but not just in a gleeful sense—being happy with their life and feeling good about themselves. Having self-respect and dignity.

When one believes in a higher power, they have a reason to think beyond their own lifetime. With this longer view, you gain a stronger set of values. From values grow standards and principles. From these grow ethical behavior. It is all connected. A simple intention to be a good person isn't strong enough to endure really tough times. We must believe in the greater good and be willing to put our own welfare on the line if necessary. Stand up for what you believe.

As the Declaration of Independence says, we are people who are "endowed by their Creator with certain unalienable Rights, that among these are Life, Liberty, and the pursuit of Happiness."

What actions will you take on this idea?

40. How Do You Know?

There is an organization called The Institute of Noetic Science, cofounded by astronaut Edgar Mitchell. They study what it means to "know" something, and how we know what we know—pretty high-minded stuff, but fascinating.

For example, take something you know to be true. Then examine how you know it. Are you sure about it? Here are some ways we conclude that we "know":

- » Personal experience—We saw it ourselves
- » Expert testimony—We heard it from a trusted authority
- » Scientific method—We tested it and proved it
- » Intuition—We know it on an unconscious level
- » Feelings—Our gut tells us it is so
- » Reason—We used logic to figure it out

None of these is a perfect source, and all could be wrong. But the more we respect each way of knowing, and the more we use multiple approaches, the more likely we are to reach a reliable conclusion. So the next time someone says, "I know this to be true," ask them, "Specifically, HOW do you know?"

What actions will you take on this idea?

41. Partnerships

I've had numerous business partnerships over the years, and I've learned that the most important part of forming a partnership is often determining how you will end the partnership amicably. This may seem to doom the relationship from the start, but that is not so.

For partners to be really effective, they must feel safe to fully commit to the relationship. If they are holding back, then someone is losing out. "All in" is good for business.

So, up front, ask yourselves, "How could we dissolve this effort with the minimum damage to either of us?" Determine who would get the assets, who would get which customers, how you would determine the value of various things, and who would get the company name. Once you are sure that you can fully commit to the task, then all your resources are empowered. Until that time, everyone is only tentatively involved.

The clearer the agreements are, the stronger the relationship is. Just as "good fences make good neighbors," so also do "good agreements make good partners."

What actions will you take on this idea?

42. Three Essentials for a Healthy Relationship

Drs. David and Vera Mace, founders of the Association of Couples for Marriage Enrichment (ACME), offered the following as three essentials for a happy marriage. I've also found them to be the essentials for a healthy business relationship:

1. Mutual Commitment—Both parties must be committed to the success of the relationship—otherwise one is carrying most of the load. Until both parties are committed, the efforts of just one will be fruitless.

2. Open Communication—Even bad news has to be okay to share. In fact, the more truthful and complete the communication, the stronger the relationship can be. We must be able to talk about the difficult and upsetting topics without attacking each other.

3. Clear Agreements—We must know what we expect from each other and what guidelines we agree to follow. Agreements should become conflict-resolving tools.

With these three essentials, any relationship will be stronger and happier.

What actions will you take on this idea?

43. Acknowledge the Value You See

In the Atlanta airport, I saw a busboy dragging himself from table to table wearily doing his work to keep the restaurant clean. He seemed so sad that even I was getting depressed! So I walked over to him and said, "What you are doing sure is important. If you weren't cleaning these tables, there would be trash everywhere, and people would stop coming in here." He was shocked. I said, "Thank you for making this a nice place to be," and I walked away.

In the time it took me to travel about 10 feet, he seemed to have grown a full six inches! He stood up straighter and wasn't smiling, but he had stopped frowning, and he appeared to be doing his work a little better. What do you bet he also felt better about himself and handled problems more smoothly?

All I had done was point out the value of what he was doing, but in doing so, I showed respect for and gave dignity to his work. All of us can benefit from taking the time to think about how our work is helping other people.

What actions will you take on this idea?

44. Learn to Chew More

Sometimes we should "bite off more than we can chew." That is how we increase our capacity. If you only commit to what you already can handle, then you may not grow. Once in a while, I think it is important to take on more responsibility than we can handle... alone. This forces us to reach out to others and to learn new ways to get much more done. People grow because they need to, not just because they want to.

So, occasionally give yourself a reason to stretch and grow. Fear of failure can be a very good motivator sometimes. I once said yes to a huge chairmanship when I had no idea how I could get it done. But I knew that others could guide and assist me, and I knew that I'd be willing to ask for their help. The net effect was that we succeeded, and I, and the others involved, all learned new skills in the process.

What actions will you take on this idea?

45. If You Can't Lead You, Don't Lead Me

Self-leadership is essential to success. If you can't lead and motivate yourself, then you will miss out on much that life has to offer. Here is the best definition of self-leadership I have ever heard: It is the ability to get yourself to do what needs to be done, when it needs to be done, whether you feel like it or not, and still do it well.

That entails a motivation to act, an understanding of the motives, a sense of urgency to complete it, and an ability to overcome your own moods and resistance.

How do you become a better self-motivator? Decide to. That's right, just make the decision to do so, and then don't turn back. Act on your decision. It's like New Year's resolutions—resolving to do them is easy. It is the actions after the mood has left that makes the difference. So learn to lead yourself, and others will soon want to follow you.

What actions will you take on this idea?

46. What Is Character?

Cavett Robert, founder of the National Speakers Association, once asked a college professor for the definition of "character." Here's what he said: "It is the will to carry out your resolve long after the mood in which you made it has left you." Not bad.

Most people let their moods manage their behavior—and most people don't get what they want out of life. I say, rise above your moods; don't let emotion drive your choices. Decide what you want, and then go after it even when you don't feel like it.

The next time you catch yourself saying, "I don't feel like it right now," let that be a call to arms for you. Add this phrase: "therefore I will take action now!" Let other people be guided by their emotions, while you become guided by your desired outcomes. Successful people are motivated more by the results they want than by the desire to have a comfortable journey in reaching those results.

What actions will you take on this idea?

47. Gracious Service Isn't Third Person

In San Antonio last week, a hotel restaurant waiter asked me, "Would 'the gentleman' like to see our wine list?" I was dining alone! I felt like saying to him, "I don't know, give me a minute to speak with 'the gentleman' in private, and I will let you know." Pardon my sarcasm, but I really think he was overplaying his role.

The waiter's intent was to be gracious and elegant, but the effect was silly. He could have said, "Good evening, Sir, would you care to see our wine list?" and the effect would have been achieved. When I speak to you directly, I acknowledge your importance as an individual, and I can show all the courtesy that is due. The aloof manners of the past are just that—past. In today's world, the best way to be gracious and elegant is to address people directly.

What actions will you take on this idea?

48. It's a Small World, and Everything We Do Leaves a Mark

Years ago, when I lived in Oklahoma, I got a last-minute call to fill in for a speaker who couldn't make it to a meeting. I was over 130 miles away but agreed to do it and drove to the meeting just in time.

Now fast-forward six years. I received a call at my new home in California from a prospective client in Belgium. The call led to my being hired for six trips to Europe and thousands of dollars in consulting work. As it turned out, the caller was the son-in-law of the man in Oklahoma who hired me as a fill-in speaker six years earlier! If I had been seeking business in Belgium, the last place I would have looked was Oklahoma.

Additionally, if I had done a half-hearted job in Oklahoma that day, the call from Belgium would never have come. Everything we do leaves a mark, so do your best, even when you don't think this one really counts.

P.S. It is now 30 years later, and I've been back to Europe for this client numerous times, even in recent years.

What actions will you take on this idea?

49. You Are Always Leading by Example

Somebody looks up to you; somebody uses you as their measure for how to do things. It is easy to discount our own value in the world—all we have to do is ignore the fact that others know we exist and that they are paying attention to us when we don't realize it.

Now, don't get paranoid and think that they are secretly watching you. That's not it. They are simply noticing you, just as you notice others. And some of them are using your example to help determine their own choices. Your children and the children of your friends and relatives surely do this. So do your coworkers, even the ones

> **HOW I MOTIVATE MYSELF**
>
> *"Whenever I have been in the mindset of "What can I get out of this?" I have always struggled. My motivation was always low. And then I started running because I wanted to be a grandpa. That was before I had a grandchild. I wanted to give my grand kids what I never had, a grandpa. I started running so I could live long enough to see my granddaughter graduate from high school, maybe even get married. I run for her. And when I don't feel like running, I run anyway. I'm going to be there and I'm going be in good health. Maybe I'll get to be a great grandpa. That reminds me, where are my shoes? I need to go for a run."*
>
> *Doug Stevenson, CSP*

you don't know by name. We can't avoid influencing each other if we are to live in society. I say, be more intentional about the examples you are setting. The better you run your own life, the better others will run theirs, because sometimes they are following your lead—even when you don't mean to be leading them.

What actions will you take on this idea?

50. Ronald Reagan

On the wall in front of my desk is a picture of Ronald Reagan. His son Michael signed it for me, and it inspires me every day. I most like President Reagan's optimism; he always looked beyond circumstances so that he could see the possibilities. He once said, "I know in my heart that man is good, that what is right will always eventually triumph and there is purpose and worth to each and every life." This statement is engraved on his gravesite. He also said, "I hope [history] will record that I appealed to your best hopes, not your worst fears; to your confidence, rather than your doubts."

Think of that attitude. Despite all the ugly realities in the world, he knew that people were fundamentally good. He believed that right would triumph over wrong, so he kept to the right path. He believed that every life was worthwhile, so he championed the causes that ennobled humanity and helped us advance. Let us do likewise.

What actions will you take on this idea?

51. "Faith in God Gives Meaning and Purpose to Human Life"

Those words were penned by William Brownfield as the opening line of the Creed of the U.S. Junior Chamber of Commerce, the Jaycees. When we believe in the existence of a good God, we see value in every life. We see purpose in living and seek to do what is right and good. It is not enough to just believe in being a good person or in karma. That limited view turns your life into a series of transactions, and there is not much satisfaction in simply winning a few hands.

I believe there is a Creator, a universal intelligence, and He knew what He was doing when He created us. This is not about debating the details of any one religion—it is about what caused the Big Bang and caused nature to evolve in such miraculous ways. The miracle of a human life is so complex that there can be no other satisfying explanation of its creation. Evolution of life forms is a proven fact, but we didn't evolve from fish or apes. We evolved from primitive versions of humans. We are not genetic accidents; we were intentional. Despite all we know, there is still no person in all of history who has ever been able to create life from nothing. Nobody, not even the greatest scientists, has brought a rock to life or created a baby. Yes, we can reproduce, but we don't determine which sperm and which egg actually become a person. Only Nature determines when and how life comes into existence. I believe that Nature can be another word for our Creator.

Look at the commonalities among all the religions of the Earth. The faiths that believe in life and a benevolent Creator all seem to have compatible fundamental principles. Even when the Creator is seen as a force or energy instead of a "person," the adherents to that faith seem to arrive at the same conclusions as to what truly matters.

My own views are Christian, but I don't feel that you too must be a Christian, or that only Christians have the truth. I just deeply believe that there is a reason you are here. There is much good that you can do. Take the time to do what you can. Make a difference, and prove to your Creator that you were a good investment.

What actions will you take on this idea?

52. "The Brotherhood of Man Transcends the Sovereignty of Nations" (The Jaycees' Creed)

When a huge earthquake hit Iran many years ago, Americans rushed to send aid, despite the tensions between our countries. When a tsunami wiped out Sri Lanka, we gave even more than we gave to the U.S. victims of the terrorist attacks on 9/11. Somewhere down deep, we know that we are all brothers and sisters. We realize that this world is bigger than us and that our petty fears and hatred are superficial. In the final analysis, we are all creatures of God, and we share the same human desires: to live a meaningful life without much pain and suffering.

We celebrate the joy of the human spirit in all countries around the world. We are, at our deepest levels, One with each other. The next time you find yourself criticizing the people of another country or faith, remember that they are doing the same thing you are: They are trying to live a useful and rewarding life so that they may rest peacefully at its end. As long as we are promoting more life, we have a common interest. Live more abundantly.

What actions will you take on this idea?

53. "Economic Justice Can Best Be Won by Free Men through Free Enterprise" (The Jaycees' Creed)

History has recorded the bones of many failed attempts to control people. The most tyrannical regimes have produced the worst net results. The economies in which central control is asserted strongly are also the least innovative and the least productive. From all these failed attempts, we have learned that control is the problem. People thrive in a free society, not an oppressive one.

Even within highly controlled societies, there are aspects of free markets. The free market always is fairer to those who produce well. A free society generates more art and beauty, more businesses and jobs, more creative solutions, and more generosity than any other society. Freedom is the key to human improvement. We are naturally suited to live abundantly; it is our birthright and our responsibility. The more we are free to pursue our dreams, the more we produce benefits to others as well.

If your family, business, or community is lacking in innovation and initiative, try expanding people's freedom to serve and contribute in the best ways they can. Free people with low taxes produce more tax revenue to their governments than heavily taxed people do. Think about that.

What actions will you take on this idea?

54. In the United States, We Are Governed by Laws, Not by Personalities

Despite any news reports or editorials to the contrary, the truth is that in America we are committed to following laws, not individuals. That is very healthy. Even when we don't admire a person holding political office, we still trust the system that they and we all follow.

Consider the most radical countries on earth. Don't you always see them parading their military weapons and huge photos of their leader? Aren't they also usually the most angry and hateful people? When we put our welfare into the hands of someone else, whom we consider more enlightened, more powerful, more significant, we should be careful to do so thoughtfully. Otherwise we give up the very thing that makes us effective: our own good judgment.

A collaborative society will almost always do better in determining their own future than any one person who rules over them. In U.S. society, each person is considered to be just as powerful as the representatives we put in office. We put them in office through our votes, and we can replace them. That means the power truly does reside in all the people, not just one individual. Use your own good judgment, often.

What actions will you take on this idea?

55. What Is the Most Valuable Thing on Earth?

Diamonds? Platinum? I believe, like the Jaycee's Creed says, "Earth's greatest treasure lies in human personality." When you measure what all other resources have contributed to the world, nothing even comes close. Look back over your own life. What were the most valuable moments of all? Your times with other people. Even your own accomplishments would be meaningless if it weren't for the presence of others. No other source holds the rewards and solutions that one personality does.

Consider that every great thing that ever existed started first as an idea in the mind of one individual. The greatest ideas, the most generous contributions to others, the largest cities, the finest hospitals, the best products, and the most beautiful works of art all began with people. You hold more potential to serve the world than anything you could own. You are a treasure.

What actions will you take on this idea?

56. What Makes You Feel Better Than Anything?

Is it a great meal, a swim in the ocean, a funny movie, a treasured belonging, a comfortable bed? Is it watching children play or being applauded by people you admire? All of these are highly appealing, and they matter, but helping someone gives you the most lasting, warm glow.

We are designed to serve each other. We are instinctively drawn toward it. So let's take more initiative to act on these giving impulses. The quickest way to overcome depression is to help someone else. When we help others, we stop thinking about ourselves and start focusing on them. The greatest societies in the world are those that continually reach out to help their fellow man. The greatest families and companies are also intensely service-oriented. Look around you for needs, and you will see opportunities each day to be of service to someone else. Take the time to reach out. You will be very glad you did.

What actions will you take on this idea?

57. How Many SNUPS Do You Have?

A SNUP is something that you do regularly that Serves No Useful Purpose. Here are some examples: following old habits, like watching extra hours of TV long after your favorite shows have ended; stacking up procrastinated paperwork so you avoid the work for now but triple the work waiting for you later; paying your bills on the day before they are overdue; putting off a dental appointment, thus increasing the amount of drilling that will be needed when you finally go; ignoring offensive or dangerous behavior in your kids, all the while knowing that there will be more of it if you don't correct it now.

None of these behaviors leads to a good result. Here are some more: saying "I can't" when you simply haven't tried yet. Telling people what they want to hear, instead of telling the truth. Sugarcoating bad news, thus leading others to underestimate the need to take action. Our world is filled with useless behaviors. So try to assure that YOUR world is SNUP free.

What actions will you take on this idea?

58. Friends

Ralph Waldo Emerson said: "A friend is a person with whom I may be sincere. Before him I may think aloud." When you are a true friend, you accept your friend as they are, warts and all. You may not approve of all their behaviors, but you accept them as a person. They know that despite their occasional missteps, their friendship with you is not in jeopardy. That means they can be themselves around you, and you around them.

It is rare to find someone like that—so rare, in fact, that most people don't have many true friends. Emerson also said, "A friend may well be reckoned the masterpiece of nature." Friends can have arguments and still be friends. They can be inconsiderate, insensitive, and even rude on occasion, while the friendship remains. That is because you accept each other's humanity and frailty. At the same time, we are committed to helping each other enjoy life and survive its threats. When we are together, we can be ourselves; we can think aloud.

What actions will you take on this idea?

59. A Child Once Said That Listening Is *Wanting* to Hear

There is a big difference between merely hearing something and truly listening to it. Listening is an active behavior; it involves seeking the message, not just hearing the words. When you truly listen, you seek the meaning in the message, and you honor the other person by doing so. Everyone loves a good listener. They console us when we are hurting, admire us when we are expressing ourselves, and learn from us when we are teaching. One of the great insults is to be ignored, and one of the great compliments is to be listened to.

Learn to be an active listener. Focus your attention on the other person, ask what they really mean, restate their message to assure that you got it, and show them that you care about what they are saying. When you do this, they will respect you even more. You don't have to agree with people to be a good listener. You simply have to work to truly understand them. So don't just hear what they say—listen for their meaning.

What actions will you take on this idea?

60. How Many Types of Friendship Are There?

I can think of best friends, business friends, neighbor friends, and community friends. The differences in each group lie in the degree of commitment between you. With best friends, the commitment is deep; with business friends, it is limited to business dealings. Neighbors may be active in our lives but not truly close to us; the same is true for others in our communities.

I believe that the essence of friendship is the acceptance of and mutual concern about each other. When I accept you as an equal or a colleague, I honor you. If I am also concerned about your well-being, then I value you.

Make a list of the friends in your life. List all of them—the ones you don't know well, and the ones you do. Then ask yourself, *Have I shown them that I value them? Do they know that I consider them my friend?* Sometimes others who would like to be your friend are simply waiting for a signal from you.

What actions will you take on this idea?

61. Honesty

Many years ago, I was considering the purchase of a collection of motivational recordings by Earl Nightingale. I didn't have much money, so I told the salesman, Harold Gash, that I would just make copies of a friend's collection. Harold inquired as to why I wanted the recorded messages, and I told him that when I listened to the tapes, I was inspired to become a better person. He then said, "Okay, you can go ahead and duplicate the recordings your friend has bought, but will you make me a promise?" I said, "Sure." He said, "Will you promise as you duplicate these copyrighted messages to listen closely to the one on the subject of honesty?"

I was mortified! Here I was trying to grow and improve, and I had naively chosen to be dishonest in the process. Self-improvement cannot be acquired by riding on someone else's coattails, or by avoiding payment for what we get. You cannot steal your way to being a better person. We each must pay our own way. When we do, we respect ourselves more, and we know in our hearts that we deserve the new success we achieve.

What actions will you take on this idea?

62.   Hold Yourself Accountable

One summer, I set a goal to run 10 miles nonstop by New Year's Day. For weeks I ran each day and lengthened my run significantly. Then around Thanksgiving, I slacked off. But on New Year's Eve at about 5:00 p.m., I remembered my goal. It was snowing outside, but I put on several layers of clothing, a ski mask, and gloves. I warmed up, then set out on the run. The cold was painful, and ice formed on my ski mask as I trudged on in the dark toward my goal.

When I got home, my wife was at the door waiting to snap a photo. Today I have the photo in my desk showing my frozen ski mask, my snow covered feet, and a smile stretching from ear to ear under the mask. The pride of accomplishment far outweighed the pain of the run, and I still take pride in the accomplishment today.

When you set a goal for yourself, don't wait for others to hold you to it. Do it for yourself. You will be glad you did.

What actions will you take on this idea?

63. What Is a Best Friend?

Not all friends are equal—some qualify as a "best friend." But what is a best friend, and how do you get one? I believe that "best friend" is a category open to everyone; it is not a contest among good friends for the top position.

Here are some of the requirements to be a best friend: You must consider the friendship to be forever, not just as long as you "get along well." You must also sustain the commitment to each other despite long periods of no contact. A best friend thinks about you and acts in your best interest sometimes, even when you haven't asked. A best friend is an extension of you; they are family to you. You include them in your victories, and you tell them your fears. You remember their attributes, and you forgive their failures. A best friend is one of the world's great treasures.

What actions will you take on this idea?

64. How Does Friendship Develop?

Friendship is a connection between people based upon trust and mutual affection. When you like someone, enjoy their company, and care about what happens to them, you are their friend. Sometimes friendship comes about because of a similarity to someone. Other times it comes from shared values, or it develops over time as you see the value in each other.

But friendship requires an active commitment. An acquaintance is simply someone you know; a friend is someone you care about.

Show your friends that you care about them. Don't just tell them—show them through your behavior. Send a thoughtful note of congratulations, encourage them when they are down, drop in on them when appropriate, and call to see how they are. Listen for what they are feeling. Accept them without requiring them to change. Praise them for their good qualities. Find ways to show that you consider them your friend.

What actions will you take on this idea?

65. There Is a Famous Acronym Known as WIIFM

It stands for "What's In It For Me?" Sales people are encouraged to think about the benefit to the other person by answering that question for them. But here's a twist that changes the dynamic significantly: Try asking yourself daily, "What's In It *From* Me?" In any situation, instead of thinking about what you are going to get from it, instead ask what you have given to it.

This is similar to John F. Kennedy's famous quote, "Ask not what your country can do for you; ask what you can do for your country." Try it today as you approach your next activity or task, ask yourself, "How can I give more to this activity to make things even better?"

What actions will you take on this idea?

66. The Strangest Secret

In the 1960s, Earl Nightingale recorded a famous album titled *The Strangest Secret*. His message taught that you become what you think about. I'd like to refine that a bit.

I have found that you are drawn toward what you think about. So if you think about a goal every day, you will be drawn toward its achievement and be motivated to attain it. If you think of yourself each day as a confident and capable person, then you will become more confident and capable. Conversely, if you dwell on the negatives and worry, you will be drawn toward what you fear.

Thoughts are things and it truly matters what we allow ourselves to think about. Those who learn to guide their thoughts away from the negatives and toward their desires are almost guaranteed better results. So what have you been thinking about lately? Focus on what you want, not what you fear.

What actions will you take on this idea?

67. The Will, Not the Skill

My friend Jim Tunney, a veteran NFL referee, wrote a book called *It's the Will, Not the Skill*. Isn't that the truth? When it comes to achieving significant things in life, the determining factor is almost always the will to achieve. In any situation where one person's motivation to succeed is greater than that of another person with higher skill, the motivated one will win.

Skill is simply latent ability. Until the will activates it, nothing happens. And having the will causes you to overcome resistance, bounce back from setbacks, and persist till you win. So don't worry if you don't yet have the skill to do what you desire; the desire alone is enough to get you started. Then, as you

HOW I MOTIVATE MYSELF

"I have very real conversations all the time with my future-self. So often that he has become my closest confidant, most focused coach and most honest advisor. When I have something that appears to be a huge hurdle in front of me I ask my future-self what it looks like on the other side. He has always been there to encourage me and assure me that the "huge" challenge in front of me was just a little bump in the road that he had no problem with. In fact, he often tells me that some of his greatest lessons were learned overcoming that challenge so I need to pay close attention as I successfully pass through to the other side."

Denis Nurmela

develop those skills or connect to the skills of others, you increase your capacity to succeed. It is the will, not the skill, that will get you what you want.

What actions will you take on this idea?

68. When It Comes to Personality, There Are Four Types

You can divide any group of people into four basic personalities. They've been called by many names over time, but I simply call them the Director, the Relater, the Socializer, and the Thinker.

Directors like to run things; they thrive on being in charge and they're motivated by results. Relaters prefer teamwork and supporting others; they are motivated by relationships. Socializers love to talk; they thrive on interaction and are motivated by activity. Thinkers seek accuracy and thrive on details; they are motivated by perfection. Directors and Socializers move quickly. Thinkers and Relaters move slowly. Directors and Thinkers focus on the task. Socializers and Relaters focus on the person.

The next time you meet someone, notice which traits they show and how they match or differ from yours. Are you a Director, Relater, Socializer, or Thinker?

What actions will you take on this idea?

69. Learn from Everyone

Ralph Waldo Emerson said, "Every man I meet is in some way my superior; and in that I can learn of him." It's true—everyone knows something you don't, even the people you wouldn't normally respect or admire. When you approach each new acquaintance with a student's attitude, the whole dynamic of your relationship is different. You value the person, and others can feel that.

Have you ever met someone and somehow just known that you would like them? How about the opposite, when you just knew something was not right between you and another person? We can tell when others don't value us, even if they don't show it in obvious ways.

So, every time you encounter another person, ask yourself, "What could I possibly learn from this person?" Then look beyond the obvious and try to sense the way that they look at the world. Even a homeless person understands life on the streets better than you do. There's always something others know that you don't. The more often you notice this, the more effective you will be. Before long, you will be eager to meet everyone.

What actions will you take on this idea?

70. Lighten Up!

Stop stressing over things that only matter to you emotionally. When life is unfair to you, get over it quickly. Take each misfortune as a mere course correction rather than as a catastrophe. And for heaven's sake, don't keep score!

When someone wrongs you, just deal with it and get on with living. Don't try to get even. First of all, you can't "get even"; you can only do more harm. And second, doing so will only prolong the bad feelings. If you lose money, or if your property is damaged by other's negligence, bounce back. Think of it as you would if a storm had damaged your garden. You wouldn't sue the weather service or spend weeks complaining about the damage or how unfair it was—you'd simply get to work to repair your garden! Do the same in all areas of your life. Lighten up! Let go so that you can grow.

What actions will you take on this idea?

71. Tighten Up!

Sloppiness in life allows more variables to creep in and spoil your plans. Stay on target, increase your self-discipline, and master the art of self motivation. When you and I neglect things and allow a mess to develop, we diminish our own self-discipline. It's like neglecting a muscle and allowing it to atrophy.

Set standards for yourself, and keep to them even when you don't have to. If you always keep a neat home or office, you will also tend to be better organized, feel better about yourself, welcome others into your world, and stay more optimistic. All things are connected—sloppiness in one part of your life spills over into other parts as well. Go clean out your closets or your garage. The best way to do this is to take action the very second that you think to do so. Don't say, "I'll get to it later." Do it immediately! Tighten up, and enjoy the extra leisure you create.

What actions will you take on this idea?

72. The Eight T's of Motivation

Here are eight words that begin with T that you can use to motivate yourself and others:

1. Target: Make sure you are clear as to what you are doing and why.
2. Tools: Without the information or equipment to do your job well, you will proceed slowly.
3. Training: Have you accessed the learning that can make you even better at what you do?
4. Time: Has there been enough time for the training to sink in through trial and error?
5. Tracking: As you proceed, be sure that you track your progress and show everyone where they stand.

6. Truth: Get the big picture, and see how everything fits into the overall plan.

7. Touch: Allow for the human factors. Make sure that everyone gets the encouragement and support they need.

8. Trust: Assure that each person is trusted just a bit more than they currently deserve. Allow room for growth, but not so much trust that you put everyone at risk.

What actions will you take on this idea?

73. Lifelong Learning

Remember your graduation day? A powerful experience, graduating. And yet, the concept of "graduation" sometimes does us a disservice once it's over. When we graduate, we assume that we are done. But life doesn't work that way—learning is never over until our life is.

A cartoon caption once said, "Lord, please don't let me die until I'm dead!" Some people certainly do—they stop learning and cease to grow. When we just withdraw from life and vegetate in front of a television or computer screen, we cease to "live." For those folks, life is pretty depressing.

Humans are intelligent creatures; we need new information and experiences. Consider your education to be never-ending. Mark each "graduation" as a "commencement" of a new phase of learning. Keep looking for things to explore, people to meet, problems to solve, experiences to gain, places to go, books to read, and lessons to learn. Stay alive as long as you live!

What actions will you take on this idea?

74. Living a Balanced Life Is a Myth

The way most people approach life balance does not work! Life is a mixture of personal, professional, mental, physical, social, emotional, and spiritual experiences. They cannot all be separated; we are whole beings, not a collection of modules. When you are at work, your home life is still part of you. When you are studying, you still have physical needs. When you do anything, the rest of you is participating.

To keep your life in balance, just make sure each part of your life gets your full attention occasionally, as it needs it. But address each one in its time. Don't multi-task to the detriment of each task. Work fully on one at a time. The spillover effect will pay off, too. Intentionally work on your physical fitness, and your thinking will improve. Learn new ways to be a better student, and your relationships and your work will improve. Develop your people skills, and you will see payoffs in all of your life.

What actions will you take on this idea?

75. Behavioral Economics

Every behavior has a value, and the lack of certain behaviors also has a cost. When you learn to think of your actions as you would think of your money, you gain much in applying yourself where the payoffs are greatest. For example, what is the value of preparation? In some cases, it is everything! General Eisenhower, as commander of Allied Forces in WWII, said, "Plans are worthless, but planning is everything."

The value of planning lies in how it prepares the planner to control things. Their written plans are often obsolete before they are implemented. It is the behaviors that have economic value. How valuable is courtesy? When we are courteous, we reduce tension, increase trust, and often gain cooperation from others. That value can be measured. So start thinking of your actions as having monetary value. Look at procrastination as a money waster. See accuracy as a wealth builder.

Note that following through on promises actually grows your reputation and builds cooperation. That is Behavioral Economics.

What actions will you take on this idea?

76. Love to Learn

Which is more valuable: getting your child to do their homework, or getting them to love to learn? If they do their homework, they are bound to learn something, but that doesn't mean that they will enjoy it. In fact, some people find being forced to study has de-motivated them from further learning. We need to cultivate in ourselves and our children a genuine love of learning. We need to make it fun and fascinating.

Look for ways to incorporate learning into everyday life. Keep track of what you learn. At dinner, ask everyone, "What is something that you learned today?" Make a ritual of answering this question daily. When it becomes second nature to ask it, it will be more likely that each person will seek good answers to it; they will seek something new to learn. Instead of making learning about getting good grades, make it about understanding new things. Don't keep a scorecard at home—leave that to the classrooms. Just cultivate a joyful attitude about learning.

What actions will you take on this idea?

77. Guard Your Mind

You are, today, the result of all the thoughts, experiences, and information that has gone into your mind. And you can control what goes into your mind from this point forward. In fact, you must, if you are to assure the future you want to have.

Notice what you read and listen to daily. Pay attention to the mix of sources you are exposed to. Calculate what percentage of it is positive and uplifting, and what percent is not. For example: Gangster rap vs. fun music; horror novels vs. biographies; soap operas vs. comedies.

Next, notice what kind of conversations you have daily. If you spend a lot of time complaining about society, the government, and other people, then your overall outlook will become more cynical. Increase the percentage of good thoughts, happy conversations, enjoyable music, useful information, and encouraging comments in your normal day. You can control your view toward the world by controlling what goes into your mind. You control it already—is it going the direction you would like? If not, make a conscious change.

What actions will you take on this idea?

78. Wheee!

Everyone loves to go, "Wheee!" You know what I mean—it is the feeling you get when you slide down a slide, skate on ice, ski on fresh snow, or surf in the ocean. It is also the feeling that comes from a bicycle, motorcycle, convertible, or private airplane. Somewhere deep inside, we are designed to love the feeling of sliding or floating or riding free. A jet ski or hang glider has the same effect for people, as do the more radical sports like bungee jumping and parachuting.

How do you get your "Wheee!" experiences? You may brush this aside as too trivial and unprofessional, but somewhere inside I know that you love it too.

The next time you are gliding across a dance floor or sliding down a banister, just stop to notice that it is a common human desire to go, "Wheee!" And life without an occasional joyful moment isn't nearly as much fun. Go for it.

What actions will you take on this idea?

79. E-Contact

In the industrial era, we were taught what I call "eye contact" skills for success in face-to-face meetings: Give a firm handshake, look them in the eye, use their name, speak clearly, and focus on their interests.

Well, today, many of our encounters are not face-to-face but rather ear-to-media or face-to-computer-screen or -smart-phone. Today we need to supplement the "eye contact" skills to become e-contact skills. Here are some quick tips for human relations via e-mail. (Many also apply to texts.)

The subject line is your appearance. How quickly you get to the point is the strength of your handshake. The degree to which you talk about their interests versus yourself is your eye contact. The way you say things in the message is your tone of voice. And whether your message is for their benefit or for your own is your courtesy. The same elements are needed in order to build trust, but they take different forms when it's via e-contact.

What actions will you take on this idea?

80. Loose Ends

One of life's great frustrations is unfinished business. Leaving things incomplete means that they are always waiting for us when we find a moment to relax. Then we have the new dilemma: Do I tie up the loose ends now, or save it for later?

Procrastination can ruin your days. I say, Resolve your unfinished business now. Figure out what you have left undone, and get it out of your way. Say your apologies, face your fears, pay your debts, express your gratitude, and clean up your messes. Either deal with it or discard it, but don't keep it lurking in the shadows just waiting to interrupt your next attempt at being productive or relaxing completely.

It is a huge error to assume that there will be a better time to finish your work. Now is the best time, and if you do it now, even though you don't feel like it, you will have it out of your way forever. Give yourself real freedom—finish your unfinished work and get on with joyful living.

What actions will you take on this idea?

81. John Lee's Four D's

Time management expert Dr. John Lee talks about his "four D's of time management." It is a way to cope with big workloads and get back into control of your life. He says the four D's are: Drop, Delay, Delegate, and Do.

First, ask, "What tasks could I drop altogether without suffering any real loss?" Much of the "work" awaiting our attention is so relatively unimportant that it would not matter if it ever got done. Drop it. Then ask, "What items could be delayed until I have more information or resources to get them done?" By now, you will have cut your workload in half. Next, ask, "What could I delegate to others so that it gets done soon and is off of my desk?" Then finally, do what is left. Do things by importance, but get them done. This should greatly reduce the workload that faces you and allow you to intelligently stay in control.

What actions will you take on this idea?

82. Charitable Giving Is Up

More people are giving more time and money to others than ever before. Despite all the cries you hear about greed and selfishness in the world, there is more generosity than ever. The types of charities that get the resources constantly evolve, but the amount of overall contributions is up.

People are fundamentally good, and when they see a need, their impulse to help is strong. Witness the huge outpouring after the tsunami that hit Indonesia and other disasters around the world. Some of us give money, some give time, some give goods, and others give influence, but all are making a difference.

What could you give? Time, Treasure, Talent, or Tools? Think of the causes and people that you care about, and then ask, "How could I give to them best?" Don't just give things; consider giving your skills or your support. Also ask, "What do they really need?" Sometimes we want to give more than others really want to receive, so make sure your help is needed.

What actions will you take on this idea?

83. What Do You Want?

Someone once said, "I can tell what you want by what you have." I asked, "How?" They said, "Everyone gets pretty much what they want—they just don't realize it."

If you want relaxation more than money, then you will have lots of time to yourself but not much wealth. If you want money more, then you will spend your leisure time working to build wealth. If you want a better job, you will be working to deserve it. If you simply idly wish for a better job, then your actions may not earn it. People get what they really want, not what they wish for. If it is not affecting your actions, then it is highly doubtful you really want it.

What do you really want? Are you working to deserve it? How could you shift your actions and wants so that the more significant ones get more of your energy and attention?

What actions will you take on this idea?

84. Who Is Managing Your Reputation?

You can decide what reputation you want and earn it within a relatively short time. Your reputation is the net result of your choices, your performance, your relationships, and your standards of behavior. Others know you by how you conduct yourself on and off the job, by what you talk about socially and how you talk about it, by the way you conduct yourself when others aren't looking, and by how you treat other people. Those items are within your control.

So decide today what reputation you would like to have a few years from now. Then ask yourself, "How would the person with that reputation do what I am doing today?" As you conduct yourself more and more like the future you, your reputation will advance, and your success will probably grow right along with it.

> **HOW I MOTIVATE MYSELF**
>
> *"Music! Certain songs help me to find my motivation."*
>
> Gerhard Apfelthaler

What actions will you take on this idea?

85. Your Relationships Define You

Your life is pretty much the sum total of your interactions with others, so the people you regularly associate with are the primary factor in defining your life. Change the people you see each day, and you change much of your life. Who are the main people in your life? Look beyond your family to everyone in your world. Where do you go each day? Who do you see and interact with there? Who do you spend time with on the weekends? Who do you turn to for advice? Who do you have fun with? Who is your best friend? Who do you consider to be someone like you?

We define ourselves by choosing who we spend time with. That determines what we talk about, because the subjects have to interest both of us. What we talk about most often determines the direction of our life. I suggest you take control of your relationships by listing everyone in your world today, evaluating what they bring to you and what you bring to them, and then choosing to grow the relationships that will bring the most value to your life on all levels.

What actions will you take on this idea?

86. Read More

Author Charles T. Jones says, "Five years from now, you will be the same person you are today, except for the people you meet and the books you read." I say, Read more! The old saying of "A person who doesn't read is no better off than one who can't read" is very true.

How much reading do you do? It has been shown in some studies that the average U.S. college graduate only reads about 1.25 books per year. Most say that they read much more: blogs, newspapers, magazines, e-mails, and occasional reports. Yes, that is true, we take in a lot of information each year. But reading books is different.

Books, both fiction and nonfiction, are structured differently from other media. More thought is given to the writing, more structure to the message. You can move at your own pace, rereading and studying them over time.

Find some books today that fascinate you. Set a goal to read a book a month, and see how much richer your life becomes. Everything you want and need to know is somewhere in print. Make the bookstore your new hangout.

What actions will you take on this idea?

87. Grandparents Are History Teachers

What are grandparents for? I became a grandfather several years ago. It is interesting to note the roles that parents and grandparents play in the family. Parents are the nurturers and guides who mold children's character and build their skills. But grandparents are the history teachers.

At first, they are the hyper-nurturers who spoil the kids and are always on their side, but as children grow, grandparents become expert guides. They teach techniques and skills; they tell stories of family history; they show the child the world in ways their parents cannot, yet.

My mother became a great-grandmother, and each time we got together with her, she shared stories from long ago that clarified who we are and how we became that way. She told of the roots of family traditions. She showed how we are all connected to the many who have gone before us. She made life more meaningful by showing us that we are part of the ongoing chain of life. I wish I could have spent more time with all my grandparents. How about you?

What actions will you take on this idea?

88. Art vs. Craft

At age 10, my son took a painting class, and I asked him if he could paint a picture of a country road in Vermont that I had seen in a magazine. He took it to school, and his teacher showed him how to paint that picture. He was very young, and his work was fairly primitive, but the finished painting was remarkably good. There was one problem though: At one point he had made a mistake, which remained obvious even after painting over it. I asked if he could fix it to look more like the photo, and he did.

His teacher, however, was appalled! She said I was stifling his artistic creativity by asking that he fix it. She missed the point that this was craft first and art second. If it had been "art," then his creative impulses would have taken priority over the accuracy of the painting.

In many endeavors, the same distinction can be useful. First we must master the craft of doing our work well, and then we can express the art of our unique contribution. Art without craft is primitive. Craft without art is dull. Both have a place.

What actions will you take on this idea?

89. What Is Value?

I once saw a globe made of semiprecious stones on a base of lapis. It was beautiful! But the art gallery wanted $3,000 for it, and I couldn't justify the purchase. A few years later, on a trip to Colorado, I saw the same kind of globe priced at $1,000, so I bought it. Last week I saw the same globe in a catalog for $297. Rats! I overpaid by $700. Or did I?

What determines the value of something? Certainly comparison is part of the buying process, but also there is a thing known as "Use Value." The value that you get from something should be the primary factor, in my opinion.

I love my globe. It is great to look at and regularly generates compliments from visitors. In use, I am getting full value from my purchase. A good way to determine the value of anything is not by just comparison-shopping, but rather by asking how useful it is to you. Art has value, tools have value, and services have value, but each must be considered in light of what it does for you.

What actions will you take on this idea?

90. Too Late to Start?

When is it too late to start something new or big? Well, ask Cavett Robert, founder of the 4,000-member National Speakers Association. He gave his first paid speech at age 61 and went on to create the professional association that today gives scholarships and education to thousands.

Norman Vincent Peale wrote his bestseller, *The Power of Positive Thinking*, at age 53. Henry Ford built his first car at age 45. Colonel Harlan Sanders started Kentucky Fried Chicken at age 65. I'd say the way to know that it is too late is by asking if you are still alive.

As long as you can generate a thought and draw a breath, you can make a difference. It is never too late to do something good. Even if others do the finishing work, at least you can get the ball rolling. What would you like to do that you have been delaying? Get started today!

What actions will you take on this idea?

91. Acknowledgment

One of my good friends grew up in a home in which her family didn't respond very openly. If you said something to them, they felt no need to openly acknowledge it. They heard you, and you were expected to know that. I'd go crazy in that environment! People like me thrive on acknowledgement.

How about you? It really is just basic courtesy to reply. By the way, it is not whether you reply that matters—it is whether the person you are responding to KNOWS that you have responded. When we don't know if someone heard us, we keep on talking or wait until we do.

Make it a habit to respond noticeably when others are communicating with you. My friend knows that I need feedback, so when I get no reply from her, I simply request, "Acknowledge please," and she does. Awkward, sure, but better than arguments, by far.

What actions will you take on this idea?

92. Advice

Most people are happy to offer advice when asked, but what about when you aren't asked? If you have advice to offer, it is very helpful to ensure that the other person wants to receive it. I am a professional speaker and consultant—I give advice for a living. In 40+ years of addressing audiences, I have found that my first job is making them want to hear my suggestions. If I were to simply get on stage and start giving advice, most audiences would reject it. But when I spend a little time conversing with them, showing them that I understand who they are, and establishing why and how I can be a resource to them, then they are eager to get my ideas.

How often have you offered advice only to have it rejected out of hand without even being considered? Frustrating, isn't it? People forget to help the listener see the value in listening. We have to sell the need for the information before people will buy what we are saying.

What actions will you take on this idea?

93. "Without Reflection There Is No Learning" –Kevin Buck

What would happen if, every day, you took time to reflect on what life was teaching you? There is wisdom to be gained from simple, daily living. If you examine the greatest moments of your life and identify what you did to make it great, you will probably discover some of your strengths.

By stopping after a movie or play to discuss its message with others, you not only observe, you also learn from it. My goal is to bring to your attention the patterns behind the circumstances—to help you notice what life has to teach you. Please take up the cause on your own. Go beyond what I'm bringing here, and seek ways to make learning an integral part of every life experience.

As Eric Hoffer wisely said, "The learners shall inherit the earth, while the learned shall find themselves perfectly suited for a world that no longer exists." Always learn, always notice, and always care.

What actions will you take on this idea?

94. Angels

If you ever wonder whether you have a guardian angel, try this exercise. Look back over your life, and think of things that you could have done, might have done, or wanted to do and then couldn't. Then look at how things turned out.

For example: I recall many instances over the years in which just a slight difference in my behavior could have produced disastrous consequences. In traffic, I often act on an impulse without understanding why, only to discover that I just saved myself from an accident. I don't know if we have guardian angels or not, but I do know that we are often protected from our own choices in unexplained ways.

Sometimes getting in your own way could have been the worst thing to happen to you. At other times, it's the opposite. Chalk it up to luck, subtle cues, or a guardian angel. Either way, we need to respect that from God's point of view, getting our own sweet way might be the worst thing for us, sometimes.

What actions will you take on this idea?

95. Anger Turned to Attitude

There were hundreds of stranded travelers, and we were all standing in lines to be rerouted by the airline gate agents. Many were venting their anger at the agents and each other. My emotions were going the same direction; my frustration was building, but then I remembered that I could control my own attitude. I took several slow deep breaths and asked myself, "How can I think differently about this?"

I decided to see it as an opportunity to learn something unexpected or meet someone who would be valuable to me later on. So I set my frustration aside and said to myself, "You are here, and nothing you can do will change that. Others are having a hard time with this, but you can be an example of calm and pleasantness. Now go do it."

It was not easy, but I did it. The gate agent was amazed that I wasn't upset. She thanked me for being so pleasant, and she let me board the next plane early. I didn't get a free upgrade (those were all gone), but I made a new friend and got treated better as well. All from one quick question: "How can I think differently about this?" Ask this question when you need a new point of view.

What actions will you take on this idea?

96. Art

I own a painting that I never intended to buy, and I love it. Paula and I were in an art gallery, passing time before dinner. We saw a nice painting, and the salesman asked if we wanted to see it in a different light. I said, "No, thank you," but Paula said, "Yes!" He took it down and moved it to a viewing area, and we gave it our full attention. Then he asked if we'd like to take it home to see how it looked in our living room. Again, I said, "No, thanks," and she said, "Yes!" After discussing it, we agreed to the trial purchase. We kept it and are enjoying it to this day.

There are three reasons we own it:

1. The salesman offered to help us examine it.

2. The salesman gave us a trial purchase with return privileges.

3. My wife wanted it, and I love my wife.

Which of these reasons was unimportant? None—all were vital to the buying decision. As Red Motley once said, "Nothing happens until somebody sells something."

What actions will you take on this idea?

97. Attitude

I like the old saying, "It is your attitude, not your aptitude, that will determine your altitude." Clearly that is true: The people who rise to the top of any endeavor tend to be those who have the right mindset and dedication to get there, not merely the ones who are smartest or best equipped to succeed.

Happily, your attitude is within YOUR control. Think of it this way—attitude is not mood, it is perspective! If you shift the way you look at something, you shift your response to it. For example, if you see a cancelled flight as a disaster, then you will spiral into despair. On the other hand, if you see it as a forced opportunity to rethink the situation, then you will look for new approaches and may even be able to eliminate the need for the trip. You might be able to have a conference call instead of the visit. It's all in how you look at the situation.

What actions will you take on this idea?

98. Authenticity

Remember Grandma's advice when you needed reassurance? "Just be yourself." That may well be just what many of us need to hear. When we stop trying to impress others with our intelligence, credentials, connections, and charm, we inevitably make an even better impression. Ironic, isn't it? By just being yourself, you will impress and charm more people than when you try to mislead them.

I recall times when others intimidated me. Those were always situations in which I thought I wasn't impressive enough. But when I recall the times I've had the greatest acceptance by others, those have been times when I was not self-conscious or trying to impress others.

The same is true for all of us. If you truly want to be accepted by others, don't try to impress them; just take an interest in them, and show appropriate respect. When you focus on them, you avoid focusing on yourself, and you will "just be yourself." After all, that is all you can be.

What actions will you take on this idea?

99. Babies

I loved a greeting card that read, "Your baby's not spoiled... they all smell that way!" Someone said, "A baby is God's opinion that the world should go on." It is in our genetic code to produce, nurture, and protect our offspring. Some people love kids, while others find them intimidating. Most people who say they don't "like" children actually mean that they are unsure how to behave toward them.

My wife loves to nurture the youngest, most helpless infants, while I prefer the kids I can communicate with verbally. I love to tell them stories and help them discover things. Now that I am a grandfather, I find that I always have a new story about my grandkids.

You and I are naturally endowed with the ability to be parents. That doesn't mean we don't need to learn more about being *good* parents, but we already have most of the basic instincts. So the next time you encounter a child, don't worry about what you need to do—just take an interest in the child. Listen to them, ask their opinion, and tell them the good qualities you notice in them.

What actions will you take on this idea?

100. Being in Business with Your Mate

Many years ago, my wife quit her outside job and came to work in my company. When she did, at first we had many awkward moments in which our marriage relationship was confused with our working relationship. Then one day we sat down to discuss her new job. Instead of focusing on our relationship as mates, we focused on the responsibilities of her new position. As we both learned to separate the marriage roles and job roles, the awkward moments disappeared!

Any time two people have a personal relationship plus a working relationship, they need to be clear as to the roles, the responsibilities, and the expectations of each. The role is what you are paid to do—the results, not just your actions. The responsibilities are areas you are in charge of. The expectations are the standards you have agreed to achieve. Clarify these, and the rest of the job will take care of itself. Remember, your job relationship isn't your marriage relationship.

What actions will you take on this idea?

101. Belief

If it is not affecting your actions, it is doubtful you believe it. I don't recall who first said those words, but they have motivated me for years. When we say we believe something, the quickest way to determine if we mean it is to check our behavior.

Do you believe that you can do anything you set your mind to? With few exceptions, I have found that to be true. We can, with the help of others, do pretty much anything we decide to do. So what do you want? Do you want more money? What are you doing with the money you earn today? What are you doing to be worth more tomorrow? Do you want to be more fit and trim? Then what are you planning to eat at your next meal? What time today will you exercise?

Everyone can find excuses, but only those who truly believe in themselves can transcend the excuses and still find ways to make things happen. Whatever your goal, ask yourself, *Do I believe I can do this?* Then ask, *Do I truly want to do this?* Now go out and do it!

What actions will you take on this idea?

102. Growing Old

When I was born, the average price of a house was less than today's average automobile price. The typical home at the beginning of the Baby Boom did not have a private telephone line, and most phone numbers were just five digits. Most families didn't own a car, and television was still a few years away.

Old, you say? Sure, but today, still many years away from retirement, I take long-distance motorcycle tours, go bungee jumping, hike the mountains near my home, and take in a few movies each month. I'm not the same kind of "old" they had when I was younger.

Our society has redefined old. Today it is more a state of mind and physical deterioration than it is one's chronological age. What age do you expect to be when you first get "old"? Personally, I may postpone it permanently. Stay alive as long as you live; look for ways to live more fully, serve more generously, and love more fondly. You may never get old.

P.S. You start to get old as soon as you detach from the responsibility to do things that matter. Find a need and fill it.

What actions will you take on this idea?

103. Bumper Stickers

If you had a bumper sticker that personified who you are, what would it say? Would it say "Proud Parent," "Baseball Fan," "Political Zealot"? Most people find it hard to come up with just one phrase that captures who they are. But most of us also tend to form quick, one-dimensional impressions of others based on their "bumper stickers," the symbolic statements we make to the world in hopes of expressing ourselves.

What kind of statement does a tattoo above the collar make? What about body piercing? How about dirty and tattered clothes? Some object, saying, "I am NOT how I dress; I'm much more than that!" I would agree. But most of the world evaluates us based on our packaging, the bumper stickers we show to them. When they see someone who cares very little about his or her appearance, then they assume that person is undisciplined in other parts of life too. So check the bumper stickers people see when they look at you. It might be time for a new one, like "A Self-Motivated Person Drives This Car."

What actions will you take on this idea?

104. Careers

Did you choose your career, or did it choose you? Was the acquisition of your job intentional and strategic to lead you closer to your life's goals, or did you just go for the money?

I recall when I got married in my twenties. I didn't have a career yet, so I decided to go into some field that would allow me to ultimately become wealthy. I chose to explore either securities (stocks and bonds) or real estate. Then I did both. First I sold mutual funds and life insurance. Then I went to work in real estate. But neither of them gave me the sense of satisfaction I was seeking. I took college courses, studied hard, and worked diligently, but the "calling" just wasn't there. Then one day my boss asked me to teach my coworkers some new sales techniques, and I LOVED it! I had found my calling—helping others to grow. That started a change in my string of jobs that ultimately led me to become a professional speaker and author. Now, almost 40 years later, I am more successful than I would have been in any other field.

When you consider your career, search beyond the obvious. Don't just look at the tasks; look for the meaning. Find how your output matters to others, then build on what you love about it. Make it a career, not just a job.

What actions will you take on this idea?

105. Dislike

Our like or dislike of someone is often not due to actual reasons but rather due to our perceptions. There are parts of our perception that are not conscious; we form opinions without being aware of why. This can be helpful sometimes, but at other times, it is destructive.

I recall a man who worked in my office building years ago. I did not like him... until I got to know him. Abraham Lincoln is famous for saying, "I don't like that man very much. I must get to know him better." To judge is instinctive, but to look beyond our instincts is wise. Give some thought to how you feel toward others, and then ask yourself, "What if I did like this person? How would I think about him then?" A change in your mindset may just create a change in your relationship.

> **HOW I MOTIVATE MYSELF**
>
> *"Coffee, coconut water, and moderate exercise geared towards strength and posture."*
>
> *Kelan John Farrell Smith*

What actions will you take on this idea?

106. Challenges

"I'd like for you to build your muscles, therefore I will start doing your exercises for you." That statement is insane, isn't it? You can't build muscles unless YOU do the exercises! We need challenges in order to grow. We need to get in over our heads sometimes. We need problems that we don't yet know how to solve. That is how society progresses. We must have challenges!

How challenged have you been lately? If you have had a period of relative ease, it may be time to find some new challenges. If you are dealing with lots of challenges right now, reassure yourself that this is the only way you will actually become more capable, more creative, and more confident. As you meet challenges, you grow in confidence and skill. So thank your lucky stars that you have challenges, and if you don't have many, go find some. Raise your hand, volunteer, take on more responsibility. You will be glad you did.

What actions will you take on this idea?

107. Change

Companies worldwide have been holding training programs on dealing with change. They teach people to welcome change, and even initiate it. But their underlying assumption is often wrong. They think that people are resistant to change. Wrong! People love change, as long as the change is for the better. We love new cars, new friends, new vacations, new movies, new everything. We don't like changes to our comfortable routines.

We know it is easier to continue our old routines than to try something new and, for us, unproven. Sometimes it makes sense to initiate change. When we are just like our competitors, it is time to change. When our results haven't improved for a while, change is due. But when it comes to high standards, core values, and commitments to others, change is not a good option.

Welcome change when it points to improvement, and challenge it when it threatens what you stand for. I remember hearing a friend say, "Don't you ever change." That's a nice compliment, but if I didn't constantly change for the better, not many people would ever say that to me again.

What actions will you take on this idea?

108. Character

My friend Cavett Robert once said, "Character is the ability to follow through on a resolution long after the mood in which you made it has left you." That pretty much captures it for me. Everyone makes resolutions to do or not do certain things; usually around New Year's, we make a lot of them. But few follow through. What makes the difference? How do you cultivate "character"?

I believe it can be intentionally developed, by merely doing what you commit to do. The more often you act upon your decisions, the more you will reinforce that view of yourself. As Dr. George Weinberg once said, "The Self-Creation Principle is this: Every time you act, you strengthen the thinking behind that act." It is easier, he said, to act yourself into good thinking than to think yourself into good behavior.

Next time you decide to do something, do it! Make the commitment and take action right away.

What actions will you take on this idea?

109. Leaving a Legacy

How will you be remembered? Don't fret over how it might go if you died today. Instead, start planning for how you WANT to be remembered. Each of us leaves a legacy, some good, some not. But if we decide in advance what we want that legacy to be, then we can make it a reality.

Try this exercise: Write down a description of what you would like your kids to say about what you did for them. Be as real as you can. Write it as if they were actually saying it. Next, write your "legacy statement" as if it were coming from your coworkers. Then write another from the point of view of your customers, and finally your community.

By combining all of these ideal statements into one overall paragraph, you will have given yourself a pretty good guide as to how to earn that reputation going forward. Be sure that you behave as the person you'd like to be remembered as.

What actions will you take on this idea?

110. Choice

Viktor Frankl wrote a book called *Man's Search for Meaning*. In it, he said that the one power each of us owns that can never be taken away from us is the power to choose. No matter what the circumstance, we still have the power to choose how we will think about it, react to it, and deal with it. That may well be the ultimate power.

My friend W. Mitchell was burned beyond recognition in an accident. He lost the ability to walk in another accident, and yet went on to become the mayor of his city, a talk radio commentator, and ultimately a professional speaker and world traveler—despite being in a wheelchair! His personal motto is "It's not what happens to you that counts; it is how you react to it."

You and I have the greatest power of all: the power to choose how we will deal with what life deals out to us. Choose wisely.

What actions will you take on this idea?

111. Common Sense

Someone said the trouble with common sense is that is not very common. What is common sense? I believe it is the capacity to do what works. If you are lifting something breakable, it is common sense to treat it with care. If you are asking for help, it is common sense to be courteous and respectful so the person will want to help you. If you are hoping for a good outcome, it is common sense to expect to earn the outcome through good actions.

I love Dr. Phil's question. On his popular TV show, he interviews people with dysfunctional lives and asks them why they are behaving as they are. Then he asks, "So how's that working for you?" Invariably, not too well. We often do things that don't make sense because we are acting out of emotion, not out of logic. The next time you are faced with a challenge, ask yourself, "What is the common sense thing to do?" It may guide you to the best outcome of all.

What actions will you take on this idea?

112. A Relationship

What is a relationship? I believe it is a connection between people in which value is exchanged. On one end of the scale, we have casual acquaintances, and on the other, we have committed partnerships. From a casual acquaintance, we just expect that the other person will not harm us. We may smile and say hello, but we don't know them, and we have no commitment to them. In a casual acquaintance, the trust and expectations are low.

But when we are "in a relationship," so to speak, we expect the other person to be looking out for us even when we are not. We expect our spouse to think about our needs as well as their own. We expect our coworkers to consider us, too. In a committed relationship, the trust is high, and so are the expectations.

List all of your relationships on a sheet of paper. Rate them between acquaintance and partner, a *One* for casual acquaintance and a *Five* for committed partner. Then think about how you can increase the level of trust with each person. The more folks you can move toward the partner category, the more possibilities and friendships you will have in your life.

What actions will you take on this idea?

113. Knowing How vs. Why

The old line says that a person who knows "how" may have a job, but the person who knows "why" will be their boss. That is generally true. The better you understand the purpose behind the processes, the more likely you will be to hold a leadership position.

So if you want to get ahead in any organization, study its reason for being. Ask, "Why was the organization formed? Why does it still exist today? Why do we focus on this particular market segment? Why do we offer this product or service? Why do we do things the way we do?"

As you grow in your understanding of these answers, you will also grow in the way you are able to contribute to and lead your organization. People become managers and leaders not just because of what they do, but also because they have learned to think like a leader. Learn to think like a leader, and the likelihood of your becoming a leader will increase dramatically.

What actions will you take on this idea?

114. Learn How to Learn

I once had a business partner who held a doctorate in marketing. One thing that impressed me about his education was that he had not only learned about marketing, but also learned HOW to learn! He knew how to research a subject, how to test conclusions, how to structure information so that it could be understood and retained better—in short, he had learned how to be a really good student. I, without a doctorate, had not acquired these skills in school. I had to learn them the long way, on my own.

Our society used to think that learning was about retaining information; if we could remember it and restate it in a test, then we were considered "learned." But that is a static education, one perfectly suited for a world that never changes. Today we recognize that learning must never stop. We need to be learners, not just learned. They say that those who simply know information are well suited for a world that no longer exists, while those who are continually learning are the ones who will lead us all.

What actions will you take on this idea?

115. Acknowledgement Increases Communication

In a consulting assignment, I once encountered a business in which there was jealousy and competition between departments. Communication was limited to one's own turf, and others were left to fend for themselves. The manager asked me to help improve overall communication.

The first thing I did was institute a new policy that applied to every employee. I required them to always acknowledge each other—when they passed in the hallways, saw each other in the parking lot, sat near others in the lunchroom. I got them to agree to say hello or at least smile and nod to each other.

The effect of this simple behavior was dramatic! When they made a new habit of greeting each other, they started to communicate more openly. They no longer thought in terms of "us" vs. "them." Instead, they saw the others as part of their team.

The same will hold true in any community or organization; the more we acknowledge each other, the more connected we feel. So look up, smile, and say hello more often.

What actions will you take on this idea?

116. A Rut Is a Grave: Routine vs. Purposeful Action

Earl Nightingale once said, "A rut is a grave with both ends knocked out." Our routines sometimes keep us from achieving more. Keep a log for a week. In it, note everything you do each day. Everything! Organize the log by times, so you can see how you start each day, what you do first, second, and so on. Notice how much time you spend on various activities, including rest and recreation. If you relax and daydream, note when and for how long.

A life filled with routine may be relaxing, but it may not be very productive. As you become more aware of your habits and routines, reflect on them to see how well they are serving you. Then rethink your patterns. Add more purposeful activity to your days, and you will add more satisfaction and achievement to your life.

Ruts are just fine, as long as they produce the results we need. If not, then they are just a way to hide from living fully.

What actions will you take on this idea?

117. Explore Your Roots—You Are the Latest Edition

You are the net result of all of your ancestors—their lives, their genes, their experiences, their achievements have all added up to the creation of YOU. That is pretty exciting. If they hadn't lived, you wouldn't, either. Little pieces of all of them, the good and the bad, are present in you.

The next question is: What are you going to contribute to the ongoing chain? Your advancements, your health and fitness, and your education will go into the gene pool of your family. Your legacy will still exist generations from now. Even if you don't have children, your contributions to society will be part of the mix. Both what you *do*, and what you do *not* do will become part of the overall picture.

I believe that each of us is given a set of gifts that can make the world better. Some gifts are relatively small, and some are huge, but all of them add up to something that matters. Please make the most of yourself, and do what you can for others. We need your contributions.

What actions will you take on this idea?

118. Can YOU Really Make a Difference? You Already Do

You make a difference. Yes, right now, at your current stage of development, you already make a difference in the world. If you weren't here, life would be different. Think of Jimmy Stewart's famous role in *It's a Wonderful Life*. He thought he didn't matter, but when an angel let him see the world without him, he found that his seemingly small contributions mattered a great deal.

The same is true of you. You were not a random occurrence; your life matters. There is a contribution you can make that has implications far beyond your ability to realize it. A kind word from you may encourage a desperate person to carry on. A compliment you give might cause someone to notice a skill they never realized, and to use it more effectively. The example you set might inspire another to do even more. We all matter, and our contributions count. Give what you can, be what you can, and do your best.

What actions will you take on this idea?

119. What Have You Learned? Pass It On

In recent years, there has been a big push to form "learning organizations." Those are groups that continually seek more knowledge, then document and share the knowledge they acquire. As organizations advance, they quickly see that the greatest assets they possess are not tangible items but rather the collective knowledge and experiences of each individual.

The longer you are with a firm, the more understanding and information you possess. The tragedy comes when this knowledge is not shared. If you learn a lot and then retire or change jobs, who benefits? Only you. But if you and others share what you know regularly, then everyone's intellect increases.

Look for ways to make sharing knowledge a part of your normal day. Tell the stories of each project or customer. Show others the techniques you have learned. Keep learning from them and with them, and on your own. But then be sure to pass it on. Keep the learning alive.

What actions will you take on this idea?

120. Luxury: What Is It? To Whom?

I remember when eating a steak was a real luxury. My buddies and I would go to a Western-style steak restaurant and get a T-bone. We were living high. I also recall when having electric windows in my car and two phones in my home were luxuries.

What do you consider luxury? Getting a day off? Having your own car? Today we often get so spoiled that our luxuries become seen as necessities. Luxuries are not just first-class accommodations or private jets. Anything beyond our basic needs is a luxury.

When you compare the ordinary lifestyle of an American to the same in most of the world, you quickly see that we live in virtual opulence!

We have our own computers, smart phones, TVs, cars, phone numbers, credit cards, and library privileges; we have twelve movies in one cinema complex, shopping centers filled with goods, car washes, medical care nearby, schools for everyone, and 911 for emergency assistance. Life here is extremely sweet. Be thankful for all your luxuries.

What actions will you take on this idea?

> **HOW I MOTIVATE MYSELF**
>
> *"In the 80s, I was trained and mentored by a performance psychologist. Permanent solution."*
> Norman A. Hood

121. Thinking Is Working!

Sometimes it is really productive to just do nothing. With all the busyness in a typical day, the one thing we often overlook is the value of silent reflection. Sometimes we need to sit and think.

The higher you look in most organizations, the more you will see people spending time thinking. Executives, scientists, researchers, inventors, philosophers, and leaders achieve much by just thinking. Naturally they act on their thoughts, but the thoughts are where the value is generated.

When was the last time you intentionally spent 15 uninterrupted minutes just thinking about better ways to do what you do? With just 15 minutes of clear thinking each day, you could generate an abundance of new ideas every week. And one or two of those ideas will be really good! It often takes just one good idea to transform a company, to turn a losing product into a bestseller, or to motivate someone to do more than ever before. Spend more time thinking. There is no telling what you will find.

What actions will you take on this idea?

122. Ronald Reagan: His Joy and Work Ethic

President Ronald Reagan used to spend his private times at his ranch in the hills above Santa Barbara. It is a rustic place with a small house and miles of horse trails. His fitness regimen included clearing brush, cutting trails, and chopping wood at the ranch. He was the leader of the free world, and yet he put on jeans and gloves and worked as a ranch hand... by choice. It kept him fit, and it kept him humble. He remembered what it was like to be covered in sweat with muscles that ached. He was also an accomplished horseman. He groomed his own horses, fed them, and rode them daily.

I really admire that about him. He could have easily delegated all but the riding to others. He could have paid to clear the trails and never gotten his hands dirty, but he didn't. He knew there was joy and satisfaction in good, hard work, and he respected the common man and woman who worked for a living and voted their convictions. I think we can all learn from his example.

What actions will you take on this idea?

123. Naïveté of Youth

When I was in my twenties, I thought I knew what the world needed and how to deliver it. I also assumed that I'd live a long life and that I'd survive any injury I encountered. The naïveté of youth is reassuring to young people but fraught with danger.

I guess the same could be said of any age. We never know all that we could know on a given subject, and much of our confidence would fade if we realized how little we actually understand. So how do we advance? I think we need to have the *humility* to acknowledge that we don't really know much and also to have the *confidence* to go boldly forward with what little we know.

The trick is to move on with an open mind, constantly learning and adjusting as we acquire new information. We are always younger than someone and could always learn from their experience. Many corporate executives have assumed that they knew more than everyone else and were above the laws of economics, as in the case of the technology market boom and bust. But there is always more to know. Keep your mind open, and listen to everyone. Some of them see more of the truth than you do.

What actions will you take on this idea?

124. Systems Replace Chaos

Data becomes information when it is organized. Information reveals knowledge when it is applied. Knowledge leads to understanding when it is studied. And understanding reveals wisdom when it is examined carefully over time.

Whenever you are faced with confusion, a good starting place is organization. For most things, helpful systems already exist somewhere. Just start organizing all the data into groupings and categories. As you do this, it will become useful information. Then you can apply that information to reveal the knowledge it holds for you.

If your finances are too challenging, then start organizing your records. Get an app or subscribe to an online service. List all the sources from which you get income. List all the bills, and then group them by type. Notice the patterns, and see what this information can teach you. You may see immediate ways to reduce expenses or to increase income. For every problem you face, there is already a system for dealing with it effectively. Look for the solutions that already exist. Systems are ready-made habits you can use.

What actions will you take on this idea?

125. Let's Be Honest vs. Telling Polite Lies

"Can I be honest with you?" When you are asked that question, doesn't it make you suspect that the person has NOT been honest with you so far? There is great value in being honest with each other. Without the truth, we cannot be confident of doing the right thing. But on an interpersonal basis, being "honest" is often misunderstood as being rude or blunt.

There is also a concept known as being appropriate. Say you think someone dresses in poor taste. Do you tell them? Why? If they are your good friend and could get bad results from their chosen "look," then you probably should advise them. But what if you don't know them or have their confidence? In that case, your "honesty" would be rude. Your point of view would offend them, and no good would come of it. If they asked your opinion, you could honestly tell them that their tastes were quite different from yours, but to tell someone what you don't like—when there is no justification for doing so—is simply inconsiderate.

Let's be honest. Wouldn't you prefer to be respected for your courtesy rather than resented for your opinion, even if you are right?

What actions will you take on this idea?

126. Where Is the Center of Our Culture?

Where is the center of our culture? Some would say in the USA it is in New York City; some say Washington DC; others say the South or the Heartland or LA. Where do you think the center of culture is, whether in the U.S. or in other countries?

I'd say it is in... our families. More than our schools, churches, governments, televisions, and newspapers, our homes form our culture and beliefs. It is the family that determines the nature of society. A woman once said, "What can I do? I am only a wife and a mother." My colleague replied, "Madam, if you don't do your job right, it won't matter what the rest of us do."

A church promotion I saw said, "No other success can adequately compensate for failure in the home." Our homes are our solid ground. That is where safety and love are supposed to live.

Look for ways to make your home more loving, more supportive, more encouraging, and more emotionally safe for all who live there. The next generation will follow your example, be it a bad one or a good one.

What actions will you take on this idea?

127. The Power of Symbols

When America was formed, we selected the bald eagle as our symbol. (Benjamin Franklin had proposed that it be the wild turkey.) Australia has the koala and kangaroo. New Zealand, the kiwi bird. Much of Asia uses the tiger or dragon; China has the panda. England has the lion. California has the bear.

Companies and countries alike have chosen animals, rock formations, rainbows, and mythical beings as their symbols in an effort to express their values. The Boys & Girls Club's logo is clasped hands, showing cooperation and assistance. My own company and personal symbol is the acorn: It represents potential and growth, and it is a natural and universal example of the possibilities that live within each seed.

What would your symbol be? Think of something that embodies the qualities you admire, the traits you'd like to develop, and the dreams you hope to achieve. Choose a symbol that expresses what you want and believe, rather than what you have at present. Then use the symbol as your personal logo or signature item.

What actions will you take on this idea?

128. Value of Rituals and Traditions

In the USA, at the beginning of major sporting events, Americans all stand for the national anthem. Before family meals, we offer a blessing. At the beginning of a school day, we recite the Pledge of Allegiance. On the fourth of July, we celebrate our nation's independence. At Thanksgiving, we count our blessings. At Christmas time, we acknowledge our Creator's gift of forgiveness. In every culture and religion there are rituals. But what is the value of rituals?

Rituals are the actions that embody our stories and express our values and beliefs. Rituals give us reassurance and reminders; they take us out of our daily routines and connect us to something greater. When children say their prayers upon going to bed, it reinforces their awareness that God exists and that they have much to be thankful for. It also activates their compassion for others when they say, "God bless Grandma and Sister and..."

Rituals matter. Sure, they can be too elaborate sometimes, and without occasional discussion, they can lose some of their meaning. But they have a place, and they deserve our respect.

What actions will you take on this idea?

129. Church Then vs. Now

In the early days of Western civilization, the center of society and the place of learning was the church. Church leaders were often the only ones who knew how to read and write. Stained glass windows that told stories were crafted to help illiterate people remember the stories and lessons. As society progressed, public schools developed, and church became a combination of our place of worship and our social network. Then, as our societies became more connected and mobile, our social network shifted, our careers gained prominence, and our churches became solely places of worship.

What does that mean? I think it means that we are more vulnerable than ever to the danger of forgetting our connection to the Creator. The U.S. founding fathers built an America that was fully based on the belief in a Supreme Being, a loving God. They said that our model of government was totally unsuited for any society that didn't believe in a loving God.

Regardless of your faith, the basis of all religions is the existence of a Supreme Power, a life source. That belief gives meaning to human existence. Without it, life is simply a series of experiences. I'd prefer to believe that there is a higher purpose to human life—how about you?

What actions will you take on this idea?

130. Service Clubs and Giving: How Do You Serve?

Around the world, you will find Rotary Clubs, Lions, Optimists, Jaycees, and many other service clubs. Throughout the 20th century, these were our primary vehicles for civic involvement. We organized chapters, planned projects, held celebrations, and built hospitals, bridges, and parks. We raised funds for scores of charities and truly made life better.

In recent years, however, there has been a decline in service club membership. Some say we aren't as giving as before. I disagree. Individual giving is at an all-time high. People are still generous; they just don't give in the same ways. Now we go directly to the charities: the Heart Association, Cancer Society, City of Hope, United Way, Boys & Girls Clubs, and more. They hold their own fundraisers—marathons, charity walks, auctions, and festivals. They have Kickstarter campaigns and other forms of outreach.

Are the service clubs still needed? Absolutely—they fill both a civic and a social function that would be hard to replace. For people who want a community network, service clubs are great. Everyone has their own way of giving, and their own needs for being involved. The important decision is for you to choose the best ways in which you can give and serve.

What actions will you take on this idea?

131. The Value of a Creed

I admire the creed of the Junior Chamber of Commerce, the Jaycees. It is the statement of their beliefs and values, and they recite it to open every meeting. Here is what the Jaycees believe; compare it to your own creed:

We believe that faith in God gives meaning and purpose to human life,

That the brotherhood of man transcends the sovereignty of nations,

That economic justice can best be won by free men through free enterprise,

That government should be of laws rather than of men,

That earth's great treasure lies in human personality,

And that service to humanity is the best work of life.

As a young adult, I recited this creed at hundreds of meetings, and as a young parent, I taught it to my son. I've never found a more compelling creed or a more inspiring way to look at the world. What do you believe in? See if you can draft a creed that captures what you care about, then read and recite it to yourself as often as you can.

What actions will you take on this idea?

132. Is the Customer Always Right?

Is the customer always right? Of course not! But, as my colleague Phil

Wexler says, the customer always has the right to be completely wrong and still be treated with dignity and respect. We need to remember that the customer deserves our courteous treatment, even when they are having a bad day or a momentary lapse of intelligence. This is not to mean that we should tolerate abusive behavior, but we should also not be anything but respectful.

The Fairmont Hotel in San Francisco once had a creed titled "Who Is a Customer?" It said a customer was the purpose of their business, a person to be treated with respect, the source of all their profits, a walking advertisement for them (good or bad), and more. It made the case that we should always remember that the customer may not sign our paychecks, but they certainly FUND our paychecks!

The customer may not always be right, but we don't have to tell them so. Honor those who honor you with their business.

What actions will you take on this idea?

133. Your Policy Manual

My friend Phil Wexler is a customer service consultant and author. Phil has what he calls his "policy manual." It is a leather-bound journal that has "Phil's Policy Manual" on the cover. He uses it for humor in his workshops, but the concept has a very serious message: Every customer should have their own policy manual, one that states clearly what they will agree to and what they won't. Businesses have them and use them all the time, but what about the customer's policies?

If the business says it is their policy not to accept American Express cards, what if you said, "Well, it is my policy to use only American Express"? Ridiculous? Yes, probably, but you see my point. We shouldn't assume that, just because one party has a written policy, that it is cast in stone. What if the other party has a different policy? Who prevails? Maybe both parties' needs should be considered.

What actions will you take on this idea?

134. Process- vs. Purpose-Driven

What drives you—the purpose or the process? In a typical day on the job, do you just follow the processes, or do you frequently think about the purpose of them? Most company policies are put into place to protect the company from losses or dishonesty. Yet most people are responsible and honest. So, sometimes exceptions need to be made.

Think about airport security checkpoints. How many people go through them each day? Millions—literally. How many of those people are possible threats? A handful, at most. So which is more important—that the security people follow exactly the same procedures with each person, or that they follow the appropriate procedures for the type of person they are dealing with? If the person does something threatening or sinister, they should take careful action, but if the person shows no signs of threat, they should show them the utmost courtesy.

A security guard at a gated community has two jobs: for guests, show hospitality; for intruders, protect the residents from them. The art is in learning to know which is which. Follow the process, but remember the purpose behind it.

What actions will you take on this idea?

135. Small Groups and Margaret Mead

"Never doubt that a small group of thoughtful, committed citizens can change the world. Indeed, it is the only thing that ever has." So said anthropologist Margaret Mead. We often think that it takes hundreds of people or millions of dollars to make a difference. Or we say, "Only those with positions of power can do big things."

But that is just not so! One person can make a difference, and with a small group of supporters, they can change the world. America's founding fathers were not a large group of people. It started with a few, and they gained support over time. Christianity grew out of twelve apostles continuing to spread Jesus' message. Granted, they were very well connected with someone in a position of power, but you get the point. Most large organizations were started by a small group of enthusiasts.

HOW I MOTIVATE MYSELF
"I try to consider each day a new adventure where I get to try something new every single day! Not only does the thought of adventure get me excited, but I have experienced a lot of new opportunities with this mindset. It can be something very small or very big - it is the action that counts! I have found this a wonderful way to motivate myself to just keep moving forward. I never know what each day holds, but I know Who is holding each day!"
Tammy A Miller

So when you have a dream or a concern that needs action, don't allow yourself to feel powerless. You have immense power when you are committed to a goal. Others catch your enthusiasm, and the number of committed followers grows. What would you like to do for the world? It is possible.

What actions will you take on this idea?

136. Just Sit and Pay Attention

There is great value in merely observing what is around you. At dinner the other night, I saw the full moon out the window behind my dinner partner. We both stopped to soak in the beauty of this sight. On a recent flight, I saw the Southern Cross constellation perfectly positioned outside my airplane window. Wow! Last month, as I relaxed on a veranda in San Antonio, I saw a chameleon descend a tree and promptly change colors to blend with its new location.

There is wonder, beauty, and happiness all around us. I love to study the behavior of my grandkids when they are at play. Their creativity and joy is captivating. The key to observation is to be still—you have to stop focusing on your busyness in order to allow the other images to reach you. Practice this right now, if you are not driving. Just be still for two minutes at the end of my message, and notice what you notice. Listen, look, feel, and experience your surroundings to see what you might have otherwise overlooked. Enjoy!

What actions will you take on this idea?

137. Beloit's Mindset List

Each fall, Beloit College in Wisconsin publishes their Mindset List. It is a list of differences between the worldview of incoming freshmen, and that of the faculty and parents.

For example: In 2016, the incoming class was born in 1999. They don't remember the first Gulf War, dial telephones, life without smart phones, typewriters, the presidency of Bill Clinton, or life without Google. After all, why would they need to? There's an app for that. They have always had PINs and computers that fit in a backpack. They have always had the Internet, e-mail, and voicemail. Most have never "rolled up" a car window, nor sent or received a fax. Long-distance phone calls have never been a big deal to them. Airports have always had security screening, and they have never seen a cassette player. DVDs came out before they were born.

Can you see how different the world must seem to them than it does to the previous generations? As we go forward, we need to allow for these differences and realize that our own point of view may need updating. In what ways are your views probably obsolete?

What actions will you take on this idea?

138. The Value of Exercise

I served for a while on an advisory board for ACE, the American Council on Exercise. That's where I learned just how valuable exercise can be. The older we get, the more our bodies need exercise. If we don't use them, they tend to atrophy and shut down.

This runs directly counter to what many people think. They say, "I'm older now, so I don't exercise as much. Besides, my back hurts, my feet bother me, I have bad knees, and I get tired too quickly." To that I'd say, "This is the very reason you MUST exercise!"

Our bodies are designed to be used, not just preserved. We need movement, and we need exertion. It is vital for us to regularly do things that stress our muscles and bones somewhat. The more resistance we encounter, the more our bones, muscles, and tissues strengthen to deal with it. Also, by forcing ourselves to move often, we keep the circulation going—that results in flexible joints, supple skin, healthy muscles, and even a better psychological outlook. The first prescription for depression is: Get out of your chair and DO something. So take a walk, use the stairs, stretch, and work. You will be happier and live longer if you do.

What actions will you take on this idea?

139. When Did You Last Set Goals?

How long has it been since you set some goals for yourself? Not just dreams, but actual goals that require you to work, stretch, learn, explore, and grow in order to achieve them. How long? Well, for most people, it's been too long. Goals are reasons. They are the stimulus, the cause for us to do more and become better. Without goals, we tend to atrophy and fall into unproductive and largely unsatisfying routines. Goals are necessary to the continuation of life.

When comedian George Burns was asked how he was able to live to be 100, he said, "I had to—I was booked for a performance that day!" He went on to explain that the most important thing for long life was having a reason to get up in the morning, having something to look forward to. Isn't it time you set some new goals? Start now to define in writing what you plan to create in your life in the following areas: family, friends, finances, career, health and fitness, intellectual growth, and spiritual development. Be specific, and get to work on them now.

What actions will you take on this idea?

140. Wouldn't It Be Good to Know Where You Stand Financially?

How much money do you have? How much do you owe? How much will you bring in over the next three months? The vast majority of people don't know the answers to these simple questions. In fact, many of them don't know how long they could survive without a paycheck.

But all of us could know—by simply taking the time every few months to determine where we stand financially, we greatly increase our control over our own money. Financial planning is MORE important when you are broke than when you are rich. If you're rich, you can get by even if you waste or lose money. When you have very little money, every item counts.

Why not take some time this week to list what you have, what is coming to you, what you owe, and what you want? With those four simple items, you can do some very valuable financial planning. The next step is to plan what you can contribute so that you earn even more.

What actions will you take on this idea?

141. When Do You Plan to Retire?

When do you plan to retire? That is, at what age do you intend to leave the active workforce? How much time is there between today and that date? If you are 50 now and retire at 65, then you have 15 productive years to earn all that you will need.

How much will you need? Despite those who say you will need less when you retire, consider that you will have all day in which to do as you choose. Chances are that your spending may actually increase! But say you are conservative in your spending—how much money each month or year will you need in order to live well and happily? That is the amount that you need to be setting aside today, minus whatever interest you could earn.

By the way, how long do you plan to be retired? How many years do you need to have a guaranteed income for? If you live a normal lifespan, you will be retired for 20 years or so. Social Security, company pensions, and home equity will probably not meet all your needs. The rest is up to you. So send some of today's money ahead to the person you will be when you retire. He or she will need it and surely appreciate you for sending it.

What actions will you take on this idea?

142. The Seven Natural Values

We are driven by our wants as well as our needs. In fact, our wants often get satisfied before our needs do. Another word for Wants is Values—what we care about. If you care about learning, then the value of knowledge to you is very high. If you care about beauty, then aesthetics have high value.

There are seven "natural values," which matter to everyone, though to different degrees. They are: Sensuality, the importance of your physical experience; Empathy, the importance of feeling connected to others; Wealth, the importance of ownership; Power, the importance of control or recognition; Aesthetics, the importance of beauty; Commitment, the importance of making a difference and doing what is right; and Knowledge, the importance of learning.

When you know someone's top values, you know what they care about most.

What actions will you take on this idea?

143. Where Do Values Come From?

There are two types of values: those we have learned, and the natural values common to everyone. Learned values include things like patriotism, religion, work ethic, relationships, and beliefs. We get these from Mom and Dad, society, church, school, and our life experiences.

Natural values are just part of who we are. Everyone cares about their physical experience, connections with others, ownership, acknowledgement, and acceptance. They also care about improving how things look and feel, doing what they think is right, and understanding the world around them. But these values hold a different importance from one person to the next. In other words, your top values might be my lowest ones.

If you understand my values, then you understand the motives that move me. Motives are the key to motivation. If I know you love to learn, I will give you a book as a gift. But if knowledge is your lowest value, I'll give you something you would like better, like movie tickets or your favorite meal. Start today to notice what people care about. It shows in what they talk about, how they use their free time, and what they defend. The better you know them, the better you can relate to them each day.

What actions will you take on this idea?

144. High and Low Sensuality

One of the basic human values is sensuality, the importance of our physical experience. It is expressed in the sense of touch, taste, and smell. Those who have a high sensuality value place much importance on the feel and experience of things. Temperature, humidity, texture, flavor... all these matter a lot to high-sensuality folks. Those with low sensuality don't react as strongly to these differences.

So, if you are taking a person to dinner and they have high sensuality, then be aware of the feel, the smell, the taste, and the comfort of the experience. Even if it doesn't matter much to you, it may matter a great deal to them.

For high-sensuality people to do their best work, ergonomics are important. Low-sensuality people can work well even with discomfort, for a while. Start to notice differences in people's sensuality values. Just pay attention to how much importance they place on physical experiences. The more you notice, the more you will know. This is just one of many ways to read people better.

What actions will you take on this idea?

145. High and Low Empathy

Empathy is the capacity to understand how people feel. The empathy value indicates the relative importance to someone of feeling connected with others. You and I both have this value. We need to feel connected with others. If this is a high value, then your life tends to revolve around your time with others. You measure each day's success by how much of it involved interacting with people you care about. You judge others by whether they are good to those you care about.

If your empathy value is low, then you put other priorities higher on your list and only connect with others once you've made progress on other goals. This can lead to very predictable disagreements: "You don't care about me! If you did, you'd put me first more often." That's a high-empathy person scolding a low-empathy mate. These differences are value differences. They don't indicate a lack of caring—they just show a differing set of priorities. The better we understand each other, the more accepting and cooperative we can be. Start today to notice each person's empathy value.

What actions will you take on this idea?

146. Wealth Value

Comedian George Carlin once said that life is about Stuff. The more stuff you have, the more complex your life becomes. Well, the amount of stuff we accumulate often reflects the value we place on wealth—ownership, that is. If owning things of value is highly important to you, then you will tend to organize your life to achieve that. (This does not include hoarding.)

Those with low wealth values choose other priorities. Have you noticed that some seemingly brilliant people never seem to accumulate much wealth, while less brilliant folks get really rich? That's because people pursue what matters most to them. They may say they care a lot about financial security, but their behaviors show you what they really value.

By understanding that some money is important to everyone but that large amounts only tend to motivate those with a high wealth value, we can see why certain people behave like they do. Everyone would love to become rich, but only those with a high wealth value are willing to work long and hard to achieve it. How important is wealth to you?

What actions will you take on this idea?

147. Power Value

I once asked my brother-in-law, "If you could have any job in the world, what would it be?" He answered, "Running something." He enjoys being in charge of a project and getting things done.

This is known in psychology as a high power value. People with high power value are the doers of the world. They organize groups, marshal resources, and get the job done. Their joy comes from making decisions, generating ideas, motivating others, and achieving outcomes. They are naturally drawn to positions of authority. Their power value draws some into the spotlight. They become performers or work hard to achieve the acknowledgement and recognition of others.

All people have this value, but for some it is high, and for others it is low. Low power value is revealed when one avoids the spotlight and prefers to work in a team or in solitude. This is not low self-esteem—it is just the natural orientation of some people. Those with low self-esteem operate from fear. Low power value is just a natural state.

How important is this value to you? Look back over your career, and see what you notice.

What actions will you take on this idea?

148. Aesthetics Value

Beauty, balance, symmetry, blend: These are all aspects of aesthetics. For people with a high aesthetics value, it really matters how things look. You can identify them by looking at their homes, cars, and workspaces. They decorate with an eye toward the right aesthetic effect. If you send them a proposal document, they will judge it by how it looks as much as what it says.

Those with a low aesthetic value hardly notice the look but focus on the content instead. Both views matter. It is important for us to understand these human differences, because this affects how well or poorly we connect with others.

Look around your own workspace. What message does it send to others about you? Does it show your good taste, your accomplishments, your relationships, or just your work? Most people's work environment tends to reflect the person who works there. If my highest value were aesthetics, how would I react to your workspace? I'm not suggesting you change your world to make others more comfortable—I just want you to notice that there is a message in how we present ourselves, and sometimes it matters a lot.

What actions will you take on this idea?

149. Commitment Value

Not everybody needs a grand quest or cause to champion, but everyone, on some level, cares about doing what they think is right. This is known as their commitment value. We each need to feel committed to something—a set of beliefs, a way of doing things, a reason behind what we do. When this value is high, you tend to be very purpose-driven. You look for meaning in what you do. If this value is low, you tend to focus more on the process rather than its purpose.

People with high commitment values love to work on a grand vision or dream. They are inspired by stories like Walt Disney's, when he created Disneyland to be "the happiest place on earth." Others simply aren't inspired as much. One with a low commitment value will not be your best choice to chair the

> **HOW I MOTIVATE MYSELF**
>
> *Two things: I take my dog for a quick walk. I have a shower because it is energizing and never fails to leave me feeling refreshed, refocused, and ready to get on with things.*
>
> *Rhoberta Shaler*

Ethical Standards committee. They'd be better at something else. Learn to notice the commitment value in people. They will show you what they truly care about.

What actions will you take on this idea?

150. Knowledge Value

Do you love to learn? Some do, some don't. We all like to know more and discover new things, but for some people, learning is pure joy. These are the people with a high knowledge value. They find discovery, dialogue, and education to be highly enjoyable. They are usually good students and like research, and even debate.

People with lower knowledge values seem to learn mostly on a need-to-know basis. They learn what they need to, but they don't consider learning to be a particularly good time. Those with high knowledge values like books as gifts, consider going to a seminar to be a treat, and treasure the ability to spend time with knowledgeable people. You can certainly cultivate your love of learning, but the value you place on learning relative to other pursuits tends remain the same. Everybody needs knowledge; the more we know, the better we can deal with the world. To a large degree, knowledge is power, but it still motivates some and doesn't motivate others. Learn to notice who loves to learn.

What actions will you take on this idea?

151. Seven Kinds of Smart

How are you smart? I didn't ask, "How smart are you?"; I asked, "How are you smart?" Everyone is smart on some subjects and in some ways. Even those with minimal IQs still may be really smart in working with their hands or in reading people.

There are at least seven kinds of smart according to researchers Thomas Armstrong and Howard Gardner. They are: Word Smart, Math Smart, People Smart, Music Smart, Spatial Smart, Physical Smart, and Self Smart. All of these intelligences can be developed. By working on your use of each intellect, you will improve its function.

Consider which smarts are strongest in you. Think about how you could use and exercise the other smarts more often, and watch your skills grow. Everyone has these smarts, and everyone can improve HOW they are smart.

What actions will you take on this idea?

152. Music Smarts

My son can figure out how to play almost any song on the guitar. I play guitar professionally, and yet his ability is far beyond mine. He can be considered Musically Smart. It's not an IQ issue; it is just a more advanced musical intelligence. All people have music smarts, but only a few have truly developed them.

There are musical gifts like perfect pitch, and the ability to write original songs, but those go beyond what I'm talking about. I have learned that everyone can develop their musical intellect by simply using it wisely. Learn to read music, practice singing your favorite tunes (alone at first), have fun with karaoke singing, or buy a keyboard and experiment with it. Learn five of your favorite tunes on any instrument.

As you use your ability for music, you will also improve your musical intelligence. Why? Because music reaches a part of us that conversation, thought, and work never touches. You will feel better and be happier with more music in your life.

What actions will you take on this idea?

153. Word Smarts

I love words! I enjoy word games and puns and double meanings. Psychologists would call that being Word Smart. Everyone has this kind of intellect, but not everyone develops it.

Words are symbols of meaning. They can carry multiple messages in just a small combination of letters. The better you become at using words creatively, the more ways you will find to communicate with others.

I challenge you to become more Word Smart. Get a dictionary and leave it out where you can pick it up on an impulse. Flip through it occasionally and explore words, any words. Each new word you add to your vocabulary will increase your understanding of other words.

Vocabulary is the great differentiator in society. You can tell someone's social status by their use of words. Power and influence are gained more easily with a mastery of language. Learn a new word today, and again tomorrow.

What actions will you take on this idea?

154. Number Smarts

Math and science seem to be the defining skills of the industrial society and the information age. When an abundance of graduates are skilled in these areas, a multitude of technological breakthroughs follow. Look at the amazing growth of the Internet, personal computers, cellular technology, and electronics in general. All are based in mathematics.

How's your math intelligence? Everyone is capable of being good at math, but it intimidates many, as well. Perhaps it's the way we were taught math.

When the occasional teacher learns to make math fun, all of a sudden we have more math majors. I believe it is time to change our approach to math. Let the teachers bring in examples and experts from fields where they have applied math to the real day to day world, like sports and poker, billiards, architecture, farming, aeronautics, software design, and chess. Let's look for new approaches to math that involve musical equations and figuring odds. When math becomes as much fun as sports, more people will pursue math. Sudoku, anyone?

What actions will you take on this idea?

155. People Smarts

Read any good people lately? There is an art and a science to reading people, and the better we learn to do it, the more successful we can be. Everyone sends out messages through their words and actions that are intended to tell others how to deal with them. Some messages are obvious; some are not. I've found that deciding to become skilled at reading people can be a valuable turning point in one's life.

Learn to read body language and its various meanings. Learn to notice and understand the different personality types. Study differences in people's values. Observe *how* people are smart, instead of judging how smart they are. Notice differences in personal velocity. Explore the imprints that a person's background has had on them. The more you notice, the more you know about how to connect with, motivate, and understand people. When you become more People Smart, doors will open to you like never before.

What actions will you take on this idea?

156. Space and Visual Smarts

My dad could always fix thing well. He understood mechanics. He also had a knack for seeing things in his head and figuring them out without actually touching them. This is known as Visual or Spatial or Picture

Smarts. It is a form of intelligence possessed by all but developed only by a few. Architects and mechanics are usually visually smart. Landscapers and interior designers share this knack.

One way to cultivate this ability is to practice visualizing. Lie on your back and look at the clouds, then find shapes and characters in the clouds. Assemble jigsaw puzzles, doodle and draw often, play drawing games like Pictionary®, sketch new ideas, and assemble things in creative ways. Study how things work, and then try to recreate what you saw in your mind. Follow the link from one part to another, and try to visualize the effect. As you improve your visual smarts, you will also improve your abilities to solve problems and to communicate. With each new intelligence we develop, we set off a domino effect.

What actions will you take on this idea?

157. Body Smarts

Tiger Woods is a golf genius. Whether you like him or not, you have to admire his mastery of golf. The people at the top of various sports are as intelligent about their sport as Albert Einstein was about physics and mathematics.

There is an intelligence known as Body Smart. Everyone has it. To develop it, we need to use our body more intentionally. Great sculptors have the intelligence to use their hands artistically. Watchmakers and musicians do, also. So did basketball player Michael Jordan, quarterback Peyton Manning, golfer Jack Nicklaus, skater Scott Hamilton, and gymnast Peter Vidmar.

The more you develop what we often call "hand-eye coordination," the more Body Smart you will be. Learn to respect your body as having a form of intelligence. Develop your awareness of each part of your body, learn how it functions, and improve your ability to use it well. You may end up being a physical genius!

What actions will you take on this idea?

158. Self Smarts

Socrates told us, "Know thyself." Daniel Goleman, in his book *Emotional Intelligence*, said that the first of the Emotional Intelligences is Self-Awareness. The better you and I understand ourselves, the more fully we will understand each other. What we see in ourselves, we will invariably also find in others.

So just how does one know themselves? It starts by merely paying attention. Our lives are filled with patterns of behavior. We have routines for getting dressed, eating breakfast, and driving to work. We usually start our grooming in the same way, brush our teeth in the same way, etc.

Keep a log of what you do this week. Note everything you do each day, then observe the patterns. Learn how you live. Next, study your reactions to others. How do you typically greet others? How do you answer the phone? What do you do when it's someone you like? Someone you don't like? How do you react to bad news? What is it like to work with you? What's it like to live with you? You will be amazed by what you learn when you endeavor to know yourself.

What actions will you take on this idea?

159. Bandwidth: You vs. Computer Chip

Bandwidth is a technology term that indicates processing capacity. If a computer has high bandwidth, then it can process many disparate items all at once. With low bandwidth, it can handle only one task at a time.

People also have bandwidths. Some folks can talk and think about five different topics all at once, while others get frustrated and confused once you add more than one. If a person with low bandwidth is selling an idea to one with high bandwidth, it is likely the "buyer" will become bored unless things move quickly. If a person with high bandwidth is selling an idea to one with low bandwidth, it is likely that the buyer will feel overwhelmed and confused by information overload. By adjusting your delivery to their bandwidth level, you can be compatible with more people—just start to notice when others become less responsive. If you increase or decrease the amount and speed of information you are covering, then you can gain greater rapport with others. Make sure your delivery of information matches their processing capacity.

What actions will you take on this idea?

160. Statue of Liberty

I recently sailed into New York Harbor on a cruise ship. As we passed the Statue of Liberty, my heart glowed with pride. This symbol of opportunity is a powerful sight to behold! People around the world may criticize the USA, but they also hope to have the freedoms we have.

But with opportunity comes responsibility. We have become the most prosperous society in history because we offer our citizens the freedom to do their best and the opportunity to fail, as well. We don't consider failure to be permanent. Failure is simply the training process for future successes.

It was once proposed that we build another statue on the West Coast called the Statue of Responsibility, thereby balancing the message of these monuments. In any culture, there is no liberty without someone bearing responsibility. The perfect state of Freedom, or Liberty, exists only when everyone, at every level of society, agrees and demands to be held responsible for their choices and actions. God bless the land of the free and the home of the brave. How can you make your world more free and responsible?

What actions will you take on this idea?

161. Southampton and the Titanic

The famous humorist and writer Erma Bombeck once said that she really sympathized with the people on the ill-fated Titanic who at dinnertime waved off dessert. We never know when our last meal will be, but we also wouldn't be very wise to eat every meal as if it were our last.

I was in Southampton, England recently, where the Titanic embarked on its first and final journey. This charming community is still thriving and launching cruise ships every day. During World War II, Southampton was bombed for days on end, and much of the city was destroyed. Yet today, the old and new parts of the city are alive and well. If you didn't know of the horrific bombing, you wouldn't suspect it had ever happened.

All of us are more resilient than we realize. Like Southampton, we have the ability to suffer powerful setbacks and still recover. So the next time you get hit by a big blow, bear in mind that you can take it. You can bounce back and continue to have a meaningful life. And, just this once, try some of those great desserts.

What actions will you take on this idea?

162. Fitness Cruise

Cruise ships are known for their food. These floating restaurants sometimes have as many as a dozen different food outlets for their passengers to visit. Travelers often complain that despite the joy of their latest cruise, they gained weight on board.

My wife and I recently took a transatlantic cruise, with six nights on the ship. We ate heartily and enjoyed the fine wine as well. And by the end of the trip, we had lost weight! This is because, before we ever departed, we agreed to make this a "fitness cruise." The ship had a fitness facility, and we committed ourselves to daily workouts. Every morning, despite some long, happy evenings, I was on the treadmill or lifting weights at 6:00 a.m. I worked out for a full hour each day and burned enough calories that I lost 1 percent of my body fat while having the time of my life. So, the next time you go on a holiday, think of making it a "fitness holiday," and add some healthy behavior to what otherwise might be a weight-gaining experience.

What actions will you take on this idea?

163. Pilots at Dinner

Have you ever watched airplane pilots as they talk with each other? They are constantly using their hands to simulate flying experiences. It is as if they had model planes in each hand. Last week, we had dinner with a group in which four pilots dominated one end of the table with stories of triumph and disaster in the air. These four did not know each other before the dinner, but because of their common love of flying, they were as connected as old classmates. The same is often true of other interests: boating, cooking, sports, etc.

Within this phenomenon lies a truth that you and I can use. When we want to connect with another person, the first thing we should do is look for what they are interested in. Find out what fascinates them. Ask what they'd do with their spare time if they could do whatever they wanted most. You may find that you share an interest with them. If you don't, use this as an opportunity to learn something new. Inquire as what it is that interests them so much. Why is that appealing? How did they discover it? Let them take you along on a hand-guided flight.

What actions will you take on this idea?

164. Partnership: Three Essentials

In any partnership, there are three essentials to keep it successful:

1. Both parties must be committed to making it work.
2. The communication must be open and honest.
3. Agreements must be clear, so both parties know what the other expects from them.

Everything else is negotiable, but commitment, honesty, and clear agreements are vital. Vital. Imagine that one of you is committed and the other is just giving it a try. The partnership is doomed. Or if only one party is fully open and honest. Or if only one party is clarifying expectations and keeping agreements. No single individual can make a partnership work. If both aren't committed to it, then there is no relationship; it is simply a temporary arrangement.

Follow this checklist the next time you talk with your partner. Ask yourselves, "Where do we need the most work next: our commitments, our openness, or our agreements?" Then work on each one at a time, and watch your happiness grow!

What actions will you take on this idea?

165. Biker Threat and Response

What would you do if you had to walk alone past a menacing-looking group of hard-core motorcycle riders in a deserted area of town late at night? Most people would find that a bit anxiety-producing. I think I'd want to move out of the "potential victim" file in the biker's head and into a file like "good guy." If someone is looking at you in a threatening way, your best bet might just be to change the way they see you.

Here's what one person did: Upon seeing a large man partially blocking her way and his motorcycle nearby, she looked at the motorcycle and said, "Nice bike! How do you get the paint to be like that?" The biker, proud to have someone compliment both his bike and his intelligence about it, explained the technique used in his special paint job. The woman said, "Well, it sure is impressive." He said, "Thanks." And then she walked away.

Try this technique in some non-threatening situations—take an interest in others, and allow them to help you understand something. This woman probably wasn't curious about the paint, but she knew how to reduce a potential threat. My friend and colleague Mark Scharenbroich wrote a book about this same concept, titled *Nice Bike!* It is now his trademark story.

What actions will you take on this idea?

166. Charity—What you give

There is a famous quote used in many fundraising meetings worldwide: "You make a living by what you get. But you make a life by what you give."

Seldom does anyone truly admire another merely because they have acquired a lot. They may admire their acquisitions, but not the person. On the other hand, almost everyone loves a generous spirit. A philanthropist gets paid in many ways—they get the satisfaction of giving, the peace of mind that comes from knowing they made a difference, the gratitude of others.

What can you give the world? How about your time? Get involved in helping others. How about your talent? Use your skills to help others achieve their goals. How about your treasure? Donate money, goods, services, or privileges to causes that you care about. Time, talent, and treasure are all great ways to give.

What actions will you take on this idea?

167. Will Rogers

Where are the opportunities today? During the Great Depression of the 1930s, Will Rogers said, "There is plenty of work to be had. There are fences to mend, trees to trim, yards to mow, fields to plow. There's plenty of work. Now you may not get paid for doing it, but you won't get paid for not doing it either." He was right then, and he's right today.

Though we aren't suffering from economic disaster nor witnessing people out of work all around us, we have plenty of people who wish they were doing something else for a living. I think we need to stop worrying so much about finding enjoyable work and start focusing on necessary work. Meaningful work. That is where satisfaction is to be found.

Look for ways to make a difference to someone. Find the parts of your own work that could be done better. Think beyond your job description, and look for ways to help your employer advance. You may not get paid for doing it, at first, but you won't get paid for not doing it either. And you may just wake up to find yourself enjoying life even more.

What actions will you take on this idea?

168. Behavioral Economics: Three Parts

Every action has a value or a cost. It is what I call "behavioral economics." The difference between a pessimistic outlook and an optimistic outlook can be measured in real dollars. Optimists try new things. Pessimists work just to protect what they have. People who think well of the customer and of their employer are measurably more productive than those who don't. The way you think really does count.

So does the way you communicate. Those who communicate well with others do more and earn more than those who don't. The ability to relate to different types of people is truly a job asset. Good work habits also have a tangible value: preparation, accuracy, follow-through on promises, courtesy, and consideration. These are habits that are worth paying for. Cultivate value in how you think, in how you relate to others, and in the habits you build. Your payoffs will be impressive.

What actions will you take on this idea?

169. Younger Next Year

I've enjoyed reading a book titled *Younger Next Year* and interviewing its author, Chris Crowley. Its basic premise is that through a lifelong habit of daily, vigorous exercise, you can stay younger, healthier, and happier.

I have found this to be true. I've decided that one of my jobs for the rest of my life is daily exercise. Since re-committing to this path, I have reduced my body fat, improved my agility, and lengthened my ability to stay alert and strong all day. I've also seen improvements in my attitude and creativity. The American Council on Exercise has long documented the payoffs of regular exercise. I've exercised for about 40 consecutive years, but this recent renewal of my workouts seems to have paid better dividends than the mere jogging and hiking I was doing before.

Give it a shot. If you are injured or badly out of shape, ask

---

HOW I MOTIVATE MYSELF

When I get up, no matter what time, I ask myself this question. "Do I choose to make this day one of happiness and see only good in what comes my way or do I choose to concentrate on the bad?" Every day, I choose to be happy. It's a choice!

Joyce Knudsen

your doctor what you could do, but do something every day. If you're in good shape, kick it up a notch. Be fully alive!

What actions will you take on this idea?

170. Hope For or Against

Let's revisit this Optimist vs. Pessimist idea. One of my friends who claims to be a "realist" is, in my estimation, showing pessimistic thinking. He says, "I'm not a pessimist—I always hope for the best." But that's not true. He actually hopes against the worst.

There is a difference between hoping FOR the best and hoping AGAINST the worst. Hope has two popular definitions: one is expecting success, and the other is wishing to avoid failure. He usually says, "I sure hope it doesn't rain!" or, "I hope we don't encounter any traffic jams." See what I mean? He hopes against the undesirable. In contrast, an optimist might say, "I'm sure glad it hasn't rained. The skies might stay clear all day" or, "What a treat! With only a few delays, we have had good traffic all the way here."

Start noticing the patterns in your own hopeful comments. See if a shift to the positive would be good for you. I think it will.

What actions will you take on this idea?

171. If I Were Brave

Nashville balladeer Jana Stanfield has a song titled "If I Were Brave." What a great title! She poses the question, "What would I do today if I were brave?" That is a very good strategy for dealing with fear. Instead of focusing on the fear, focus on what you would do if you had confidence and strength. How would you act then? This question takes us beyond the emotional barrier of fear.

Try it on yourself or with your kids. The next time someone is afraid, ask what they'd do if they were not afraid. Get them to just consider the alternative. In doing so, you break the stranglehold of the fear.

I tried something similar when I was facing a bungee jump once off of a very tall bridge in New Zealand. I asked myself, *If I didn't have this fear, what would I do?* I decided I'd take the first step. And it worked! What would you do if you didn't have fear of doing it?

What actions will you take on this idea?

172. Lucky 13

Is there such a thing as a "lucky number"? How about an unlucky one? Some hotels have gone so far in catering to this superstition that they no longer have a 13th floor—the 12th floor is immediately below the 14th. The floor is still the 13th, but most people don't think about it.

Shakespeare once wrote, "There is nothing either good or bad, but thinking makes it so." That is certainly true of luck. Luck is a concept fabricated in the mind, built upon ignorance and superstition, but it sure is a popular concept! Many ancient cultures were guided by numbers as omens of good or bad, but numbers are just numbers. It is the thinking that makes a difference.

There is no denying that there are "lucky streaks," when things just seem to go in your favor. But these "streaks" are highly dependent on your mindset. People who think they are lucky tend to be luckier than those who don't. Likewise, those who think themselves unlucky tend to be so. The mindset creates the reality.

Catch yourself whenever you talk about luck. Make sure that you use the psych-out strategy that will help you, not one that will reinforce your fears and doubts. The way you think shapes the way you are. And YOU can control the way you think!

What actions will you take on this idea?

173. Convention Dance

I was inspired recently by watching members of the National Speakers Association at a dance. Of 4,000 professional speaker members, about 1,500 had attended the convention, and about 500 of those attended the dance after the awards gala. On the dance floor, I saw young and old, tall and short, handicapped and able, average and odd, all dancing happily to the tunes.

There were three people on the dance floor in wheelchairs, dancing with able-bodied people. A little person was dancing with a young man twice her height. A blind man was dancing with his sighted wife. It was a true inspiration. All were enjoying the music, and nobody was put off by the limitations of the others. That is true acceptance. Diversity at its finest. Races, abilities, genders, and, ages all blended in the happy celebration of the joy of music. Rock on!

What actions will you take on this idea?

174. Handicapped Clerk

What a different world I live in than the one I was raised in! When I was a youth, people with physical challenges were considered weak and not included in normal activities. It wasn't just my parents and teachers who thought this way—everybody did. It was the norm.

But last week, my wife and I were shopping for clothes, and the clerk who served us was a delightful lady with deformed arms. She clearly had the intellect to do her job well and the attitude to go with it. All she lacked was the usual ability to use her arms as most people do. It put us off for a second, but when we saw that she accepted her condition, so did we. In fact, I took pleasure in seeing how well she adjusted to the limits of her limbs.

I've come to believe that the way we react to other people's difference tells us more about us than it does about them. If we are afraid of or offended by them, it is our restrictive attitude that is the problem, not their condition. All people deserve human respect and dignity. When we treat them that way, the differences seem to disappear.

What actions will you take on this idea?

175. Oxford Professor

I had the privilege to attend a lecture series with an Oxford professor recently. Something she did in listening to her students truly impressed me.

On occasion, one of us would ask a question of her that was out of the ordinary line of our discussion. Instead of struggling with an answer, she often replied, "It appears that you may have some thoughts on this matter. Would you mind sharing them with us?" This almost always caused the questioner to smile and say, "Yes, I'd be happy to." Then they would go on to elaborate on an idea they were hoping the professor agreed with. She used the reflective question to probe further into what the person was concerned about, and in so doing, she made the lecture more interesting for all of us.

The next time someone asks you a rather large question, try her technique. Simply say, "What are your own views on this topic?" You may learn something useful.

What actions will you take on this idea?

176. You Matter

A boss of mine once refused to promote me to a position I felt well qualified for. He thought I was overestimating my ability. This caused me to double my efforts and earn the new position. He wasn't trying to motivate me, but he did nonetheless.

Jim Thorpe was one of the greatest natural athletes of all time, but we might never have heard his name had it not been for Pop Warner, who coached him. Somebody taught the great pianists of the world to play the piano. Someone coached and encouraged each of us before we truly excelled. Everyone matters. Even those who seem to harm us are often a stimulus for us to take a totally new direction.

Consider this—without all of your life's experiences, both good and bad, you wouldn't be who you are today. A person who only gets encouragement will probably overestimate their abilities and not judge risk accurately. A person who only gets discouragement will underestimate themselves. Both the good and the bad make a difference, so when given a choice, be a positive influence.

What actions will you take on this idea?

177. Who Do You Measure Yourself By?

When asked how you are doing in life, who do you measure yourself by? Your parents, friends, relatives, classmates, coworkers, high achievers? Who? The person or standard by which you measure yourself says a lot about where you are headed.

As a youth, I wanted to achieve even more than my father. As a young professional speaker, I wanted to be accepted among the successful veteran speakers. As a veteran speaker, I want to be valued by my audiences and readers. As a father, I want to be a positive influence on my son and grandchildren whether they value me right away or not.

As you and I progress in our lives, we see that the real value in a person comes from their being a force for good—a contributor, not a taker. Think about what you want most to achieve at this point in life. Now think bigger, think beyond your own ego, and ask, "How could I make the world a better place?"

What actions will you take on this idea?

178. Ferrari Factor

Joe and Steven argued for hours over which of them would get to buy my new Ferrari. I called them to announce that I had gotten a Ferrari in the mail from one of my clients. (Clearly something was odd about it arriving in the mail.) But they didn't notice my little joke, and they assumed I had a full-sized car and that they *didn't* have one. So they decided to buy it from me, and they argued as to which of them would buy it.

The reality was, my car was a 1/25th scale model, but I lured them on. Finally Steven announced that it was settled—*he* would buy my car! I told him it wasn't for sale, but he persisted. I told him it was 1/25th the size of a normal car, but he brushed that aside, saying "All Ferraris are small." I told him the engine didn't work. He said it could be replaced. He wanted my car! When he finally realized his error, he was mortified! Later he said to me, "Jim, you got me good." How often have you wasted energy worrying over what someone else has that you do not? Wouldn't it be more productive to compete with your former self rather than with others?

What actions will you take on this idea?

179. Preparation: External

The Boy Scouts' motto is "Be Prepared." That is not a bad personal motto for you and me. Those who spend time in preparation find that they stay in control of things. Those who don't prepare are controlled by circumstances and by others. You've heard the old line: Proper Planning Prevents Poor Performance.

Here is another way to think about it: Failure is a form of practice. John Ruskin once said, "People have come to fear failure far too much these days. It is the practice necessary for success." If you can experience your failure during the planning process, then you won't fail when it comes time to execute the plan. The more we think about all the ways something could unfold, the more possibilities we see. The person who sees the most possibilities has the most options open to him, and the person with the most options in any situation usually wins. Dwight D. Eisenhower said, "Plans are worthless, but planning is everything."

What actions will you take on this idea?

180. Preparation: Internal

Someone once complained that every time opportunity knocked on his door, he was out back taking out the trash. I know the feeling. Most people miss opportunities because they didn't prepare for them to arrive. But if you are not ready, then it is not your opportunity.

I like to think about becoming an "eligible receiver" of opportunities. It is a form of "becoming lucky." You can increase your own good fortune by simply getting ready for windows of opportunity, whether they arrive or not. It is not a waste of time, even if things stay the same—because YOU didn't stay the same, you intentionally got better!

One way to prepare for your opportunity is to look internally at your world and yourself. What information could you access that would help you? What publications could you read to find opportunities? Who could you associate with more often? What skills could you develop? Think of this: If you were to learn a new language, wouldn't it follow that you'd soon find opportunities to use your new skill? Those who don't speak Italian don't get offered free trips to Italy in return for serving as an interpreter. Get ready; your opportunity is coming.

What actions will you take on this idea?

181. Self-Preparation: Mental

The importance of mindset cannot be overrated. How we think about what we are doing has an impact on the outcomes we achieve. Each day we get to choose our attitudes. As we start the day with optimism, we increase our energy. As we meet a new person and look for the good in them, we open the relationship. Also, when faced with problems, we can fight against them, give up and get depressed, or consider them a new starting point.

A friend of mine didn't get a job he wanted, and I observed that despite missing this job, he had been the "topic of the day" among the executives in his company headquarters. I suggested that this could lead to some very good future opportunities. At first he brushed my view aside, but a few days later, he was informed that an even better position would soon be offered to him!

You might say, "But what if that weren't true?" You tell me—which is a more pleasant way to face the day: depressed about a past loss, or looking toward a future win? You choose your mindset every day. Choose well.

What actions will you take on this idea?

182. Self-Preparation: Physical

As you prepare to meet the day, think about this: You will have a better day if you are ready for it. What items do you need to have with you today? Your scheduling calendar, smart phone, laptop, notepad, some vital information or file, a specific tool? How do you need to be dressed today in order to make the most of things? Who might you see today? What could you learn about them in advance?

If you are meeting someone special, where would be the best place for a really good meeting? Where will you eat breakfast, lunch, and dinner, and why? How could you use these events to your advantage? When will you start the day? When will you retire today?

What will you listen to as you drive, exercise, and relax? How could you turn these into learning times? Who would like to hear from you today? How could you easily connect with them? Be ready for your opportunities today.

What actions will you take on this idea?

183. Targeting: Who (Markets and Groups)

Let's assume that you are starting a new business. Who already buys what you sell? The best way to go to market is by contacting those who are already sold on your product or service, but are currently buying from someone else. In this case, your task is to "rescue" them from the other provider and give them a better product or better service, or even a better price.

> **HOW I MOTIVATE MYSELF**
>
> *Give yourself accolades and act as if they are coming from a stadium full of cheering people.*
>
> *Bob E. Spurgeon*

On the other hand, if you are offering something that nobody else is offering, then you need to determine who wishes they could have the benefits of your product or service. If you are selling a new computer application, then your best prospective customers will be those who already buy computer applications of similar types. Whatever you offer, go after the folks who already buy something like it. They will be your natural prospects.

What actions will you take on this idea?

184. Targeting: Who (Individuals and Centers of Influence)

In ancient times, when one army faced another larger army, one of their best winning strategies was to eliminate the opponent's leader. By doing this, the other army would be less likely to oppose you. (Think David and Goliath.)

You can also apply this principle in a positive way by gaining the approval or support of the leader. In every community there are one or more people who influence the opinions of others. If we want to gain acceptance in that community, then our best starting point is to win the support of the "centers of influence." Some of these are obvious: the company's president, the city's mayor, the church's pastor, the family's patriarch. But others are more subtle.

Get into the habit of noticing who listens to whom. Start tracking where opinions come from and how they are formed. Sometimes you can present a thought to the right person and have doors open for you all along the way. So notice who the centers of influence are in all your relationships, then pay attention to how attitudes and opinions are formed. The next time you need to gather support for something, you will know the best place to start.

What actions will you take on this idea?

185. Targeting: How (Strategies)

Consider this: Your local Boys & Girls Club needs to raise funds, and you have been chosen to chair their annual festival. How do you gain popularity and support for your event? Use the same strategies that good businesses use to sell their latest product or service—target the most likely buyers. Who already believes in youth clubs? Parents. Who else? Teachers. Who else? The police and the school system.

Now ask yourself, *How do I reach these people?* Determine what they read, what TV shows they watch, where they get their news, who they listen to, who they avoid, and what they do with their spare time. With these answers, you can easily design a plan for where to place your advertisements, who might display your posters, and whose endorsements might cause lots of people to participate. To find support, always look for the natural supporters who already believe in your cause.

What actions will you take on this idea?

186. Targeting: How (Tactics)

Strategies differ from tactics. A strategy is an overall approach to something, whereas a tactic is a specific application within the strategy.

If you wanted to sell a new breakfast cereal for kids, your strategy might be to generate demand for it among the kids by advertising during cartoon shows and at children's events. You might think, *If I get the kids to want it, then the parents will buy it for them.* This is often a better strategy than convincing the parents first. Your tactic, on the other hand, would be how you went about winning over the kids. You might give out samples, create a cute cartoon character to be your advertising hook, or develop slogans that make your product sound great to kids.

Choose your strategies wisely, then apply yourself to your tactics diligently. Success will follow.

What actions will you take on this idea?

187. Connect with the Head—Credibility

Are you believable? When you talk with others, do they trust what you say? Part of their reaction to you is based upon your credibility. If something is "incredible," that means you don't believe it.

How do you develop credibility? For one, your reputation for telling the truth tends to follow you. If you have always been known to tell the truth, others trust you. If you are a gossip, others suspect that you might also gossip about them. If you criticize others, it lessens your own credibility. They say, "If you are throwing dirt, you are only losing ground."

One way to gain credibility is to be more intentional about what you say. When you state something as the truth, make sure it is really so. Opinions, when overstated as if they were truths, usually lead to skepticism and a lack of trust. Another way to be credible is to only cite sources you know are reliable. Don't just repeat the opinions of others: Check your sources, and prove your claims. Think like a news reporter; check things out before you announce them to others. Be more credible. This is especially true when it comes to e-mails that are forwarded by others. Many of those have distorted the truth. Check your sources.

What actions will you take on this idea?

188. Activity—Are You Doing Enough?

One way to tell why someone is successful or not is to examine their activity. Look at how much they do. Some folks complain at their lack of results but don't ever increase their actions enough to become successful.

If a salesperson is good at selling but is not making many sales, the chances are that they aren't calling on many prospective customers. Assuming that they really can sell, the more people they see, the more sales they will make. If a person hasn't gotten a job despite several interviews, they might just need to schedule more interviews. Or they may need to handle the interviews better.

Often, it is a simple matter of increasing the activity to get a corresponding increase in success. Babe Ruth was one of the greatest baseball hitters of all time, but he was also the greatest at striking out! He swung the bat more often than others.

So ask yourself, "Am I trying often enough to get the outcomes that I want?" To get more, give more. Increase your activity, and the results will follow.

What actions will you take on this idea?

189. Connect with the Heart—Relationships

When I give a convention speech, I always seek to connect with people on an emotional level as well as an intellectual one. I don't simply want to "make sense" to them—I want them to care about what I'm saying. To do that, look for what *they* care about. Listen to what people say, and watch what they do. If they truly care about the quality of their product, the history of their company, the value they provide to their customers, or the pride they take in their work, then I can acknowledge and compliment them on that. The more they see that I value what they value, the more of a connection they feel with me.

The same applies to you. As others sense that you share their values or respect their commitments, they will accept you into their world. Get into the habit of noticing what matters to others. Therein lies the key to connecting with them.

What actions will you take on this idea?

190. Connect—Trust

When tension is high, trust is low. Relationship tension, that is. In any relationship there is tension. When two people are in harmony, the tension between them is low and, consequently, trust is higher. To develop more trust with anyone, manage the relationship tension.

Look for ways to be more compatible with them. Adjust your speaking speed to be similar to theirs. If you talk slowly and they talk fast, speed up a bit, but be natural. If they are talking about specifics, don't ramble on about concepts—give more examples. If they move around a lot, don't sit still; move around a bit as well. If they are being ultra-careful, take care in what you do, too. Once they see that you are careful like they are, they will trust you more. Some people like to move quickly, others prefer to take their time. Learn from them, and follow their lead. By adapting to them temporarily, you will reduce the tension between you, and trust will follow.

What actions will you take on this idea?

191. Assess the Situation—Probing

How good are you at asking questions? The better you are, the more quality answers you will get. There are two general types of questions: open-ended and closed-ended. A closed-ended question asks for a specific answer: "What time is it?" "Three o'clock" is the end of the answer.

An open-ended question asks for more information: "What do you think about the new office décor?" You could answer briefly: "I like it." Or you could elaborate for half an hour on what you like or don't like about it. I once heard someone ask an employer, "How many people work for you?" (a closed-ended question), but he answered, "About half of them work for me. I'm having trouble motivating the other half" (an open-ended answer).

Have some fun with this concept. Develop a handful of open and closed questions to use today. See how people respond. Practice becoming a better questioner, and you'll get better answers.

What actions will you take on this idea?

192. Assess the Situation—Analyzing

Your 10-year-old comes to you complaining that her brother won't let her join in the game with him and his friend. What do you do? On the surface, it seems a simple case of getting the kids to play together. If you command the brother to include his sister, you may get compliance, but did you do the right thing? The only way to know is to analyze the situation a bit more.

By looking at more aspects of the situation, you may learn that what they are doing and what she wants to do are totally different activities—she's just feeling left out. Or it could be that the game is only suited to two people, as in chess or checkers. It might be a matter of ability, if they are passing a football and she's not up to their level of skill. Or the boys are being mean to her, and she wants revenge. There are a thousand possibilities, and you can only know what is happening by exploring a bit.

This is true in all situations—there is the *What* is happening, and then the *Why*. Seek the Why before taking action. Don't just react to symptoms; find the underlying cause.

What actions will you take on this idea?

193. Assess the Person—Understanding

It is so easy to focus on behaviors and ignore the reasons behind them. Say a child has just done something better than he or she has ever done before, and they come to you saying, "Look at what I did!" On the surface, that may seem to be bragging, but underneath there is probably a yearning for feedback and acknowledgement. We need to hear the reactions of others and to have someone with whom we can celebrate our good works. Without such a person to share experiences, we feel somewhat abandoned. Take a moment to help others celebrate their wins, and you will find them smiling deep within.

Also, many of the arguments people get into day-to-day are not about what they seem to be. Often they are rooted in the desire for acknowledgement, the need for a simple apology, the feeling of not being understood. Learn to step back and notice what is behind the comments, and you will often be able to improve the situation quite easily.

What actions will you take on this idea?

194. Assess the Person—Empathizing

Two words I'd like to explore with you are Sympathy and Empathy. Sympathy is feeling as others do; Empathy is understanding how others feel. When people seem to want sympathy, they often really want empathy. We can best help and nurture others, not by feeling as they do, but by understanding what they are feeling, and by caring enough to show them that we understand. Often when others seem to want you to solve their problem, they may just want someone to understand their difficulty.

Being a good listener helps immensely. Try asking, "How does that make you feel?" or saying, "That must have been really difficult for you." Don't assume that you know what they are feeling—probe and ask them to help you understand. Display genuine concern. Your empathy will be valued more highly than your sympathy. Show them that you care.

What actions will you take on this idea?

195. Three Points and a Poem

A friend of mine jokes that all public speakers just tell "three points and a poem" in their speeches. That may be true for some, but it's actually not a bad formula for all of us. No, you don't really need a poem, but if you have to give a presentation, consider breaking your message into three easily remembered main points, and then close with an appeal for action. In country music, they say that the secret to good songwriting is three chords and the truth—a simple melody with a profound story or message.

A simple structure makes the speech easier to deliver and easier to remember. By having only three points, it is fairly easy to find a story or example to illustrate each point. Then, when you summarize the three points at the end of your speech, you can conclude by saying, "What this means to you is..." then explaining what action they can take to benefit from your message.

Try it next time you have a speech to deliver. And now for my poem... just kidding.

What actions will you take on this idea?

196. Solve Their Problem: Relevance

All of us are occasionally salespeople. When you are explaining the value of your offer, take a moment to complete this sentence: "What this means to you is..." If you are selling cell phone services, explain the wide coverage area, but remember to tell me, "What this means to you is, no more missed calls." When telling your children to come to dinner on time, explain to them, "What this means to you is, everyone will be happy when you arrive, and you won't generate the bad feelings others get when everyone has to wait for you." The more often we use this, the more persuasive we will be.

Earl Nightingale once told a story of a woman who was buying a stove. The salesman told her about the energy output and the fuel consumption, and finally she interrupted with the question, "Will it keep me warm?"

What actions will you take on this idea?

197. Give Yourself Away

David Dunn wrote a book titled *Try Giving Yourself Away*. It is a delightful short book filled with stories of what happened when he started looking for ways to be helpful every day. He'd pick up trash he hadn't discarded and spontaneously help others everywhere he went. He never sought thanks or rewards for his efforts—but he received them anyway! People would stop him on the street and say, "I saw you give up your parking space for that family in the van. That was very generous of you." Or they'd simply trust him more because they witnessed his giving attitude.

Why not try it for yourself? Starting right now, look for some ways you could help another person today. Start small: Hold open a door, lift a package for someone, drop a note of congratulations, acknowledge someone's hard work, thank someone for being patient or generous, look for something to compliment ("You are a good listener," "Your smile just fills a room," "People seem to admire you," "You are a good role model").

The more you give yourself away, the more the world will give right back to you in ways you never would've expected. Start now.

What actions will you take on this idea?

198. How to Be Creative

Creativity grows from using different frames of mind. For example: If you want to think of new ways to generate money, try applying these creativity-stimulating words:

1. Magnify—How could I do MORE of what I do and, in turn, earn more money?

2. Minify—How could I take the smallest things I do and make some of them more productive?

3. Reverse—How could I let others do something they want to do and earn money from it? Do I have tools or property or tickets I could share with others?

4. Accelerate—How could I do things faster?

5. Slow Down—How could I be more meticulous about what I do?

6. Do Less—What actions could I eliminate to free up my energies for more profitable activity?

7. Delegate—Who could I get to do things for me for a fee, or even for free?

8. Think Future—Assuming that today's work is already handled, what could I do next that might produce some income?

9. Think Past—What have I done before or stopped doing that might be beneficial now? The more you change how you look at things, the more new ideas you will see.

What actions will you take on this idea?

199. How to Give

Give people what they value, not what you value. If you want to be generous with someone, look first to determine what they care about. Learn what they admire and enjoy, then choose your gift. Too often people spend time and money on gifts that they think are wonderful, only to find that others don't agree. That's because they are thinking only from their own point of view.

If someone is very physically active, they might enjoy receiving a spa treatment, or sports tickets, or a recreational gift. A person who is more cerebral might be happier with a book or lecture recording. People who are highly social may be happiest with a lunch with friends or attendance at a party. Those who are money-oriented might like to get a gold coin or subscription to a financial magazine. Those who are competitive might like sports items or behind-the-scenes access to people they admire. Artistic people may enjoy a visit to an art gallery or a decorative item that matches their tastes.

When you want to give, ask first, "How do they like to receive?"

What actions will you take on this idea?

200. I Don't Feel Like It!

What would the world be like if we always had to wait until we felt like doing something before we actually did it? I've been told that maturity is being able to get yourself to do what needs to be done, when it needs to be done, whether you feel like it or not—and still doing it well.

HOW I MOTIVATE MYSELF

When I am down or lacking energy the quickest fix is good music, preferably Motown! And you should see me dance....even in the car!

Camille Valvo

A friend of mine said that is the case when changing a baby's diaper. He explained: You must get yourself to do what needs to be done (change the diaper), when it needs to be done (it cannot be saved for later or rescheduled to fit your desires). And it doesn't matter whether you feel like doing it or not—it still must be done. Finally, it must be done well. If you don't do it correctly, there will be bigger problems later on.

How often have you said, "I don't feel like it" or, "I'm not in the mood to do it"? These are understandable statements, but they are not justification for not taking action. Practice eliminating the "don't feel like it" factor from your life. Do what needs to be done, and do it now.

What actions will you take on this idea?

201. Solve: Personalizing

I got a letter yesterday from a business I know. At the bottom, there was a handwritten "Hello" from an acquaintance who works there. The difference between my reaction to the business letter itself and my reaction to the business letter with the personal note was dramatic! Because it was personalized, I took the time to read the entire letter and act on it. Without the personal touch, I might have set it aside or discarded it.

How can you add more personal touch to each contact? In an e-mail, you can best do it with your subject line or the opening sentence or a photo attachment. In a mailing, you can make a handwritten note on the outside or on the letter. In a phone message, you can add a personal greeting or comment. In a gift, you can add a message to the card or leave a note inside. When leaving a note at home for your family members, add a smile or personal comment. Just these little personal touches can make a big difference in the response to your communication.

What actions will you take on this idea?

202. Solve Their Problem: Involving Others

If there is a problem to solve, the quickest way to reach a solution is often to involve others; and people tend to support that which they help to create. The next time you face a dilemma, instead of just handling it yourself, reach out and ask for opinions. Seek the advice or input of others. In doing so, you honor their ability to help, and you show respect for their perspective. Just because you reach out doesn't mean that you are forced to accept their answer, but seek it nonetheless. People love to help, and they enjoy being asked for their input.

Also, if you offer your opinion to someone, don't *require* that they follow it; otherwise, they'll stop seeking your ideas. A reply that comes to mind is the formal statement "duly noted." When someone says, "Duly noted," they indicate that your idea was heard, it will be considered, and you are thanked for offering it. If participation is encouraged and ideas considered, then everyone feels valued.

What actions will you take on this idea?

203. Negotiation

A negotiation can either be a debate between adversaries or a collaboration among problem-solvers. It's often is up to you to decide which one it is. If a salesperson approaches selling a car as a power struggle, then the buyer will surely feel manipulated. But if the seller treats the buyer with respect and honesty, they will usually make a fair offer on the car. The same is true in office negotiations, conflict resolution, and parent-child disagreements.

At age 22 I was a bill collector, and I found that I got more payments when I treated the other person with dignity. The man who took over after me approached the job as an enforcer of the contract. He also ended up in the hospital from a beating a past-due customer gave him.

Sometimes good negotiations can be a very important skill. Respect the other person, be honest, be fair, and be firm.

What actions will you take on this idea?

204. Negotiations: Summarizing

When you are discussing an agreement with someone, remember to summarize occasionally. We tend to forget the finer points of discussions once we get to the next part in the dialogue. So, once in awhile, just stop and recap what you have resolved and agreed upon. Putting things in perspective this way will reduce subsequent disagreements and solidify understandings.

In selling real estate, it might go like this: "Let's recap what we've done so far. You said that a large family room was important to you and that the size of the yard wasn't a priority. That eliminates some of the homes I would have shown you. But price remains a concern, so let's look at less expensive properties where you might later renovate to build a larger family room. Is that fair?" In this case, the seller is respecting the desires of the buyer and bringing out other possible approaches to the desired result—an affordable home where the family room can be made larger.

Here's another example: In planning family holiday trips, you might say, "Okay, we have agreed to spend equal time with each family this year. We've specified two visits to my side of the family and four to yours so far." Then you can proceed with the awareness that both families are being fairly considered in your plans. Summarize often, and agreements go more smoothly.

What actions will you take on this idea?

205. Confirm: Asking

Two friends of mine once wrote a book titled *If You Don't Ask, You Don't Get*. How true. Asking for what you want is the only way to assure that your desires are known and your intentions are clear. We expect this from each other, and rightly so. Any time you are selling an idea or product, be sure to ask the other person to buy. Tell them what you want: "If you will sign this order form, then we can get started right away" or, "Do I have your approval to go ahead now?" The other person is often waiting for a cue from you that now is the time to commit.

Inexperienced sales people often make compelling presentations and then wait for the customer to say, "I'll take it." The trouble is, the customer is usually waiting for the salesperson to ask for the order. If both of them assume they are going to "think it over," then nothing will get done.

It is not bold or aggressive to ask someone to commit—it is simply the next logical step in solving their problem or taking action. Ask for what you want.

What actions will you take on this idea?

206. Confirming the Agreement

In the field of selling, the biggest area of concern is the part known as "closing the sale." Customers resist it, and sales people fear it. Often the salesperson will present the product and then defer to the sales manager to close the sale. This indicates a weakness of the selling process and a misunderstanding of what needs to be done. Sales managers often call me for help in getting their salespeople to become better "closers." But there is a problem with that: Closure is not needed; commitment is.

I tell them not to close at all. Instead, CONFIRM the sale. This is not just a play on words—it is a different focus. When we CLOSE something, it is shut, finished, over. When we CONFIRM something, it is official, agreed upon; it is a beginning, not an ending. A confirmation is a commitment. It is the initiation of a buyer-seller relationship, not the end of it. So think in terms of confirming agreements rather than of closing sales. Tension will dissolve, and cooperation will improve.

What actions will you take on this idea?

207. Assure the Customer Is Satisfied: Review

When you and I buy something, we expect that we will be happy with it. But many business people don't take care to assure that this happens. They assume that since you saw the product or heard their presentation that you know the benefits of ownership. The trouble is, our memories are not all that sharp. We forget some of the key points and recall the last thing we focused on.

So anytime you are the provider, take time to review aloud what the buyer is getting. Review their interests and concerns, the problem they were seeking to solve. Show them once again the benefits and special features of your product or service. Remind them of how good their decision was to buy from you, and assure them that you will deliver what they wanted. Say to them, "Let's recap what you wanted and how this meets your needs."

When we refresh their awareness after they have made a purchase, we strengthen their satisfaction and increase their loyalty, as well.

What actions will you take on this idea?

208. Assure the Customer Is Satisfied: Follow Through

Follow-through may be the largest problem area in business. It is easy to make promises, come to agreements, choose goals and strategies. The hard part is making it happen.

Think of your own experience; how often have you encountered a problem with someone else's follow-through? You buy a product, but it doesn't perform as you wished; you call their service department and get stuck in "voice jail." You agree to meet at a certain time and place, and then the other person doesn't show or, even worse, doesn't call.

Consider these: A prospective client asks you for information, and you send the materials, but you don't call to convert their interest into a purchase. Someone offers to send you some information and never does. You discuss something with your child, agree on a new household rule, and then you don't enforce the new agreement. Things return to the way they were before.

Follow-through is where things happen. Commit today to instant and constant follow-through.

What actions will you take on this idea?

209. To Build Customer Loyalty: Up-Serve Them

There is a concept in business known as Up-Selling, which gets the customer to buy more. For example, in food retailing, the server may ask, "Do you want fries with that?" By asking, they increase the likelihood that you will order more food. This is also known as Add-On Selling. The problem is that the customers sometimes resent it, and the sales people just don't do it.

I say we change the game entirely. Stop Up-Selling and start Up-Serving. Don't just change your words, but change your actions. Up-Selling is about a bigger sale. Up-Serving is about greater satisfaction.

Look for more ways to serve the customer. Find better solutions to their needs. When you seek to increase their *satisfaction*, often you will get even larger *transactions*, a bigger sale. When you are no longer seeking to persuade them, you are seeking to help them. When you put your focus on serving, the selling will surely follow.

What actions will you take on this idea?

210. To Sustain Good Relationships with Customers: Master the Recovery

A study once showed that most customers leave their providers not because of dissatisfaction, but rather because they felt the company was indifferent to them. Another part of this study showed that a customer who has had a problem with your company that was quickly and properly resolved is MORE likely to remain loyal to you than a customer who never had a problem at all. Isn't that amazing? This is because by resolving the problem, we show them that we care, that we value them as customers.

The process of recovering from a customer's problem has a few critical steps:

1. Show them that you understand their problem by listening to them without interrupting.

2. Apologize for the inconvenience this has created (even if you weren't the one to blame).

3. Correct the situation.

4. Check to make sure they feel the problem has been solved.

Master the recovery process, and you will gain more loyal customers.

What actions will you take on this idea?

211. Manage Your Resources

In times of great need, often there are plenty of resources available that we can't access very easily. During the disaster recovery after Hurricane Katrina in New Orleans in 2005, tons of supplies were sent to the city, but many people still went without until ways were found to get the supplies to the people. The problem wasn't resources; it was distribution.

The same is true for you and me. We often have the information and support we need, but we aren't organized enough to access it, or we forget that we have it. How many times have you gone to the store for an item only to learn upon getting it home that you already had the same item in your cupboard or garage? Once in a while we should just explore our own inventories to see what we have. Check the files, cabinets, and storage areas to remind yourself of what is there. You may already have the things you feel you need. Likewise, occasionally remind yourself of who you know and what they do. Sometimes the solutions, suggestions, answers, and helpers we seek are already within our circle of friends and acquaintances.

What actions will you take on this idea?

212. Manage Your Information

It is not what you know that counts—it is what you remember when you need it. Often when we are faced with a challenge, we forget what we already know and consequently don't bring our best solutions to the problem. Have you ever thought of a great response to something long after you needed it, perhaps on your way home after the event? I've been in debates, business conflicts, and sales calls over the years in which my best ideas came to me after the moment had passed. I didn't lack the intellect or right strategy; I just came up with it at the wrong time.

One solution to this is forethought. When you know that a possible challenge may arise, review your information in advance. Get the key information out of your memory files, and put it on the desktop of your mind. Review your notes, scan your files, visualize the event in your mind, and think of possible solutions. Those who fare best when the heat is on are those who have already rehearsed the event in their minds.

> **HOW I MOTIVATE MYSELF**
>
> *All you have to do is 10 minutes and if after that point exercise feels terrible you don't have to do more. By that point it feels good, you're warmed up and your respiration has finally caught up with your breathing! The endorphins start almost immediately so by then you're hooked!*
>
> *Debra Atkinson*

What actions will you take on this idea?

213. Manage Yourself for Continuing Growth

An organism that stops growing has begun to die. The nature of life is growth and advancement. We are organisms, and as long as we grow, we continue to thrive.

Advice columnist Ann Landers once told of a couple who had drifted apart after many years of marriage. The woman was committed to a career in nursing, constantly learning and improving. The man had ceased his studies and settled into a dull routine. For this relationship to revive, he needed to re-engage his life, break his routines, and start again to grow, learn, and improve.

Make a commitment today to never stop growing. Keep your interests alive, get outside your routines, and connect with others, even when you don't feel like it. There is always more to learn and more living to do. The more active you are, the more fun you will have—even when you don't feel like it. Remember those times you did something despite not being in the mood, yet having a great time. Don't let inertia rule your life. Take charge, and keep on growing.

What actions will you take on this idea?

214. Manage Yourself, Motivate Yourself

How do you know if you are self-motivated? If you can get yourself to do what is needed, even when you don't feel like it. The operative phrase is "when you don't feel like it." Most anyone can motivate themselves when the motives are already active, but that isn't self-control—it is just following impulses. The people who master their lives and control their own destiny are those who spend a lifetime learning how to direct themselves in productive ways.

What is it that gets you to take action? Are you competitive? Do you seek the approval of others? Is it pride of workmanship or being of service that lights your fires? Take time to find out. Start today to study your own patterns. Learn to notice what it is that gets your interest and holds it. The best students of all are not only students of their craft, but also students of themselves. Know yourself, and then you will be in a better position to grow yourself.

What actions will you take on this idea?

215. Living in Fast Time

In the 20th century, times were slower than they are today. With instant communication and Internet accessibility, we are connecting more often, collaborating more openly, and creating more change than ever in history. As my friend Leland Russell says, we are living in "fast time," when the change around you is greater than what you can keep pace with. We used to occasionally get "caught up", but today we are never truly caught up—we are always obsolete on some subjects and out of date in many other ways.

To cope with Fast Time, we need to pay more attention and expand our awareness. The more often we tune in to the rest of the world and our own profession, the less likely it is we will miss important developments. Also, the more we broaden our exposure to areas we wouldn't normally study, the more options we see, and the more possibilities we will have. So stay alert and reach farther in your exploration. The world is expanding in fascinating and wonderful ways. What could you study today?

What actions will you take on this idea?

216. Think Strategically

When we think strategically, we advance more quickly. Strategic thinking means thinking with the end in mind. Focus on the outcome you want, visualize the ideal results you seek, and then make all decisions in ways that advance your cause. Strategic thinking has three elements: forecasting, goal setting, and self-improvement.

As you think about the future, identify the factors that exist today and how they might affect you in the future. Plan for those influences. For example, if you were in the telephone business several years ago and you didn't forecast the impact that cell phones would have, you'd be out of business today. If you had a successful fax machine business years ago, you'd be unemployed today if you didn't change with the technology of the times.

Once you think about the future, clarify your goals into a clear picture of what you want, and keep it before you every day. We are drawn toward what we focus on, or, as Earl Nightingale once said, "You become what you think about."

Next, ask yourself how you will need to improve in order to bring about the future you want. The more you anticipate the future, motivate yourself toward your goals, and improve your ability to achieve them, the more likely your desired future will be.

What actions will you take on this idea?

217. Future Factors

When you see the big picture of what is coming, you are better able to make its effect work *for* you rather than *against* you. Learn to continually scan your world to assess the current reality, then explore future possibilities as well. I regularly read *Futurist* magazine and Daniel Burrus' Techno-Trends newsletter for just that purpose. I want to know what is coming in many fields, not just my own. I also want to learn about the strategic issues that are likely to affect me. In his work *Leading in Fast Time*, futurist Leland Russell explains that knowing your options begins with knowing what is coming.

Become a student of your industry and our society. Read trade journals, explore Websites, and tap into knowledge that goes beyond your usual sources. The more you know, the more possibilities you will have. Expand the number of sources from which you gather information. Seek views that don't agree with yours. See all sides of the situation before you settle on the one that feels right to you.

Your future will be a result of the factors that are in the hands of others and the responses to them that are within your own hands.

What actions will you take on this idea?

218. Future Picture

If you don't know where you are headed, it is assured that you will miss your goal. When Walt Disney first envisioned Disneyland, he was in Tivoli Gardens in Copenhagen with his friend Art Linkletter. He said to Art, "Someday I'm going to build a place like this for families." Walt Disney went on to crystallize his "Future Picture" so well that hundreds of others joined his efforts to create the happiest place on earth. Today all of us have been touched by the Disney magic.

What is your future picture? What do you want to be, have, experience, or do in the future? The clearer your picture becomes, the more you and others will be motivated to make it a reality. Spend some time writing a description of what you want. Make it clear, go into great detail, create a vivid description that anyone can see.

To paraphrase an old line, When you SEE it, you will achieve it! Don't wait for the hard reality to exist before you go to work on your goal. Create a new reality in your future picture, then turn it into a fact that all can see. When you see it in your mind, you will achieve it.

What actions will you take on this idea?

219. Future Conduct

If you keep doing what you have always done, you will keep on getting what you have gotten so far. It is your conduct that changes your future! What do you want to do or achieve in the future? Get clear on that picture, then ask yourself what new behavior will bring it into reality. *How do I need to conduct myself in order to have the future I want?* Will Rogers once said it is not what you know that counts—it is what you do with it that makes the difference. Behavior is the key to success.

Clarify the actions, the daily behaviors of the person who would achieve your goals. Be specific: How would they work, study, communicate, handle problems, keep themselves fit, balance their personal and professional priorities? Make this picture as complete as you can, and then live it! Begin to advance your own behavior to the patterns of the person you will need to be. Then you will start getting what you want.

What actions will you take on this idea?

220. Think As If

Would you think differently if your dreams had already come true? Of course you would. If your marriage were perfect, would you think differently about your family and your life? If you were at the top of your profession, would you think differently? If you had won the lottery, would you think differently? The biggest challenge in advancing your life is not in advancing your circumstances—it is in advancing your thinking.

Unhealthy people who get into good shape sometimes fall back to old habits because they still think in unhealthy ways. People who suddenly become rich often become poor again because their thinking didn't change their financial behavior. Well, this works in reverse as well. You can change your thinking first, and your circumstances will follow. If you desire to become slender, start thinking like slender people. Don't make food the center of your day; just eat when you need to. Don't dread exercise—enjoy it! Don't plan to be tired, plan to be full of energy. Your attitude will select your reality.

What actions will you take on this idea?

221. Act As If You Couldn't Fail

What would you do if you knew you could not fail? What would you try? What goals would you pursue? Often fear and doubt keep us from pursuing our dreams. We assume we won't make it, so we don't even try.

Let's reverse that process. Start to assume that you CAN do almost anything you set out to do: It just might be true. Approach your life as if you cannot fail. This is not "unrealistic"—it is merely optimistic, in advance of having proof to back it up. After all, failure is only a permanent state for those who accept it as such. Successful people see failure as a momentary state, and they get right back to work on their goals. Act as if you cannot fail. You may surprise yourself by achieving more than ever before. What do you want most in the world right now? How would you go after it if you knew that you would ultimately succeed? Go for it.

What actions will you take on this idea?

222. Failure Is an Experience, Not a State

There are those who are broke, and there are those who have no money. The difference is in the word "broke". When something is broken, it doesn't operate properly. Now, most people would fix it, but people with a failure mentality simply adjust to the new reality and stay "broke." That is the poverty mentality. Lots of us have been without money in our lives, but we didn't become poor. Poverty is despair, helplessness, a state of giving up, no longer trying.

But in poverty, there are always a few who don't accept their state as a lasting one. They look for new ways to work, new things to learn, new solutions to problems. These folks become successful despite their humble beginnings. This is usually not because they are gifted or got a break. It is because they refused to stay poor and did what was necessary to overcome it. You see, failure is simply a temporary situation.

If you lose a race, you haven't lost all races—you've just lost this one. If you are bankrupt, you haven't lost your ability to earn and save money. You have simply had a bad financial experience. Take your setbacks as starting points, and never accept limitations as being permanent. You can do what you wish to do.

What actions will you take on this idea?

223. October 2004 *National Geo* Article

In October of 2004, Joel K. Bourne, Jr. wrote an article published in *National Geographic* titled "Gone with the Water." In this article, he described in alarming details the hurricane and flooding disaster of Katrina along the New Orleans coast. He even described the panic and confusion that followed. **All of this was one year in advance of the actual event**.

No, he is not a psychic; he is a journalist and researcher. He determined exactly what the vulnerabilities of New Orleans were and predicted the results if a large hurricane were to strike. My point is that people knew this could happen. They knew this long before Katrina was even a tropical depression. They didn't act to prevent it because very few people believed it was ever likely to happen—but Joel Bourne did.

In all our lives, there are warnings like this. Sometimes it is a persistent pain that warns us of a health risk, or a recurring argument that tells us our relationship needs attention. It may be a business problem or a high credit balance that never goes down. But the warnings are there. Don't let a Hurricane Katrina occur in any part of your life before you take action to prepare. Let the lesson of the Gulf Coast be a cautionary tale to get you started in preparing to meet life's challenges with confidence.

What actions will you take on this idea?

224. Rebirth Begins in the Mind

The Gulf Coast, specifically New Orleans, has gone through the process of rebirth since the hurricane destruction at the start of this century. The rebirth was not in their tangible circumstances alone, because rebirth begins in the mind. If people continue to think as they have in the past, they will recreate past circumstances. Rebirth requires new thinking.

Poverty, for example, is situational and attitudinal. The situation, a lack of money, can be easily corrected by giving money. But the poverty attitude requires much more. Poverty mindedness is a form of helplessness. People who think this way consider themselves incapable of improving. The tragedy is that they are NOT incapable; they just think they are, and that's enough to immobilize them.

So what can we do to help people advance? Give them hope, show them examples of how others have made it, tell them stories of self-improvement, facilitate discussions with optimistic people, reinforce the positives all around them, and transcend the negatives.

A rebirth can be achieved from even the darkest of circumstances and often has been. But first there must be a decision to change. Let's show others that they can do it too!

What actions will you take on this idea?

225. Meaning and Purpose Aren't Found in Things or Places

If only I had a home of my own. If only I had a better job. If only I didn't live around so many losers. If only I were healthier. If only, if only, if only. Hey, break the pattern! A good life isn't found in things. It is found in actions. Get outside of yourself, start helping others in some way, and voila! You will experience a sense of satisfaction and fulfillment. The quickest way to feel good about yourself is to do good for other people.

Do what? Do anything that is useful. Pick up the trash others ignore. Help a stranger. Volunteer to assist a school, Boys & Girls Club, or community center. If you are not physically strong, help in the office or on the phone. If you are not well educated, help stock shelves and greet guests. Look beyond your circumstances, and fill the needs. You may not get paid for doing these things, but you don't get

HOW I MOTIVATE MYSELF

I do this too but say 5 min, lol.
Works every time!

Amy McIlwain

paid for avoiding them, either. Try to find two things you can do before the end of this day that will help someone—just two.

What actions will you take on this idea?

226. Things and Places Have Value ,Too

When I go home to Arkansas, I have feelings that can't be replicated anywhere else. There is something special about "home" that resonates deep in one's soul. You remember the tree in your family's front yard, the day your neighbor built a new porch, the smells of the first day of autumn, the days before the streets were all paved, the times when you'd sneak into the ballpark. All these moments come flooding back in subtle ways. Home matters.

And yet as the song says, "anywhere you are is home." Each day we make new memories, build new connections, and find new friends. Wherever we stay for a while starts to become a home to us. It is good to honor our home, and it is good to occasionally let go so that new homes can be created. We are nest builders, yes, but we are also explorers. So honor both parts of your nature. Never stop growing.

What actions will you take on this idea?

227. Usefulness and Self-Esteem

I remember a silly poem from when I was a kid: "Nobody loves me, everybody hates me. I'm going to just eat worms." Silly, yes, but some people actually carry that attitude through life. They accept the worst life has to offer, because they don't feel worthy of anything better.

Personally, I believe that everyone deserves the best life can offer. And a good way to get others to expect more from life is to help them become more "useful." When you do something that matters, you feel needed. The more you feel needed, the more you feel worthy of good things. So, to increase self-esteem, do something worthwhile.

I once asked a psychiatrist what was needed to assist a deeply depressed friend. He answered, "Action, any action. By doing something, your friend will feel more useful and therefore have more hope." So, when you or anyone you know is depressed, do something. The bolder the better, but get up and make things happen.

What actions will you take on this idea?

228. Traveling Strategy: Reduce the Variables

I've been traveling constantly for over 40 years. I've flown, driven, and ridden over much of the free world, and I've learned a few travel strategies that all of us can benefit from.

First: Reduce the variables. If you have two stops to your destination, get to the first one as early as you can. If your flight is at 10:00 a.m. and you can get to the airport early, do so. Go through the security screening as early as practical, and then relax with a cup of coffee or your cell phone near the gate where you will depart. Then, if anything changes, you will be the first to know and the first to be able to book an alternate route.

Second: Pack lightly. Wear the same jacket with two outfits, pack a set of dress shoes, and wear your casual shoes to travel. Avoid checking luggage if you can.

Third: Enjoy the travel. See the scenery, explore the airports, watch the people, sample the foods, take an interest in the other travelers (especially your seatmates), but don't bother them unless they really want to talk. Some people prefer to withdraw while they travel. Find your style of travel, and have fun.

What actions will you take on this idea?

229. Praise Somebody If You Like What You Are Getting

One evening while dining with friends, my friend Joe not only paid for our dinner, he also stayed behind to speak with the manager. I asked what he said, and he told me how happy he was with our server. He said, "I told the manager specifically what she did well so that he could acknowledge her and teach the others to do likewise. She learned our names and used them when she came back to the table. She heard us mention a birthday, and she brought a cupcake. She cared!"

When you like what someone is doing for you, tell them about it. Good works, when not acknowledged, tend to stop after a while. Good works when appreciated openly get repeated. So tell people what you like and how you feel. It is rare for praise to be shared and common for complaints to be made. Spread your praise wherever you go. People will start looking forward to your arrival.

What actions will you take on this idea?

230. Tell Yourself the Truth

Ever been accused of "kidding yourself"? Most of us, on occasion, are guilty of not telling ourselves the truth. To avoid a problem we don't know how to solve, we act as if it isn't a problem. All the while we know in the back of our minds that it is waiting for us "someday." Like financial planning—when you don't feel competent at handling finances and you fear that you don't have enough money to do any planning, then no planning is done at all. Later on, of course, financial problems arise, and by then it is often too late to do anything to avoid them.

But you plan for things before they become a reality. You plan for wealth while you are broke. You plan for fitness while you are out of shape. You plan for education while you are ignorant. Starting today, tell yourself the truth more often. Take one category, like finances, and find out exactly where you stand. Then begin to plan how to make things better. Seek resources and people who know what you need to know. Keep on learning, and you'll keep on earning.

What actions will you take on this idea?

231. Hope Is Only Found in You

When things look hopeless, remember that it is YOU who is lacking hope, not your circumstances. Don't say, "There is no hope"; instead, say, "I have no hope... yet." There is almost always a better way, somehow. Never give up hope. But also, never confuse hope with wishing. Hope requires an optimistic outlook and action. Wishing is passive.

When you feel despair, a good starting point for hope is Situation Analysis. Take stock of exactly where you stand. Consider all aspects of the situation. Don't lapse into depression; stay actively involved in defining where you are right now. As you do this, you will start to notice little opportunities, options you hadn't thought of before. By exploring these, you may open up whole new vistas for solutions within your grasp. So keep the faith—things will get better as long as you get better, too. Accept what you can't control, control what you can, and reach out when you need assistance. Others are eager to help.

What actions will you take on this idea?

232. Why Don't the Rich Give More?

A large number of people believe that Robin Hood had it right: Take from the rich, and give to the poor. It's a simple concept, I agree. But in most cases, the rich are already giving to the poor, at least here in the USA. Our society is the most generous society in history. We give in unprecedented numbers. Both the rich and poor alike are a giving people. We also have structured our tax laws to encourage even more giving. When we find a cause that is good for large numbers of people, we offer tax incentives for contributing to them.

Many people decry the income gap as if equality were a good thing. It doesn't matter how much the most successful people make—it doesn't diminish what the poor can get. This is not a zero-sum game. The more anyone earns, the more they will use it, which creates opportunities for those who have less. It is easy to see a huge home or large income figures and say, "They have so much, they should give even more."

Maybe so, but taxing the rich doesn't usually produce more money for the poor—it takes money away from the rich. Okay with you? Not with me—I want them to stay rich! When people are rich, they create more work for others, because they buy things and hire others to do things they can't do for themselves. That means that jobs are created, stores are kept busy, families are fed, and our economy works. Let's create even more rich people. Then let's be among them.

What actions will you take on this idea?

233. Manage Your Intent Rather Than Your Content

If you were giving a speech, would people care most about your content or your intent? The content is your words and details, the examples and proof you offer. Your intent is your purpose, the "why" behind your words. I have found that if your intent is to impress people, they probably won't be impressed. But if your intent is to help them, they will admire you.

The next time you have to address a group or make a sales presentation, work on your intent. Seek to truly be of service first, then look for clever or profound ways to say things. One of the most admired and quoted speeches ever was a very short commencement address delivered by former British Prime Minister Winston Churchill. He told the assembled graduates, "Never give up. Never, never, never give up." And then he sat down. Not much content, but huge on intent. And people still remember it.

What actions will you take on this idea?

234. Aristotle on Trust and Eloquence

Aristotle is quoted as saying that eloquence will not move people nearly as well as trust. Having the right words, being able to deliver them with power, and developing a powerful voice all might serve you well, but... If people don't trust you, they won't act on your message. Trust is first among the factors that generate action. We follow people we trust. We trust people who have our best interests in mind.

So, if you would have others follow your lead, make sure you are leading them where THEY would like to go. Look for the benefits to them in what you are suggesting. That's how you will develop followers. Even something as simple as asking for money can be made more appealing by describing how the other person may feel when they have given the money. Charities often quote the following: You make a living by what you earn, but you make a life by what you give. Eloquent, sure, but more importantly, if said by someone you trust, that is all the reason you need to give more generously.

What actions will you take on this idea?

235. Spend Your Life Learning to Motivate Yourself

I've been a motivational speaker for over 40 years, and people often ask me, "Who motivates the motivator?" Well, the answer is: the motivator does. Every highly motivated person I've ever known is, most of all, SELF-motivated! They don't wait for others to get them started; they make a lifelong study of how to become and remain SELF-starters.

Self motivation is pure gold in the business world. Every employer is looking for people who are highly productive and low-maintenance. By low-maintenance, I mean those who don't require constant reminders, incentives, threats, and encouragement in order to do their jobs. What motivates you? In other words, what are your motives? What do you want? Why? How can you get yourself to go after it? When you get depressed, how can you get yourself re-motivated? Learn to manage YOU, and the world is yours.

> **HOW I MOTIVATE MYSELF**
>
> *Bribery. When I finish this task I am procrastinating on I get to buy myself a guilt free chocolate shake.*
> Brian Walter

What actions will you take on this idea?

236. Be Thankful for the Imprints Others Left on You

I've met some people who are mega-rich, billionaires, they have more money than most people could count. Without exception, they were very poor at some point in their lives. The imprint of poverty was essential to their continuing motivation to succeed. I know people who were ignored and criticized as kids, yet went on to become substantial leaders and solid citizens. Why? Because the imprint of their tough times provided the motivation to overcome them.

We tend to be motivated by what we lack or fear, more than merely what we want. So don't fret about your hard times or former abuses; accept those imprints as part of who you are. Find within them the motivation to transcend your hurts and truly succeed. Become the kind of person who never again would have to go through such experiences. Be a person of substance, a giving, caring person, who helps to make the world a better place. We will love you for it, and you'll like yourself better, as well.

What actions will you take on this idea?

237. People You Meet and Books You Read

Carl Sagan once commented on the unique power of books to allow us to enter the minds of others both alive and dead, near and far. The colorful and wonderful Charlie Jones, author of *Life Is Tremendous*, said that you will be the same person five years from now that you are today except for two things: the people you meet and the books you read.

We grow through interaction. In books, we can interact with the wisdom of the ages and the lives and stories of great people. By forming the habit of reading something every day, we enrich our lives, advance our minds, and discover new solutions to old problems. Make reading a priority in your life. Start with what you enjoy most. Make a habit of devoting part of each day to reading. Then explore new topics. Visit bookstores often, and explore the shelves. You will find more books you wish to read than you have time to devote to them—so start with one or two. Go to the library and learn what they have. Stay a while and read. Explore the wonderful information that others have written for you.

What actions will you take on this idea?

238. The Cost of Not Learning to Use E-mail

Grandma won't try to learn to use e-mail, so she doesn't get to see the digital pictures that the rest of the family shares every week. Bill won't learn to use the directory on his cell phone, so he has to carry a written phone directory in addition to the phone. Brandy has a new oven that virtually cooks your meals for you, but she uses only the functions that she knew on her older, standard oven. Jane still uses a paper ledger because she's intimidated by the idea of learning to do online banking. Jack has a security system at home that he's never read the manual for, so he leaves the house unarmed when he is away. Willie has the same problem with DVD player at home. He's still using VHSs so that he doesn't have to learn more.

What's the cost of not learning to use new technology? More than most of us realize. What learning have you been avoiding? How long do you think you can put it off before the cost becomes too high? Consider how little joy you get from avoiding the learning process. Then project how soon you will learn the basics you need. Isn't it worth the temporary discomfort of learning something new? You will only have to learn it once—then you can use it every day.

What actions will you take on this idea?

239. Master One Part of Life, and the Others Will Follow

A friend once asked me, as he patted my chubby tummy, "What is that about?" I said, "It is evidence that I have a lot of projects going on and not many of them getting completed." Until he asked, I hadn't thought about why my eating discipline was lagging. How could that be? When we are struggling in one area, we tend to neglect our other needs. So stay in balance where you can; everything is connected.

When your business is struggling, be sure to eat right and work out often. When you are out of shape physically, take control of your finances. If you have relationship problems, make sure you read inspirational books and hear uplifting lectures. In other words, all of your life is connected, so take care of what you can, even if you still have problems in another category. When you improve one part of your life, the others often follow. Discipline and motivation tend to transfer well from one part of life to another.

Naturally you should also address your primary needs in the best ways that you can. But take heart and know that any form of self-improvement will have good spillover effects. Get to work on you, and things around you will start showing progress as well.

What actions will you take on this idea?

240. Elsie's Recovery Factors

When my mother-in-law had heart surgery many years ago, I remember wondering what would have the biggest effect on her recovery: the care the doctor provided, her physical fitness and genetic strength, the love and support of her family, or her own attitude about her recovery? What do you think?

I'd say all of them matter a lot. Her optimism about recovering was vital to her well being. Doctors used to call it the "will to live," or in her case, the "will to heal." All those other factors mattered greatly as well.

We are a system of connected systems. Our thinking, our fitness, our genetics, our relationships, our nutrition, and our support network—all are part of the overall system. When we appreciate their connectedness, we are more likely to act in ways that sustain our well being.

What actions will you take on this idea?

241. What Would You Save in a Crisis?

The tornado was at the end of my driveway, or at least it looked that close. So I quickly decided to abandon all the photo albums in the house and return to the people I loved who were sheltered in the basement. That was a defining moment in my life. Never again have I felt strongly attached to my belongings; I care most about the people I love. My "stuff" can usually be replaced—and even for the irreplaceable things, I'll be okay without them.

This hit home again on a recent motorcycle tour of the Alps. I had been taking photos each day and had captured some wonderful images of famous and beautiful places. Then we dropped the camera, broke it, and lost all the images. I was crushed! It took me half an hour to process the emotions and get back to normal. When the disappointment subsided, I came to the conclusion that my most valuable take-away would be the memories, not the photos. So I spent the rest of the trip truly enjoying every moment. Then we bought some nice photo brochures to take home.

What would you save in a crisis?

What actions will you take on this idea?

242. Things That Are Measured Tend to Improve

Years ago, management consultant Peter Drucker stated that "things that are measured tend to improve." This is also known as The Hawthorne Effect, based on behavior changes noted at a factory where production measurement was posted daily. And it applies to virtually everything.

If you measure your daily food intake, you will tend to eat more wisely. If you measure your exercise daily, you will exercise more. If you measure every dollar you spend, you'll spend more carefully. You don't necessarily have to have a plan or a goal; the mere fact that you are measuring your actions causes you to think about them more carefully. One thing you will notice about superior athletes is that "winners keep score." They always know their numbers, and they can always tell you the score of the event.

> **HOW I MOTIVATE MYSELF**
>
> *I ask myself this question, "What do I owe my future self... NOW?"*
>
> *Dave Jensen*

So what would you like to improve in your world? Begin by measuring some aspect of it. Keep a log or a chart to show the daily fluctuations. In other words, keep score.

What actions will you take on this idea?

243. Courage

What does it mean to be courageous? I think it means that you face your fears and take action anyway. Courage is not the absence of fear; it is acting despite your fears. Without fear, what need is there for courage? It is courageous to openly admit weakness when you feel you will be judged. It is courageous to speak up for what is right, especially when others don't. It is courageous to show that you care when you are surrounded by cynics who pretend they don't. It is courageous to stand up for someone who is weak. It is courageous to live by your principles and values, even when others don't agree with those values. Daily living takes courage. It takes courage to do what is necessary, especially when it is not admired.

Courageous people are not people who are not afraid. They are people who do what is right and needed, despite their fears of embarrassment or pain. Where does courage come from? From the inner knowledge that by doing what is right, sooner or later things will work out—and from the knowledge that you will respect yourself more by doing what you know is the right thing.

What actions will you take on this idea?

244. Jason Said, "Grandpa, I'm Very Happy!"

The sun was setting, and you could follow its progress by watching the shadows rise on the surrounding hills. My grandson Jason was with me there in our backyard. I told him that the stars would come out soon, and then we saw the first ones faintly appear. He was 4 at the time. He said, "I have to put on my pajamas now," so I let him go into the house. I told him, "Come back in a few minutes, and I'll show you something very special."

When he returned, all ready for bed, I picked him up, and we walked outside into the dark. He looked up and saw a brilliant display of stars. It was a perfectly clear night. He exclaimed, "Wow, Grandpa, they are everywhere!" Then he paused, looked at me, and said, "Grandpa, I'm very happy!"

My heart almost melted. Whew, what a moment. I said, "Jason, I'm very happy too!" Even today, when I think of that experience, I become "very happy."

Treasure the moments with people you love, and help them discover the wonders of this world. You will be very happy you did.

What actions will you take on this idea?

245. Reading a Book: Sometimes One Third Valuable and Two Thirds Boring

I took a cruise recently and read a book while on board. The book was fascinating... for about a third of the way through. The rest of the book was not very well written and was mostly boring. But the book served me well nonetheless. I got many good ideas from it, and I'm glad I read it. Even the dull part had some value.

There is value in most every resource. So when you pick up a book, don't require that the entire book be valuable—just look for what it has to offer you, and appreciate the value it offers. Some books will change your life, some will touch your heart, some will put you to sleep, and some will expand your mind. It is said that those who don't read are no better off than those who can't read. Pick up a good book today, or even one that is not so good. Spend some time reading, and find the value it brings you.

What actions will you take on this idea?

246. What's Important Now? (WIN)

I love my friend Joe Willard's simple question: "What's Important Now?" He writes the initials WIN to remind himself to ask this. In any situation, it is not the situation that matters most, because that is already history. What matters most is "What's important NOW?"

Say you are in an auto accident and are alone by the road with a bleeding injury. You may be tempted to groan from the pain or worry about the wreck, but what is important NOW is to stop the bleeding. If you don't do that, there will be no future. I learned this as an Army medic years ago. First Aid demanded that first you stop the bleeding. Then you clear the airway so the person can breathe. Only after that can you protect the wound and treat for shock.

In business and at home, the same question will serve you well. Whatever happens, get into the habit of asking, "What's important now?" When you arrive at a restaurant and they overlooked your reservation, what's important: chastising them for the error, or finding a way to get your party some dinner? If we asked WIN more often, we'd probably spend less time blaming and arguing and more time actually making things happen.

What actions will you take on this idea?

247. What Would the "Person of the Year" Be Doing Now?

This is a bit of wisdom from my friend and mentor Joe D. Willard. As a young salesperson, he aspired to become the "salesperson of the year." So he asked himself daily, "What would the salesperson of the year be doing now?" This caused him to use his time more productively and to constantly think beyond his current situation and focus on advancing toward his goal. Not surprisingly, he quickly became the salesperson of the year, and sustained this level of success for several years.

What is your goal? Think of yourself as the person who has already achieved it and ask, "What would that person be doing now?" When you experience a setback, ask what the person of the year would do. When you achieve a success beyond what you expected, don't just bask in the glow—take it to the next level. Everyone, no matter how successful, has good and bad experiences. The difference between successful and unsuccessful people is in how they respond to those experiences. No matter what comes, ask yourself: "What would the person of the year be doing now?"

What actions will you take on this idea?

248. How to Know What to Give to Someone

How do you know what gift to give someone? How can you be sure they will like it? I'd say, "Ask them!" No, I don't mean necessarily that we should announce our generous intentions in advance. I just mean that the best source of information about what someone would like to receive is the person himself.

Learn to observe people creatively. Look at what they like and don't. Look at what they do with their spare time. Listen to what they talk about with enthusiasm. Notice what they do when they have some extra money. Pay attention to the stories they tell and the comments they make. They will show and tell you what they care about. Then, when it comes time to buy or give them a gift, choose what they would most enjoy. The problem with much gift-giving is that it is done from the giver's perspective rather than the receiver's. We should be giving what they'd like to get, not merely what we'd like to give.

What actions will you take on this idea?

249. How to Express Sympathy

Years ago, when my father died, many of my friends expressed their sympathy. Months later, I was reflecting on the experience, and I noticed the many forms of expression. Some were unsure what to do so they just said, "I'm so sorry." Others showed up and greeted me warmly but silently. Still others recounted stories of how much my father had meant to them. Some sent sympathy cards with their signature. Others sent cards with notes and memories included. Some showed up with food, and some offered to send thank-you notes on behalf of our family. Some just left us alone and later on said, "I was sorry to hear of your loss."

This told me not what they said, but how they felt toward me and my dad, and how they expressed their sympathy. This is hard for all of us. I've decided to:

1. Always do something to let the person know I care.

2. Be specific—mention a memory or express a feeling or just let them know that even if I don't know what to say, I want them to know that I care.

3. Not make the message about me. It is their moment.

What actions will you take on this idea?

250. Acknowledging a Religious Holiday

Happy Ramadan, Happy Lunar New Year, Merry Christmas, Happy

Hanukkah... All these are expressions of good wishes. But often we are criticized for saying them because they aren't "politically correct." I say, "Get over it!" For crying out loud, all we are doing is passing on good wishes. When someone says Happy Birthday, do you apologize to all who are present for whom today is NOT their birthday? Of course not! Let's stop being hypersensitive.

Wishing everyone a Merry Christmas on or about December 25 is simply spreading cheer. It is not selling religion, nor is it in any way judgmental. Saying Happy New Year is in many ways the same. If you are Chinese and it is not New Year's Day to you, just accept the good feelings and say thank you. The same holds true for us Christians. Let's start respecting all religions and stop worrying about who believes what. If everyone tries to say the exact right thing, people will just do nothing.

I say, let's keep the good wishes alive. So Happy Groundhog Day to you. My family doesn't celebrate groundhogs, but maybe you do.

What actions will you take on this idea?

251. How Long Will You Live? Life Expectancy: Yours and Statistics (RealAge)

How long will you live? According to statisticians, the normal U.S. life expectancy is now approaching 80 years. Wow. A century ago, the average life expectancy was less than 45 years. That sure puts the age-65 retirement model in question, doesn't it?

How long you and I live depends on variables, but many of those are in our own hands. We know that people stay healthier longer when they have: good relationships, healthy eating habits, regular vigorous exercise, ways of reducing stress, and a sense of purpose and meaning in their lives. So how long will you live? Well, if you have none of the above, then it may not be very long. But if you decide to live a long, full life, the ways to do it are known and doable.

One interesting exercise is the questionnaire online at RealAge.com. It shows you your age in the context of your genetic history, medical history, and lifestyle. Try it out. It may change your perspective. As Spock used to say on *Star Trek*, may you "live long and prosper."

What actions will you take on this idea?

252. Age Wave: Redesigning Our World for the New Old

When I was growing up, "old age" started at 65. Today we often see 75-year-old people skiing, surfing, and lifting weights. "Old" isn't what it used to be. Our world is being redesigned so that sports cars, fitness clubs, and even movie seats are becoming more accessible to the new, vital, fit seniors. Newsprint is getting larger for older eyes, and much of our world is evolving once again to suit the Baby Boomers. The 78 million people in the Baby Boom are now reaching retirement age (at the rate of over 10,000 people a day), but they aren't retiring. Instead, they are retooling for a new life or lifestyle.

> **HOW I MOTIVATE MYSELF**
>
> *Condition myself to three words- DO IT NOW. My deal w myself is that I NEVER stray from that- I say it I do it. So that takes time to develop. Start by doing anything simple and easy but preface it with DO IT NOW. Repeat that till it becomes a habit on all things easy. Then NEVER deviate.*
>
> *David Corbin*

When do YOU expect to become "old"? It is more of a decision than a fact. You become old when you stop expanding your life. Make plans now never to become "old." Keep on looking for ways to live more fully with each passing year. You are as young as you think. Your body may be older, but exercise can change much of that. Decide to stay young for as long as you live.

What actions will you take on this idea?

253. Family Traditions—Honor the Old and Start the New

Some cultures have strong family traditions; some don't. As a youth, I saw families who always honored the rituals and practices distinctive to their heritage or religion. It was my impression that my family didn't have these. Then, as an adult, I realized that we did, in fact, have our own traditions and rituals. These traditions all started somewhere, and I recognized that I could start my own traditions for our family if I wanted to.

Whether you have a traditional family or not, you do have a group of people you feel connected with. These are your family. What traditions could you start with them that would strengthen your bonds and reinforce your values? How about always sharing what you are thankful for as you enjoy Thanksgiving dinner? Or having a time each week when you discuss the lessons you learned from this week's experiences? How about doing something to communicate your strongest values to all the succeeding generations? Give it some serious thought. What starts today as an event can becomes a tradition and leave a legacy for future generations.

What actions will you take on this idea?

254. Know Thy Neighbor—A Foiled Attempted Kidnapping

One of our neighbors was almost kidnapped recently. Her family had been targeted by a disturbed individual, and he coerced her at gunpoint to leave her house and get into his van. He didn't count on the fact that she knew her neighbors. When a neighbor saw the look on her face, she went indoors and called the police. Then the kidnapper got distracted, and our friend ran back into her home and locked the door. He jumped in the van and sped away, only to be apprehended by the police.

Now, before you get caught up in the drama of this story, I'd like you to notice why he was apprehended. It was because our friend knew her neighbor. The more we connect with those around us, the stronger the sense of community, which increases our safety. We ARE our neighbor's keeper in many ways, and we can watch out for each other. If we don't know each other, we may not even suspect anything is wrong. Get to know the people who live near you. You may need them, and they may need you. Besides, there are some nice people out there.

What actions will you take on this idea?

255. Boys & Girls Clubs: A Positive Place for Kids

I've been a long-time leader in the Boys & Girls Clubs movement where I live. What impresses me about this organization is its 100-year history of providing a Positive Place for Kids before and after school. In a supervised environment, they provide a place for fun, friendship, learning, homework, and the development of character. In an otherwise chaotic world, they offer kids a Positive Place to go each day.

What causes do you care about? Chances are good that an organization near you is working on exactly that same need—and they need your help. You may only be able to assist once in a while, but they need you. They need volunteers, temporary workers, committee leaders, supporters, sponsors, guides, referral sources, people who can lend them needed resources, and more. Look for a place to invest your energies to make the world a more positive place for all of us. As my friend Cal Johnston says, kids may be only 30 percent of our community, but they are 100 percent of our future!

What actions will you take on this idea?

256. International Youth Foundation—At Least One Irrationally Committed Adult

The International Youth Foundation has committed itself to fostering at least one adult per child who is irrationally committed to the welfare of that child. *Irrationally committed to their welfare.* Isn't that a great goal? Who would you go beyond expectations in order to help? Who would you put yourself on the line to protect? We need more of that.

We need a sense of duty to protect and assist each other. Nobody makes it through life alone. We need the streets others build, the water others provide, the buildings they build, and the foods they produce. We need their friendship and goodwill. We need them to take away the trash and clean up our surroundings. We really all need each other. Keep that in mind the next time you see someone working. Whatever it is that they do, you probably benefit from it somehow. Take a moment to thank them for doing their part. Let them know that we need them.

What actions will you take on this idea?

257. Study What Works, and Don't Stop Doing It

What is the last thing you did that saved you money? What did you do to attain your ideal weight in the past? What is the best thing you ever did to reconnect with someone you had a conflict with? How did you get into a great mood? Well, for heaven's sake, do it again! Don't give up on the strategies that work; take note of them and repeat them. Make habits out of them.

So often people will do something that works and then go blissfully onward as if they learned nothing from the experience. Your best life coach may well be your own past experience. Learn to learn from yourself.

Do the same for others—help them notice what they do right. Catch them in their successes, and point out what worked. In business, be sure that you form a regular habit of After Action Reviews, where everyone notices what worked and what didn't. The keys to your future success are already present in your past successes. Just make time to learn from your own experiences, and then start learning from the experiences of others as well.

What actions will you take on this idea?

258. What Does Your Space Say about You?

Would you like to become better at reading people? Then learn to study their surroundings. We have long known that a person's office reflects their values and interests, but did you also know that all of our surroundings speak volumes about who we are?

One of my friends always keeps his car immaculate. It is filled with tools such as global positioning systems (GPS) and high-end satellite radio equipment to maximize his driving experience. Contrast that with my friend whose car is a total mess. She has food scraps on the floor and crumbs in the cracks of the seat. There are receipts on the floor and mystery materials under the seats.

Which of these people would you trust with your estate planning? Their space may not tell you for sure how tidy their lives are, but how would you prefer to bet? Look at your own life—your home, your closets, your car, your office, the interior of your briefcase. Maybe organizing each one of those would be a good place to start organizing your life.

What actions will you take on this idea?

259. Emotional Bank Account (Covey) and Points (Wexler)

Dr. Stephen Covey often talks about how we build "emotional bank accounts" with others. Our good deeds and our bad ones constitute deposits and withdrawals. My friend Phil Wexler tells of how we earn "points" with people based on the image we project and on our behavior.

Both concepts are within your control. You can consciously make more deposits with people, and you can intentionally earn more points with people. Then, after you have done these good deeds, when the time comes for you to make a withdrawal, to ask for a sale or seek a favor, there will be a big enough balance in the account to cover it.

What could you do today to earn more goodwill with your colleagues and customers? What will it cost you? I'll bet you can build your deposits without costing yourself a cent. Just by noticing ways to do good for others, you will find easy and much-appreciated actions that can fill your account to overflowing. You might just get rich!

What actions will you take on this idea?

260. Rethinking Week

Between Christmas and New Year's, I usually devote the entire week to rethinking my life and business. It's my annual thinking retreat. It could be done at any time of year, but I prefer that one, because most businesses are only half awake during that week, and the phones tend to be quiet.

I devote each morning to thinking about one key part of my life: finances on one day, family on another, health and fitness on another, and so on. As the week wears on, I shift to reviewing my goals, my successes, my frustrations, and my dreams. By the last few days I focus on planning, on identifying the specific steps I plan to take to make each part of my life as I want it to be.

This review and planning process has served me very well over the years. I step back at first and just look at each part of my world. Then I study the patterns of success and challenges. Next I set my goals for each, and finally I map my path to every goal. From that point, I have my action plan to create the world I want. You can do this. Give it a try.

HOW I MOTIVATE MYSELF

I read my previous motivational articles and watch videos of me speaking. Sometimes I read motivational books too.

Rosemarie Rossetti

What actions will you take on this idea?

261. The Precious Present (Spencer Johnson's concept)

Spencer Johnson is a brilliant thinker and one of the world's top authors. He once wrote a book called *The Precious Present*. He said that the most precious gift, or present, we could give another is our presence in the present moment with them.

What a beautiful thought! People are starving for sincere personal attention. They risk their lives to get it, they break laws to achieve it, they spend time and money to accomplish it.

We all need to know that we are noticed and that we are loved and valued. Why not save folks all the effort and just start giving more of your attention to them now? Start at home with your partner and kids. They are starving for quality attention. Take an interest in them. Really listen to them without judging. Spend time just focusing on what they care about. Then do the same at work. You will find that others start valuing you more. They'll become interested in your priorities, too. Give them a precious present today: your presence in the present moment.

What actions will you take on this idea?

262. Dad's Workbench (My Dad's 100th Birthday Remembrance)

In our garage there was a workbench that my father had built for himself. He spent hours out there fixing, building, and improving things. I'd often stand at his elbow and learn from him. The smell, the sound, and the feel of that garage lives with me to this day.

My dad would have turned 100 in 2015. I wonder if he knew how important those moments were to me?

How about you: Do you know when you are creating moments like these for the people in your life? Often we are not even conscious of how important our actions are to others. Everywhere you will find people who are seeking a guide, coach, or mentor. When we find them, we treasure their presence in our lives. While you are thinking about this, how about telling your mentors how much you appreciate them? Just let them know that you consider them important and that you have learned from them. It's amazing how powerful that awareness can be. We all love to help, and we all need to be appreciated. Give them a call... today.

What actions will you take on this idea?

263. What Causes You to Feel Loved?

When I was little, my grandmother used to let me sit in her lap, and she'd rub my back. Even today, when my wife rubs my back, I feel safe and loved. That's just one of scores of ways people show each other that they care. When my son seeks my advice or my friends come to me seeking my perspective, I feel valued.

People tend to show their affection in the ways that they prefer to receive it. If a person's father made them feel loved by teaching them a skill, then they assume others will react similarly when they teach. But that's not necessarily so. Everyone is different in how they feel and why.

Some folks assume that straightening up the house or doing chores is a way of showing their love. Others find those to simply be responsible forms of behavior. Some cook to show love, some bring home paychecks—but these are only loving behaviors if the recipients understand your intent. It may be that your efforts to show others you care are missing the mark. Until you know how they determine whether you care, you can't really be sure they are getting your intentions. What causes you to feel loved?

What actions will you take on this idea?

264. Openness: Vulnerable Sharing Versus Angry Sharing

One endearing human quality is openness. Sharing your feelings and thoughts can go a long way to drawing others to you. But be careful not to confuse venting with sharing. When you start your comments with, "Let me tell you what I think," you can bet you are not drawing people toward you. First, "Let me tell you" is a demand, not a request. Second, if you want to tell me what you think, just tell me. You might start with a softer opener like, "In my opinion" or, "As I see it" or, "From where I sit…" Each of these is presented as offering another perspective instead of making an aggressive declaration.

Without openness, we don't get to know each other. And if all we get to know is strong opinions, then we don't get to know the person behind them. People don't connect with each other just because they agree with their positions. They connect when they agree with their feelings. If you care about what I care about, we are kindred spirits. As Zig Ziglar says, "People don't care how much you know until they know how much you care."

What actions will you take on this idea?

265. What Do You Need to Learn Next?

As you look over your life, what do you think will be your next big challenge? Wealth issues, health issues, relationship challenges, career choices, philosophical concepts? Why not get ready for it before it arrives?

Just ask yourself, "What do I need to learn next?" Then start today to prepare for it as if it were already scheduled to appear. They say that many of the lottery winners quickly squander their newfound wealth and become poor again. That is because their thinking didn't change—only their bank account. If you knew that you'd soon come into a lot of money, wouldn't it make sense to learn how to manage money better? If you knew you had a big challenge coming with another person, wouldn't you sign up for some webinars on dealing with difficult relationships? The time to learn life skills is before we need them. Think of how your life may unfold, and start today to learn what you will someday need to know. When you are ready for them, your challenges transform into opportunities.

What actions will you take on this idea?

266. The Gratitude Brigade

I recently chaired a big charity dinner and auction that involved almost 500 people. As we prepared for the event, months in advance, I informed my committee that after our event I wanted them to stay together as a "gratitude brigade." The hundreds of people who supported our event would need to be thanked—but more important than thanking them was assuring that each person *felt* thanked.

Saying thank you has no effect unless the other person senses your gratitude. We decided to keep a database of participants and to assure that everyone received three different forms of thanks. One might be a personal letter or note. Another might be a token gift. A phone call or in-person visit might be the third. An e-mail message, an invitation to another celebration, a drop-in with news of the outcome, a news clipping, a snapshot taken at the event, a short story of how the charity had helped people. Each of these can be conveyed in a way that says, "Thank you very much." When people go out of their way to help you, assure that they feel the gratitude and see the results of their generosity.

What actions will you take on this idea?

267. The Ability to Apologize Is a Strength

Once I was reviewing a big project with a colleague. The project was a success. My colleague was brilliant in her role. Many problems had cropped up, but all in all, things went very well. As we reviewed the event, she was praised for her accomplishments. But when we examined the aspects that didn't go well, she made excuses.

She could have just admitted that she was overwhelmed and stretched too thin, but she didn't. Her fear was that any show of weakness would hurt her in the eyes of others. In fact, the exact opposite was true. If she had acknowledged both her weaknesses and her strengths, then strategies could have been developed for coping better. But she sustained her defensiveness.

Ultimately she almost lost her job. Not because of mistakes—everyone makes mistakes, and when they are made with good intentions, then criticism isn't required; correction is what is needed. She almost lost her job because she was unwilling to say, "I handled that poorly. I need to find a better way of dealing with situations like this." With that simple statement, she would have been seen as strong and mature.

What actions will you take on this idea?

268. Just One More Tree

When I jogged during the first year of trying to get into better shape, it was difficult for me to go very far. Instead of accepting the limits of my fitness, I decided to push the envelope just a little. On the jogging trail near my home, I'd reach the end of my comfort zone and, instead of stopping, I'd say, "I'll jog to the next tree or street sign." This "just one more tree" habit led to being able to run five miles without difficulty.

Today, decades later, I ran and hiked 6.2 miles of mountain trails in 102 minutes—and I'm in my late 60s! The same concept applies to making one more sales call or completing one more paragraph of a report or reading one more page of a book. How about sending one more thank you note? Just one more before you stop.

What actions will you take on this idea?

The Self Motivation Checkup

A proven, action-oriented system to help you optimize your success in every area of life.

WHAT THIS CHECKUP IS DESIGNED TO DO

THE SELF MOTIVATION CHECKUP IS LIKE AN AERIAL PHOTO OF YOUR life. It identifies your current mode of operation in the eight overall areas of your life, then leads to a prescription for each area to improve your awareness and/or performance. This is the beginning of a lifelong exploration. Cathcart Institute is committed to being your continuing resource for insights into your nature.

This is your assessment; it is confidential. It is not to be used as a comparative tool among people, only for you to assess yourself.

HOW IMPORTANT IS SELF AWARENESS?

In an interview with commentator Bill Moyers, author and thought leader Dr. Peter Drucker was reportedly asked, "What would you advise kids to do to get ready for the next [21st] century?"

He replied, "Know your strengths. That's the most important thing, to know what you are good at. Most people only know what they are not good at."

Daniel Goleman, author of *Emotional Intelligence*, said that the most important of all the emotional intelligences is self-awareness. And, of course, Socrates said it most succinctly: "Know thyself."

People who are self-aware are better listeners, less self-conscious, less judgmental of others, and more willing to admit their mistakes. The also tend to produce better quality work, and to experience fewer interpersonal problems.

WHAT THIS CHECKUP IS DESIGNED TO DO

It's a lot like getting your car serviced. Most people wait till something breaks before going to the mechanic. When you bring your car in for service, they may have a specific 21-point checkup. Why do they do this? To help prevent more costly problems. The average person manages their life through crisis, not by design. When you do a checkup on yourself, making sure you are operating on all cylinders, your life will run smoothly. Bottom line? It's better to spend time on the checkup instead of the breakdown.

HOW TO REVIEW YOUR RESULTS

Don't expect a grade or a clinical analysis. Expect instead to gain a series of glimpses into who and how you are that will help you make better decisions, know a good choice for you when you see it, and help you remain at peace with yourself while continuing to grow.

This is a map for your future exploration and personal growth, but this is *today*'s assessment. All

> ### HOW I MOTIVATE MYSELF
>
> *I have a strong belief to always do what I hate or find hard to do first thing in the morning so I can work, play, ski, ride all day after! So "Get over it and jump at it" morning mindset saves my day and sanity because it is worse to put it under the cover and feel bad all day long after.*
>
> *Sylvia Perreault*

of these observations are "for now." They are stop-action snapshots, not full-action movies of you. Just as a medical checkup shows your current state of health and fitness, this self motivation checkup shows how well you are *currently* directing your life in each area. Remember, you can change your actions.

Don't try to change your Nature. Instead learn to Nurture your Nature. Complete this checkup again whenever you are in a period of transition or life change, i.e. new job, new home, family milestones, or career changes. As your circumstances evolve, so will your priorities and operating modes.

NEXT STEPS: HOW TO GET THE MOST OUT OF YOUR FEEDBACK

Review your findings and see if you feel they are true. Write out your initial reactions in pencil and date them; discuss them with others, and experiment with and test these observations. See if they are valid. Remember that all of these observations come from the answers you give. If your answers change, so will the assessment's observations.

DISCLAIMER

This assessment is something that you are doing for yourself. The benefits are limited to the information you have provided. If you ranked yourself unrealistically high, you will not receive the appropriate descriptions and prescriptions for your current state of living. If you ranked yourself unrealistically low, you will find that the feedback in this report is more appropriate for someone with lower awareness, performance, or both, than you. The checkup bases its results on the assumption that the information you provided was realistic and an accurate portrayal of how you feel you are currently doing in each area of your life.

THE PERSONAL PRIORITY WHEEL

Here's a way to help keep your life in balance. Draw a wheel with eight spokes. Then label each spoke as follows: Mental, Physical, Spiritual, Emotional, Family, Social, Career, and finally Financial. Consider each of these spokes to be a rating wheel. Now ask these questions.

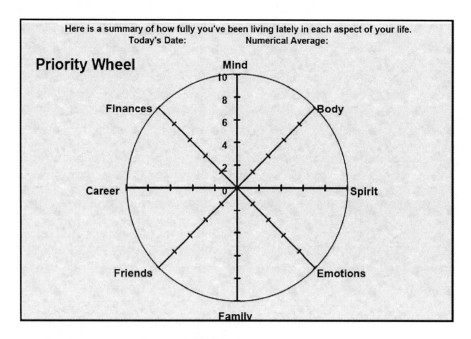

THE PERSONAL PRIORITY WHEEL

Answer the following eight questions with respect to how active you are currently within each of the listed areas in your life. In other words, how fully are you living in this part of your life right now? A score of 0 is equivalent to hardly living at all, being completely dissatisfied in an area, while a 10 is living so fully that it would seem impossible for you to be more effective. Rate each of the eight areas separately.

MIND

1. Your mind is capable of learning, memory, problem-solving, creativity, music, poetry, art, writing, brainstorming, and much

more. How fully have you been using all the parts of your mind lately? How effective have you been in keeping your mind active lately? How have you challenged it? **Choose a number from 0 to 10 as to how fully you have been using your mind lately:** _____

BODY

2. Your body has myriad functions. Consider these aspects: breathing, blood flow, sensory perception, muscular strength and coordination, balance, overall flexibility and agility, aerobic fitness, nutrition, sex, and healing. Also important to your health are avoidance of poisons such as drugs, nicotine, and alcohol, and the use of your body in recreation and sports, plus relaxation and repair of the parts of your body that aren't functioning as they should. Do you purposefully take care of your body? **Choose a number from 0 to 10 as to how fully you have been using your body lately:** _____

SPIRIT

3. Your spirit or soul is the essence of who you are. It's the entity that dwells in your body and uses your mind, the inner you. The spirit awakens and lives through joy, love, inspiration, dreams, vision, and commitments. It is nurtured by noble thoughts and inspiring words; it thrives on helping others and on creating things of beauty, works of art. It communicates through prayer and meditation. It honors life. **Choose a number from 0 to 10 as to how fully you have been exercising your spirit lately:** _____

EMOTIONS

4. There's a multitude of emotion in everyone. These include happiness, fear, sadness, joy, compassion, anger, pride,

exhilaration, laughter, peace, curiosity, and satisfaction. Are you feeling all these emotions? Or do you suppress many of them? We're designed to experience a full range of emotions, not just a controlled few. Naturally you need to express emotions in appropriate ways, but they need to be experienced and not suppressed. **Choose a number from 0 to 10 as to how fully you have been experiencing your emotions lately:** _____

FAMILY

5. Family is the word we use for the people closest to us. It can include those who are related to us and those to whom we choose to have a close relationship. In this context, refer to the people you love most. Think of the quantity of contact you've had with them, and then think of the quality of those contacts. **Choose a number from 0 to 10 as to how fully you have been engaging with your family lately:** _____

FRIENDS

6. Your personal community is made up of your friends. Ralph Waldo Emerson said, "A friend is a person with whom I may be sincere. Before him, I may think aloud." We have all levels of friends in life: best friends, neighbors, co-workers, sports buddies, club members, social friends, playmates, and casual acquaintances. Each has their place in a balanced, full life. **Choose a number from 0 to 10 as to how active you have been with your array of friends lately:** _____

CAREER

7. Your career can be called your livelihood. It's often the source of your primary contributions to the world and the source of most

of your income, monetary or otherwise. Is your livelihood lively? Relate it to your knowledge, skills, credentials, achievements, notable contributions, and overall effort. Do you work to your potential? Do you work with purpose? **Choose a number from 0 to 10 as to how fully you have been pursuing your career lately:** _____

FINANCES

8. Tangible wealth is usually only important to the degree to which you don't have it. Whether you are interested in money or not, it is essential to your survival. Our property and our material possessions also make up our tangible wealth. Do you know where your wealth comes from—all of it—and where it all goes in your life? Have you been learning more and more about the use and management of your money? Do you ignore money, or stay acutely aware of it? Focus not on how much money you have but on how fully you have been living in relation to directing the flow of money in your life. **Choose a number from 0 to 10 as to how active you have been in handling your finances category lately:** _____

THE PERSONAL PRIORITY WHEEL SUMMARY

Take the numbers from the eight ratings above, and plot them on this wheel. Place a dot on the line that indicates each spoke of your life's wheel: Mental, Physical, Family, Friends, Spiritual, Career, Emotional, and Financial. Once you've marked each scale from 1 to 10, then connect the dots around the wheel.

Each of the eight spokes in this wheel is a 1 to 10 rating scale. The center of the wheel is zero, and the first dot away from the center is a one. The outer perimeter of the wheel represents a 10, or fully living in that part of your life.

When you have connected the dots within the wheel, you will no doubt notice that your shape is no longer a circle but rather some geometric mutation within the circle. This new shape shows you only one important thing—where you have been placing your emphasis lately. It cannot show you where you are strong or weak, because you didn't rate that factor. The parts of your life that are fully expressed will be rated toward the outer rim of the circle, and those that you have been ignoring will be ranked closer to the center hub.

You'll now see where you need to place more emphasis in order to help balance your life. Note that the areas you neglect will not bother you at first; after a while, though, they will start interfering with the other parts of your life.

It is surely impossible to live a constantly balanced life, but we can certainly learn to shift our focus from time to time to assure that no part of our life is neglected. Make time to be fully alive—otherwise, you will be forced to find time for illness, relationship problems, depression, or bankruptcy. So living a well-balanced life means shifting your attention and energy from one spoke to the other again and again at the appropriate times so as to never neglect any of them. *In the illustration that follows you'll see that this person ranked Family, Body, and Career the lowest. If this persists, then there will be relationship, health, and business problems soon. It's a good wake-up-call assessment. Now they can use the Thought Diet™ to strenghten each area.*

> ### HOW I MOTIVATE MYSELF
>
> *I moved to the location I felt the most productive in my late 20s, so getting up at 4:45am to work out is never a chore. Life happens by design. On days I'm tired, I put my workout clothes ready to jump into next to the sink (sometimes I've worked out with clothes inside out) but when you are happy/thankful first, the rest falls into place.*
>
> *Andrea Samadi*

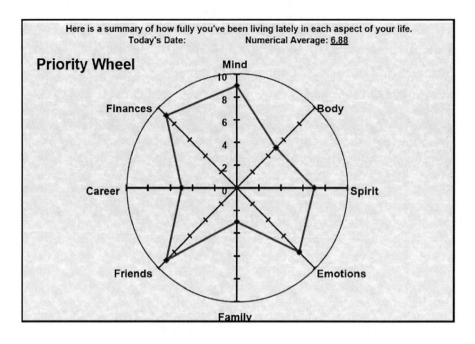

The Personal Priority Wheel is a comparison of the eight primary aspects of your personal life to show which areas have been getting the most attention lately.

UNDERSTANDING YOUR PERSONAL PRIORITY WHEEL

1. Note the individual numbers on each scale. The distance between each of those numbers and the number 10 represents the amount of living you could improve by in that area. If you got anything less than 10s all around, then there's plenty of room to grow.

2. Next, notice which numbers were highest. Those are where you've been putting your emphasis lately. That's probably where you are most comfortable.

3. Now, note which numbers were lowest. Those might represent the areas you avoid or tend to put toward the bottom of your to-do list. The low numbers often represent your most important homework.

Looking over the numbers, you might not see the balanced picture you'd like. In fact, most people do not come up with a balanced circle very often. More often than not, we put our energy into one of the four *external* areas: family, friends, work, or finances. We work toward making sure our family is safe, or our job is safe, or our wealth is safe, and then we think we are living fully. Or we may spend lots of quality time with our friends and assume that we have a full life. This is not a safe assumption.

You might be just the opposite, dedicating yourself to the four *internal* areas: mind, body, spirit, and emotions. Some people put all their energy into making sure they have the body they want. Or they only feed their mind, or nurture their spirit. Others explore and express a multitude of emotions. The areas that do not get enough of your attention will eventually create distress and demand more attention. Any areas that you neglect will soon interfere with the rest of your life until they get the attention they need. So learn to shift your emphasis continually from one area to another. All of the life areas are important, but advancement in one will not necessarily produce advancement in another.

GROW EACH ONE

If you don't like your ratings, you can change them. Simply start by doing more of what you are capable of in each area. To live fully, all eight need to be occasionally nurtured and kept generally in balance. How can you achieve this state?

Since we already know that "a journey of one thousand miles begins with a single step," I'm thinking that adage might hold the clue. Just put on your running shoes and go out to the curb...

MIND

Take a look at the many ways you use your mind, and select one or two for emphasis and development. Then choose a simple starting action to get you headed down the path to growth. For example, if you want to be more creative, use brainstorming or a computer game as a daily exercise for a week, then expand from there. To develop your learning, select some material and commit five minutes a day to its study. You will usually spend more than the five minutes with it, but even five minutes is great. Get started—in doing so, you'll develop and use more of your mental abilities.

BODY

In regard to your body, the main thing is to be active. Like the functions of the mind, it's a "use it or lose it" proposition. Be active; move your body more than you're used to, no matter what your age. Even if you just do sitting-in-your-chair exercises, move! Movement brings more oxygen to the brain so you'll even think better. Feed your body better than you're used to feeding it. Stretch your body, and try to do some things that you haven't done in the past; live up to a higher standard when it comes to physical ability. Look to the guidance of organizations like the American Council on Exercise*, and find out what you can do reasonably for your age and your fitness level to become more healthy as time goes on. Read the book *Younger Next Year* by Crowley and Lodge.

SPIRIT

For more inner peace and joy in your spirit, acknowledge yourself for the unique person you are, and start to praise others more often. Develop a generous spirit; give more of yourself to other people, selflessly. Show more gratitude for what you've received. Dedicate more time to learning about what you believe, studying the scriptures or the foundations of the philosophy that you believe in.

EMOTIONS

When it comes to your emotions, if you want more fun, more fullness, more joy, or more peace in your life, then express more of those emotions. We often isolate ourselves from the rest of the world and only express a fraction of the emotions within us. That may be a very comfortable, safe thing to do, but it's not very rewarding or fulfilling—and it certainly inhibits your growth as an individual. Look for ways to adjust your life so that you experience and express more of your emotions, expanding your range of experiences.

FAMILY

To have more in the area of family, show more closeness and love. Listen to the other members of your family. Show them more attention; find some little ways to let them know that you care about them. Make some time for them each day. It's amazing how little time we spend with the people we care most about.

FRIENDS

In the area of friends, they say that to have a friend, you need to be a friend. Be a person who's fun to be with. Lighten up, and take an interest in what other people are doing. Don't be self-absorbed. Look for ways to support what other people do and to connect with them more. If you want to have more mail, send more letters. If you want more praise from other people, give more compliments to others.

CAREER

From a career perspective, if you want more pay, then first give your employer or customer a raise—do more than you're required to do. Look for ways to add a little bit extra to every customer interaction or to every task that you perform. Acknowledge other people for the good job they do. Let your supervisors know what you like about what they do, and how they could be even more effective in managing you. If you want more responsibility, take on more responsibilities, and behave more responsibly in what you do right now.

FINANCES

When it comes to your finances, you have to take the money and resources you already have and allocate them more wisely. Or invest your energies in a more financially rewarding way. Think more often about money—more responsibly and systematically—and you'll find ways to save or earn more. In either case, you'll have more money as a result.

NURTURE YOUR NATURE

As you *give* more energy to each of these eight areas of your life, you will *have* more life in those areas, and have it more abundantly. It's your nature to live all aspects of your life fully, skillfully, and with more enjoyment. You may need to merely rethink some of your existing life patterns in each area in order to release your potential for growth.

In the exercise after the Personal Priority Wheel, we will identify your Mode of Operation (M.O.) and plot it on the Awareness/Performance (AP) Grid. There, you will see whether Education (Information/Skill) "Knowing" or Motivation (Action) "Doing" is needed most at this time. Use this tool to help you decide on your next best actions.

MODE OF OPERATION

Once you know which parts of your life will need more attention soon (personal priorities), then you can pause to look at which Mode of Operation (M.O.) you are in for each spoke. You want to know whether you need more Knowing or more Doing in order to rank higher in each category.

The four Modes are: Passenger, Critic, Competitor, and Leader. The natural assumption is that "Leader" is the best mode and that you should always be in that one. Not true. There are times and places for each of them.

For example: When you are in seat 14A on an airline headed to Los Angeles, the best Mode you can be in physically is Passenger, because you literally are one. It would be entirely inappropriate for you to be taking a Leader posture or voicing your Critic point of view or asserting your Competitor Mode to somehow win over others. But you could certainly take advantage of the passenger experience to focus on learning, relaxing, communicating, creating, writing, researching, or reflecting about the other parts of your life. *You can choose your Mode, but you can't always choose your circumstances.*

So when you are editing or consulting or coaching, then your Critic Mode might be the best. When you are in a competition, your Competitor Mode will serve you best, and when you're able to exert initiative and make a difference, Leader Mode is the one for you. Mode must match the situation and your intended outcomes. Ken Blanchard calls this "Situational Self-Leadership®."

THE M.O. GRID

AWARENESS + PERFORMANCE = MASTERY

INTRODUCTION

NOT ONLY DO WE NEED AN AVENUE OR DIRECTION IN WHICH WE CAN express ourselves, but we also need a vehicle, or process, with which we can develop ourselves. To develop new skills and not have a chance to use them is frustrating; and to have a great opportunity to use a skill that you don't yet possess can be downright depressing. Self-development and self-expression bring us to the M.O. Grid. It shows your Mode of Operation, and it is based on two basic elements: *Awareness* and *Performance*—how you think, and what you do, Knowing and Doing. Self-development is begun through increased *Awareness* of where you are right now and what is needed in order to grow. Self-expression is how you *perform*, what you do. The basic principle of the M.O. Grid is that high Awareness (A) multiplied by high Performance (P), equals Mastery—and Mastery yields fulfillment.

Two Things That Determine Your Life: How You Think, and What You Do

AWARENESS+PERFORMANCE

Awareness in its simplest form is Knowing. Performance in its simplest form is Doing. When you change either of these, in some ways, you change your life.

> **HOW I MOTIVATE MYSELF**
>
> *Caffeine+alarm+commitment. Don't over think. Just do it. There will be LOTS of pain and crying.*
>
> *Sarah Idriss Miller*

Your Awareness determines how you think. The more you know about a subject, the more possibilities you can see. But when you learn only *how* things work, then you're stuck with the processes, doing it that way all the time. If you keep on doing what you've always done, you will keep getting what you've always gotten. Here, you will focus on how to increase your Awareness to improve your life.

AWARENESS: PROCESSES & PURPOSES

Let's simplify. *Why* is the Purpose. *How* is the Process. Which do you focus on most? We need to know *why* we do what we do: what we believe in, and what we stand for. We need to know the purposes behind the processes that we're following, and then we need to apply our performance to our purpose. The difference between processes and purposes is bridged by principles. If you learn the purposes behind someone's actions, then you can see which principles apply and which processes make the most sense. When you know purposes, you can make better decisions. The more you're stuck with processes, the harder decisions are.

PERFORMANCE: REQUIREMENTS & EXTRAS

The first factor in our equation was Awareness (how you think). The second factor Performance (what you do). To bring about your future growth, think about doing more. "Doing more?" you may reply. "There aren't enough hours in the day already!" Simply put, we do not grow unless we stretch. In any situation, if you just ask, "What is required? Now, what else can I do?" then you will be programming yourself to stretch, to grow, to find new alternatives. Then you can make a difference, and your difference can help make the world to become a better place. If all of us did only what was required, the status quo would exist forever—things would never change. Nothing grows until somebody does more than they're paid to do, more than they're required to do.

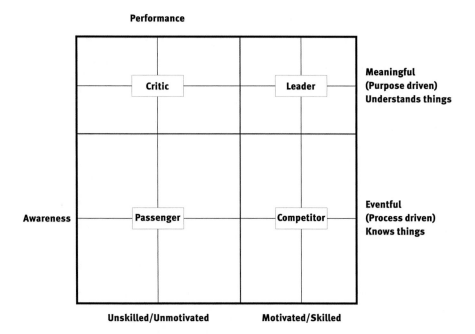

YOUR M.O.: THE GRID

The vertical axis is Awareness, which measures how much you know in a specific area. More than that, it involves raising your level of thinking in any situation—the ability to think about the bigger picture. This scale ranges from complete ignorance (not knowing anything) at the bottom, to total enlightenment (knowing everything) at the top. The four stages are: facts (knowing only the facts), information (knowing how to organize facts into information), knowledge (applying information to create knowledge), and wisdom (exploring the principles in the knowledge to acquire wisdom).

The horizontal axis, Performance, ranges from doing nothing at the far left, to exhibiting world-changing behavior on the far right. On the left, you are simply doing the job and no more, what is required (or less). On the right is high performance—doing more than is required, overfilling your space, stretching yourself, growing, contributing something extra. The four stages are: doing less than is required, doing only what is required, doing more than is required, and doing much more than is required.

YOUR OPERATING MODE

Your operating mode (Modus Operandi, M.O.) determines the quality and quantity of outcomes you produce in each aspect of your life. In this model, the resulting four quadrants help us identify four modes of operating: Passenger, Critic, Competitor, and Leader. Your operating mode will be different from one aspect of your life to the next. Every one of us finds ourselves in each of these four modes at one time or another in all categories of our life. You can always change your operating mode by merely changing your Awareness or Performance.

HOW I MOTIVATE MYSELF

When I have to do housework or yard work or book work or work work I rotate stations every hour or so through the day so it goes faster and I don't get bored with the dishes or weeding or filing. My friend like you is a writer and she just finished writing a review, she finished her Facebook post by saying "Now I am off to the movies to reward myself." I reward myself too. Sometimes with food or a musical break sometimes like now with a Facebook break. Break's over now, back to work.

George Honn

MODE OF OPERATION: THE M.O. GRID

The next step is to evaluate your current position on the M.O. Grid for each area of your life. This process will result in a comprehensive diagnosis of where you are on your path to success and fulfillment. The two dimensions used for measurement and placement on the grid are Awareness and Performance (Knowing and Doing).

A—Awareness is measured by knowing the processes as well as the purposes and principles, the *why* of things. More than that, it involves raising your level of thinking in any situation, the ability to get more information or think about the bigger picture. This scale ranges from complete ignorance, not knowing anything (a **"0"**) to total comprehension, knowledge, and understanding (a **"10"**).

P—Performance is measured by how closely are you meeting your optimum capability with respect to effort. It ranges from doing nothing (a **"0"**) to demonstrating world-class effort (a **"10"**). On the lower end of the scale, you are simply doing the job and no more. On the upper end is high performance, doing more than is required, overfilling your space, stretching yourself, growing, and contributing more.

Use the descriptions from the Personal Priority Wheel section to better understand what each area of your life includes.

MIND

A. How much do you know and understand in this area of your life? Do you know what you need to know in order to grow intellectually? Choose a number from 1 to 10: _____

P. Compared to what you could do under current circumstances, how well are you performing with regard to your mind? Are you challenging yourself mentally? Are you spending time to expand your mental capacity? Choose a number from 1 to 10: _____

BODY

A. How much do you know and understand in this area of your life? Do you know what you need to do to be at your best? Do you know about proper nutrition, rest, or your weight? Choose a number from 1 to 10: _____

P. Compared to what you could do under current circumstances, how well are you performing with regard to your body? Are you exercising, eating properly, and getting proper medical and dental care? Choose a number from 1 to 10: _____

SPIRIT

A. How much do you know and understand in this area of your life? Do you know what you believe? Do you understand your spiritual nature? Choose a number from 1 to 10: _____

P. Compared to what you could do under current circumstances, how well are you performing with regard to your spirit? Are you spending time developing yourself spiritually? Do you surround yourself with people who challenge and nurture you spiritually? Choose a number from 1 to 10: _____

EMOTIONS

A. How much do you know and understand in this area of your life? Do you know what triggers your various emotions? Do you understand how different aspects of your life impact your emotions? Choose a number from 1 to 10: _____

P. Compared to what you could do under current circumstances, how well are you performing with regard to your emotions? Do you often talk to those close to you about your emotions? Do you express your emotions in an appropriate manner? Are you living "out loud," or are you suppressing your feelings too much? Choose a number 1 to 10: _____

FAMILY

A. How much do you know and understand in this area of your life? Do you stay up on the events in the lives of those you love? Do you feel you know what it takes to have a close family? Choose a number from 1 to 10: _____

P. Compared to what you could do under current circumstances, how well are you performing with regard to your family? Do you call, write, or e-mail your family members on a regular basis? Do you often spend quality time with them and invest in the lives of those you love? Do you really listen to them? Choose a from number 1 to 10: _____

FRIENDS

A. How much do you know and understand in this area of your life? Do you stay up on the events in the lives of your friends? Choose a number from 1 to 10: _____

P. Compared to what you could do under current circumstances, how well are you performing with regard to your friends? Do you call, write, or e-mail your friends on a regular basis? Do you often spend quality time with them and invest in the lives of your close friends? Choose a number from 1 to 10: _____

CAREER

A. How much do you know and understand in this area of your life? Do you know what type of work you enjoy doing? Have you identified your strengths and weaknesses? Do you effectively utilize your time? Do you keep track of current trends and information in your industry? Choose a number from 1 to 10: _____

P. Compared to what you could do under current circumstances, how well are you performing with regard to your career? Are you delighting those you work with and your customers? Are you taking classes or attending seminars to continue your skill development? Choose a number from 1 to 10: _____

FINANCES

A. How much do you know and understand in this area of your life? Do you know where your money comes from and goes to? Do you know what you are spending/earning on interest or investments? Choose a number from 1 to 10: _____

P. Compared to what you could do under current circumstances, how well are you performing with regard to your finances? Do you budget and prioritize your expenditures? Do you make educated and responsible decisions about your finances? Choose a number from 1 to 10: _____

This may feel like a repeat of what you did on the Priority Wheel, but it gives a different reading. This shows you not only where you are on the wheel but also what Mode of Operation you are currently employing. You'll soon see whether you're in Passenger, Critic, Competitor, or Leader mode in each area. Your mode will reveal whether you need more information/education or more action/motivation in order to advance.

SELF MOTIVATION CHECKUP RESULTS

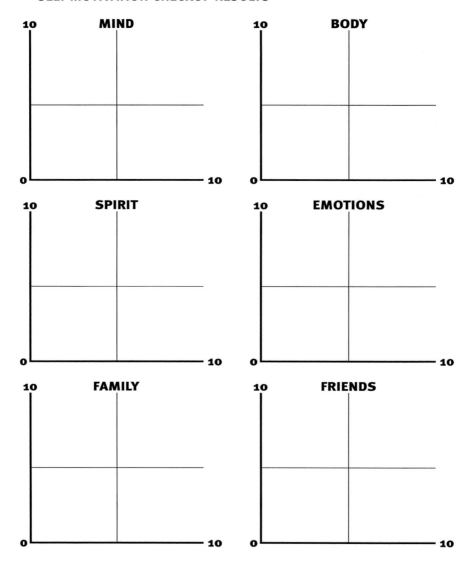

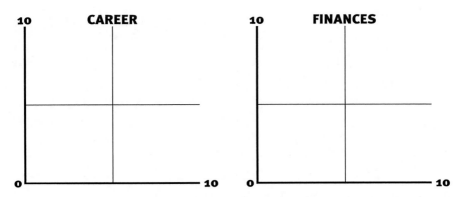

These rankings show clearly which areas of your life need your attention next, and whether you need more knowing or doing in order to improve them. Use these as your guide for setting priorities about where to focus your energies next. Return to this exercise every several weeks, or anytime you're feeling out of touch or overwhelmed.

An example of how to use this grid follows. It assumes certain readings on your assessment and gives corresponding prescriptions for how to improve yourself. Though these may differ from your ratings, please use this as an example and apply those recommendations that fit for you.

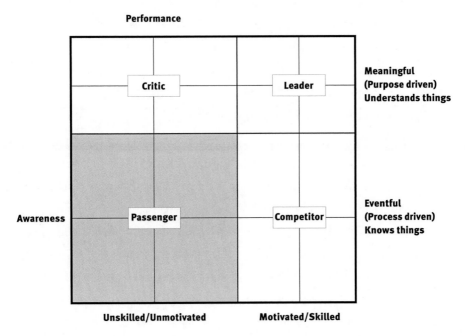

PASSENGER

If you are low in awareness and low in performance, then you fit into the lower left quadrant. A Passenger, in this sense, is someone who does things

> ### HOW I MOTIVATE MYSELF
>
> *I give myself a time deadline, such as fully up & dressed by xx:oo.*
>
> Janice Schooler Litvin

without question. If you asked a Passenger, "Why do you do that?" their answer would be, "It's my job. It has to be done. Somebody has to do it. Besides, that's how I was told to do it."

Since they are not very self-aware in this area of their life, Passengers constantly wait to be motivated by someone else. However, as they move up on the performance scale, their operating mode will change. If they regularly get outside of their comfort zone, they will start to stretch, grow, and do more than is required. They will need less motivation and simply need to be empowered with good information, the right kind of tools, and the situation in which they can control the outcome as much as possible. People in the Passenger mode don't seem to think on a very deep level in this area of their lives. Passengers don't have the energy or motivation to question the process or authority in this life area; they also tend to be confused about it much of the time. They are passive, waiting for orders or permission in this area. They rarely feel confident enough to take a leadership role. In this life area, they tend to think as victims.

If someone wants to get out of this Passenger mode, how can they do it? They can start asking more questions, start expanding their awareness. Like a 3-year-old, they should ask, "Why?" to everything! As they progress up that awareness scale, they become more and more enlightened and valuable to organizations and relationships. The Passenger quadrant is an area in which an individual needs both meaning and action. People in this quadrant tend to be underachievers; they tend to experience emptiness, depression, fear, and a feeling of entitlement. Their awareness and performance are both relatively low.

Individuals in the Passenger quadrant have lives that are more eventful than meaningful, and they are on the unskilled and unmotivated end of the spectrum. These people have room for a great deal of improvement in both their awareness and performance. This area of their lives needs attention to live up to their maximum potential.

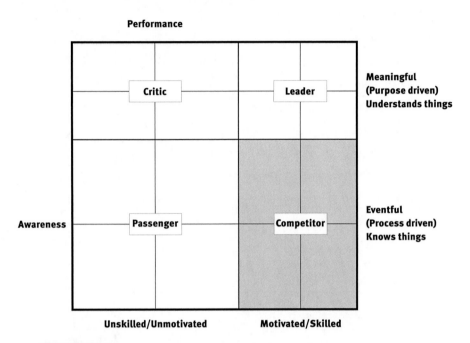

COMPETITOR

When you start to increase your performance, but not your awareness, then you move into the lower right quadrant, which is the Competitor. Competitors tend to be workaholics. It's as if they're running on a treadmill, trying to win a race that doesn't exist. They keep turning the speed up, thinking that somewhere in the distance, they're going to win. Well, it's not going to happen; all they will get is calluses on their feet! They're in danger of burnout—they're operating from fear.

They're afraid that they're not going to be first or most or best or biggest. They're constantly looking over their shoulders, watching other people to see where they stand in relation to them. In a word, they're *competing*. And that's a hyper-tense, uncomfortable way to live, because there's no satisfaction in it, no fulfillment. There is a small momentary win in saying, "Yes! I was number one," but then a moment later, you say, "I've got to get back on that treadmill again."

> ### HOW I MOTIVATE MYSELF
>
> *I'm generally pretty motivated. However, I find that when I'm not motivated, it generally means I'm tired - even if I don't realize it. Silly as this may sound, after a nap, my motivation is back in full bloom!*
>
> *Nancy Hightshoe*

The Competitor quadrant is an area in which an individual needs meaning. People in this quadrant tend to be driven and overburdened in this area of their lives. They are achievers, but the satisfaction is short-lived. These people need to internalize the statement, "If there is not much meaning in what you do, there is not much value in what you do." If you begin to find meaning in your performance, you will move closer to fulfillment.

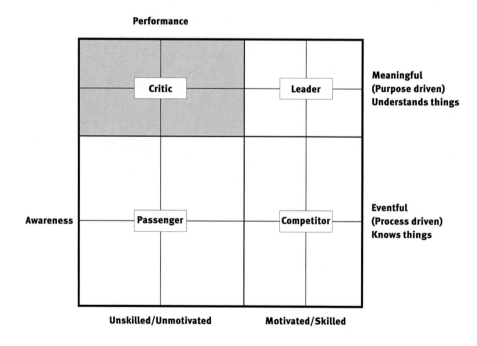

HOW I MOTIVATE MYSELF

In the eighth century a great Jewish mystic Rabbi Hillel said, "If not me who? if not now when?" I moved a couple of mountains behind that one. Being a Reverend and coming from the restaurant business I realized the church time was once a week not like the restaurant twice a day. So my phrase to pick up the pace around here was pedal to the metal spirituality. I don't have time to waste so let's get going.

George Honn

CRITIC

Up the awareness scale, in the upper left quadrant, is the Critic. The Critic mode does only what's required but thinks about it a lot more. They've figured it out; they understand some of the reasons. A lot of times, they slip into the mode of being merely a spectator, a backseat driver. They sit in the stands at the stadium and call out the instructions they think are right—but of course none of the people on the field hear or care what they're saying.

They may know themselves very well, but they take no action to grow. If all we do is seek more enlightenment, but not let it affect our behavior, we end up as an armchair quarterback in a very lonely situation. Most Critics tend to become cynical and skeptical in this area of their life, and they tend to become an articulate incompetent. They talk a great game but seldom play in it.

What does a Critic need to do to move into the realm of leadership? A Critic needs to do more than is required, such as not just doing the work but actually solving the problem, putting in whatever effort is necessary to achieve the needed outcome. The Critic quadrant is an area where an individual needs action. People in this quadrant tend to experience loneliness and a feeling of separation with respect to this area of their life.

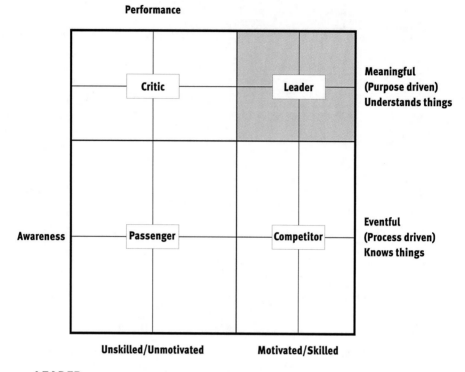

Performance

		Meaningful (Purpose driven) Understands things
Critic	Leader	
Passenger	Competitor	Eventful (Process driven) Knows things

Awareness

Unskilled/Unmotivated   Motivated/Skilled

LEADER

If a person simply improves their performance while staying focused on the goal and purpose, they will attain a new level of mastery. That's when we enter the quadrant in the upper right corner, the Leader. That's where life becomes fulfilling. Leaders are contributors; they make a difference in the world, and they experience a sense of personal fulfillment. Life matters to them, and they feel great about the changes they bring about.

The Leader quadrant is the only mode in which you will find a person achieving fulfillment. Personal fulfillment begins the minute you start doing more than you have to do, and the minute you start focusing on why you're doing it. If you're purpose-driven and you're exceeding the requirements, you respect yourself more. Once a person learns the fundamental principles, then they can figure out the processes easily.

This assessment has led you through the process of increasing your awareness of yourself. But those who are only self-aware aren't fully in the game. Without also mastering the art of self motivation, your situation never improves. When you can both understand and motivate yourself, then you leave the Passenger mode and graduate into the mode of a Leader. A purpose-driven personality combined with high performance is a perfect formula for fulfillment.

***

Now that you have become familiar with the M.O. Grid, you can easily reflect on what your level of Knowing and level of Doing are in any part of your life. By doing this, you will reveal your current Mode, be it Passenger, Competitor, Critic, or Leader. If the mode you are in is appropriate to the situation, then no change is needed. But if there is a disconnect, and if the mode doesn't suit the circumstances, you can change by focusing on either gaining more information (Knowing) or taking more action (Doing).

HOW I MOTIVATE MYSELF

I always do a visualization and feel what the end result will be like. I do this over and over and make it as real as possible until it becomes ingrained. Sometimes I do the same thing for not taking action and how that feels - I make it as uncomfortable as I can. Then I go back and feel the end result of taking action. This has gotten me through all kinds of situations even seemingly impossible ones.

Taylor Kay Stephens

Okay, now you've read a book, but will it really impact your life?

Here is a review of this book. Let's see how much of it will stick with you.

> » How many of the video clips linked throughout this book have you viewed so far? If none, please go back and view some of them to bring these messages to life for you.

> » Did you actually write some answers in the "How can I use this idea?"

> HOW I MOTIVATE MYSELF
>
> *"I have always set my goals higher than I thought I could possibly achieve. My philosophy was that even if I didn't reach those lofty goals the end result would most likely be more than acceptable. It has worked out pretty well for me. I set goals for owning a big boat, running a marathon, writing a book, and building my company."*
> Tom Miller, author, business owner

spaces after each of the hundreds of thought stimulators? Do one more of them right now. I'll wait.

> » Of the 68 ways to motivate yourself, how many are you already using? Take a moment and count them. Write the number here:

> _____

> » Which parts of your life showed the need for more attention on your Personal Priority Wheel? Write the top three on a separate sheet of paper to work on next.

> » On the M.O. Grid, which mode were you ranked in the most often? Passenger, Critic, Competitor, or Leader? Do you need more Knowing or more Doing in order to stimulate your growth and advancement?

> » What is the one thing in your life that needs for you to just get started on it more often (e.g. Just put on your shoes and go out to the curb)?

» If you only did one thing from this entire book, what one action would make the biggest contribution to your success?

» Do you have a written picture of the Future You? That's your magnet. Make sure the description is compelling to you.

» And finally, let me ask you just one question: What Do You Want?

» Go get it!

Epilogue

A Personal Message from Jim Cathcart

AND NOW THE FUN BEGINS... You have graciously invested many hours of focused attention on this book in an attempt to make your life better and to discover ways to help others do the same.

I sincerely appreciate the commitment you've shown to your growth.

You deserve to feel very good about reading this far, and especially good about the exercises you have completed. The number of people who truly commit to self-improvement is so small as to be hard to measure. Yes, lots of people buy the books and go to the lectures, but very few of them do what you've done.

For that reason, I am convinced that you will help to make this world a better place. It is the group of people like us, who take the effort to change ourselves, that causes massive evolution. Society doesn't change until individuals do. I'm talking about you!

Thank you for improving yourself and for seeing the world in optimistic ways. I am proud to have you as a new friend in growth.

Please stay connected with me via our websites, and let me know what you need as you grow. I'll continue to grow and explore personally, and all that I discover will be made accessible to you. So put me on your team. If you need my direct, personal involvement in your company or organization, let us know. I take on a few special clients each year, and I'd love for you to be one of them.

"God said, 'Build a better world.' I asked, 'How? The world is so big and complicated now. I'm so small and limited. What can I do?'

Then God in all His wisdom said,

'Build a better you.'"

–Author Unknown

In the Spirit of Growth,

Jim Cathcart

Since 1977, Cathcart Institute, Inc. has been helping people succeed by bringing them insights, resources, and skill development.

Jim Cathcart, our founder, is one of the world's most award-winning professional speakers and authors. He travels the world delivering seminars and keynote speeches, as well as serving as a personal advisor to many senior executives and entrepreneurs.

Cathcart.com is our primary website. It contains more than 700 pages of articles, resources, videos, and recordings that are free for you to download. There is also a store on our website where you can obtain Jim's award-winning books, assessments, recordings, and training materials. For any needs that aren't met by the posted resources, simply give us a call or drop us an e-mail at info@cathcart.com.

Our partner organization, Thrive15.com, through its founder Clay Clark, has recorded more than 100 interviews and short lessons by Jim Cathcart. These are available to you via direct links embedded throughout this book and by going directly to their website. The code word "acorn" will give you 30 days of free access to all 1,000 of their videos.

Among the 18 books authored by Jim Cathcart, there are two that represent major resources for you in addition to this one: *The Acorn Principle* and *Relationship Selling*.

THE ACORN PRINCIPLE™ BY JIM CATHCART

The Acorn Principle guides your exploration into the areas of your life that hold your biggest payoffs. You'll enhance the most important relationships in your life and career, isolate the strengths that bring you success, and learn to use your limitations as guides for better decision-making. If Socrates' wisdom is "Know Thyself," then Jim Cathcart's is "Grow Yourself." Self-aware self-starters are pure gold in business. *The Acorn Principle* will bring out the wealth potential that sleeps within you right now. 240-page book. Go to Cathcart.com/shop to order it.

RELATIONSHIP SELLING™ BY JIM CATHCART

Learn to increase your Sales IQ with this book. There are eight stages in the sales cycle and eight sets of skills that correspond to them. These skill sets, known as "competencies," are the framework of this book and its related videos, audios, and workbooks. This is the latest edition of the original *Relationship Selling* book that Jim Cathcart wrote in 1985, the book that popularized the concept. It is available worldwide in both print and eBook via Cathcart.com/shop. There is also a series of eight short eBooks on each competency.

To contact us:

Cathcart Institute, Inc.

Executive Office

117 Greenmeadow Drive

Thousand Oaks, CA 91320-4182 USA

Phone: 1-805-777-3477

Website: http://cathcart.com

E-mail: Info@cathcart.com

On social media, simply search for "Jim Cathcart" or "Cathcart Institute."

For speaking engagements, contact us directly or through your favorite speakers bureau.

Created by Jim Cathcart. Copyright 2016. All rights reserved.

Acknowledgements

Thank you Paula and Jim. Paula Cathcart and Jim Cathcart Jr. deserve my gratitude for tolerating and enduring all of the weirdness of my growing process. While I was trying to figure out how to get me to do what needed to be done, especially when I and (and they) often didn't feel like it, they were having to put up with my insistence on doing things that didn't seem to matter much at the time. I appreciate their tolerance. It made a true difference.

Thank you Tony Alessandra, Dan Clanton, Sam Gross, Bill Bell, Bill Gillespie, Rupert Robertson, Jimmy Gillespie, Charles Lee and my other best friends throughout the years. I am a reflection of your imprints and I treasure that. Thank you Don Varnadore, Harold Gash, Marsha Field, Carol James, Bill Johnson, Nido Qubein, Terry McCann, Kathy Cathcart, Doug Reynolds, Cavett Robert and Bill Gove for your belief in me at times when my own belief in myself was weaker. Thank you Gary Goranson, Joe Willard, Leo Hart, David Chu, Dennis Madden and Rodger Bland for giving me the opportunity to contribute to your organizations' success and for your continuing faith in the value of my input. Thank you Carolyn Johnson Brown and Pamela Stambaugh for helping me grow Cathcart Institute. Holly Duckworth, Jan Payne and Darrell Davis deserve my special thanks for helping to refine this manuscript.

Thanks Mom and Dad for guiding me into this amazing life.

Dear Reader, the power of acknowledgment is immense. When others openly cite the value of our actions we are lifted to a higher level of self esteem and our inner lips smile more broadly. You have this amazing ability right now. You can increase the positive energy in yourself and others by making sure to acknowledge what they have done. Please accept this as a duty and a privilege. Take time to thank and mention others. It really does matter when we do, and when we don't. Add to the joy of the world, share the spotlight by shining it on others.

To learn more from **Jim Cathcart**, view his entire library of online-training courses at Thrive15.com.

Sales IQ Plus

The Ultimate Sales Skills Assessment
for Professional Trainers & Coaches!

Rated Top National Sales Speaker 5-years Running!

SalesIQ.us

Video Lessons

O N THIS PAGE ARE 35 VIDEO LINKS TO FREE TWO- TO THREE-MINUTE clips from dozens of video interviews and lessons from Jim Cathcart as a faculty mentor for entrepreneurial training on Thrive15. com.

Readers can get 30 days of free access to all 1,000 video lessons on this site with the use of the code word "acorn."

No subscription is required for these; just click the link and watch at your leisure from your phone or computer.

- Success: How Fully Are You Living Now? - Jim Cathcart - Purpose
  https://www.thrive15.com/preview/Success How Fully Are You Living Now

- Goal-Setting Mastery - Jim Cathcart - Purpose
  https://www.thrive15.com/preview/Goal Setting Mastery

- Changed Mind, Changed Life - Jim Cathcart - Mindset
  https://www.thrive15.com/preview/Changed Mind Changed Life

- Get Vaccinated From The Entitlement And Justification Epidemic - Jim Cathcart - Mindset
  https://www.thrive15.com/preview/Business Mentors Get Vaccinated From The Entitlement And Justification Epidemic

- Managing People You Can't Fire - Jim Cathcart - Mindset
  https://www.thrive15.com/preview/Managing People You Can%27t Fire

- Self Motivation: The Key To Success - Mindset
  https://www.thrive15.com/preview/436

- Self-Discipline And Persistence - Jim Cathcart - Mindset
  https://www.thrive15.com/preview/Self Discipline And Persistence

- Steps To Keeping Yourself Motivated - Jim Cathcart - Mindset
  https://www.thrive15.com/preview/Steps To Keeping Yourself Motivated

- The Daily Thought Diet - Jim Cathcart - Mindset
  https://www.thrive15.com/preview/The Daily Thought Diet

- You Have Greatness Within You - Jim Cathcart - Mindset
  https://www.thrive15.com/preview/You Have Greatness Within You

- Learning To Fly With The Eagles - Jim Cathcart - Networking
  https://www.thrive15.com/preview/Learning To Fly With The Eagles

- The Art Of Self-Promotion - Jim Cathcart - Marketing/PR
  https://www.thrive15.com/preview/The Art Of Self Promotion

- Practice Up-Serving To Increase The Satisfaction - Jim Cathcart - Sales
  https://www.thrive15.com/preview/Tulsa Community College Continuing Education Practice Up Serving To Increase The Satisfaction

- Eight Competencies Of Relationship Selling - Jim Cathcart - Sales
  https://www.thrive15.com/preview/Eight Competencies Of Relationship Selling

- Jim Cathcart's 15 Sales Moves - Jim Cathcart - Sales
  https://www.thrive15.com/preview/Jim Cathcart%27s 15 Sales Moves

- 14 Ways To Increase Sales This Year - Jim Cathcart - Sales
  https://www.thrive15.com/preview/14 Ways To Increase Sales This Year

- 7 Natural Values: Reading People - Jim Cathcart - Sales
  https://www.thrive15.com/preview/7 Natural Values Reading People

- Powerful Moves To Grow Your Business This Year - Jim Cathcart - Sales
  https://www.thrive15.com/preview/Powerful Moves To Grow Your Business This Year

- Determining And Managing Different Personal Velocities - Jim Cathcart - Management
  https://www.thrive15.com/preview/Management Training Determining And Managing Different Personal Velocities

- Teaching Your Team To Think Accurately - Jim Cathcart - Management
  https://www.thrive15.com/preview/Teaching Your Team To Think Accurately

- The Key To Promotion: Reputation And Favor - Jim Cathcart - Human Resources
  https://www.thrive15.com/preview/The Key To Promotion Reputation And Favor

- Self-Leadership - Jim Cathcart - Leadership
  https://www.thrive15.com/preview/business mentors Self Leadership

- Invest In Yourself: It's Worth It! - Jim Cathcart - Personal Development
  https://www.thrive15.com/preview/TCC Business School Invest In Yourself It%27s Worth It

- Self-Empowerment: The Eight T's - Jim Cathcart - Personal Development
  https://www.thrive15.com/preview/TCC Business School Self Empowerment The Eight T%27s

- Public Speaking: The Out Of Body Experience - Jim Cathcart - Personal Development
  https://www.thrive15.com/preview/Public Speaking The Out Of Body Experience

- ➡ Acorn Principle - Jim Cathcart - Personal Development
  https://www.thrive15.com/preview/421

- ➡ The Purpose Of Ongoing Education - Jim Cathcart - Personal Development
  https://www.thrive15.com/preview/Tulsa Community College Business School The Purpose Of Ongoing Education

- ➡ Uncapping Your Growth Potential: The Art Of Organization - Jim Cathcart - Personal Development
  https://www.thrive15.com/preview/Uncapping Your Growth Potential The Art Of Organization

- ➡ Focus On Core Tasks Until Success - Jim Cathcart - Personal Development
  https://www.thrive15.com/preview/Tulsa Community College Business School Focus On Core Tasks Until Success

- ➡ Climbing The Ladder Without A Degree And No Obvious Opportunity - Jim Cathcart - Personal Development
  https://www.thrive15.com/preview/Climbing The Ladder With A Degree And No Obvious Opportunities

- ➡ Learning How To Develop A Pleasing Personality - Jim Cathcart - Personal Development
  https://www.thrive15.com/preview/Climbing The Ladder With A Degree And No Obvious Opportunities

- ➡ Learning The Art Of Concentration - Jim Cathcart - Personal Development
  https://www.thrive15.com/preview/Tulsa Community College Business School Learning The Art Of Concentration

- ➡ Don't Be Overwhelmed; Create The Habits You Need - Jim Cathcart - Personal Development
  https://www.thrive15.com/preview/Tulsa Community College Business School Don%27t Be Overwhelmed Create The Habits You Need

➡ Staying Motivated: The Work Game Of Learn, Earn, Return - Jim Cathcart - Personal Development
https://www.thrive15.com/preview/Staying Motivated The Work Game of Learn Earn Return

➡ Public And Professional Speaking: Confident Communication - Jim Cathcart - Communication
https://www.thrive15.com/preview/alternatives to Lyndacom Public And Professional Speaking Confident Communication

ENDORSEMENTS

Game changer! You don't read this book, you experience it and live it. Jim Cathcart walks you through his life journey to help you see first hand the power of self-motivation and backs it up by providing specific insights to make it happen."

Mark Hunter

CSP, "The Sales Hunter", http://thesaleshunter.com

Outstanding as Usual! Perfect timing for such a Book. Every 20 & 30 Something should Read it and Heed it and Work For Success...Just Like the Author Did!

Kurt Kilpatrick

www.KurtKilpatrick.com

According to a Gallup poll, about 70 percent of U.S. employees are either not engaged or actively disengaged in their jobs. I wish they would read Jim's book so that they could find their drive again!

Dr. Gerhard Apfelthaler

Dean, School of Management, California Lutheran University

Jim easily describes the benefits of how motivating oneself can bring about personal fulfillment and success. His teachings in this book is the kind of motivation one needs on their journey to achieving all that they want to achieve.

Adrian N. Havelock

http://www.adrianhavelock.com

Do you feel limited by your current obligations, relationships, physical challenges or financial difficulties? With the tools Jim shares with you in this amazing book, YOU can take control of your current set of circumstances and transform your life. Your current results DO NOT DICTATE your future... your current thinking does. Thank you Jim!

Jan Payne

attractingpossibilities.com

The Self-Motivation Handbook is like Wheaties for your body, mind and soul. The choice to become a champion requires you to take big and small actions daily to get your closer to your goals. No matter what your goal this book give you powerful stories and a daily dose of motivation to get you to the finish line. Don't just put this book on your bookshelf put it by your computer, in your gym bag, the kitchen, in your car or anywhere you need a little push to get you to your dream.

Holly Duckworth

http://www.hollyduckworth.com

My 40 years of business experience, reaching multi-million dollar revenues have taught me exactly what Jim Cathcart says we should always be asking ourselves: "How would the person I'd like to be, do the things I'm about to do?" The best motivation we can get is from that person we will become. Jim knows the secrets of self motivation and is on a personal mission to not make them secrets any longer with the entire world!

Denis Nurmela

DenisSpeaks.com

Jim Cathcart has helped me and many others through the years with great ideas, motivation and powerful insights. Make your life better and get this information - then use it! You will be glad you did!

Terry Brock

http://terrybrock.com

Jim Cathcart's *The Self-Motivation Handbook* is your ultimate guide to discovering the highest and best version of YOU. Do exactly what Jim says in this book and when you look back upon your life you will hardly recognize where you started from.

Ray Stendall

http://www.raystendall.com

Jim Cathcart is an international authority on public speaking. The tools and techniques outlined in this powerful practical book helps you excel as an accomplished speaker. I wish I had this book long ago.

Professor M.S.Rao

Author of 30 books including the bestselling
21 Success Sutras for CEOs

Having been in the arena of motivation and its many facets I learned that true motivation is self-motivation. In *The Self-Motivation Handbook*, Jim has actionable steps and teachings to help the reader discover his or her internal drive to become self motivated. Like *The Acorn Principle* in self-awareness and growth, this will become the manifest for anyone wanting get going in any endeavor and have the motivation to see it through, whether it's in fitness, business or beyond. Great work Jim!

Bob Choat

https://bobchoat.com

This book, like all of Jim's books, should come with a highlighter. Impact-FULL reading.

Dean Lindsay

http://deanlindsay.com

Jim Cathcart didn't get to where he is by slacking off. He's motivated himself to outstanding achievements and hundreds of thousands of others as well. When he talks about self-motivation I listen. You should too!

David Corbin

http://davidcorbin.com

We're born without a handbook for success. Maybe, just maybe, this is the book you've been waiting for to get you going.

Victor Antonio

Host of Life or Debt

http://www.victorantonio.com

Self-motivation is the essence of achieving what you want in life. Without it, you're spinning your wheels in wasted time, effort, and lost opportunities. You have a limited life span. Optimize it!

Ken West

Jim Cathcart can and will make a difference in your life. This book should be by your side for 90 days and watch your life and bank account get better!!!!!

Coach Ron Tunick

http://www.coachrontunick.com

Jim Cathcart provides bite size morsels of wisdom to help readers navigate the trials and tribulations of living a inspired life on ones own terms. If you are serious about stepping into your greatness than this handbook with Jim's teachings on self motivation is the one to reference again and again.

Robert Stack

http://famecoach.com

Self Motivation is the key to becoming independent. There is no "off" button. This book is the roadmap you'll need to stay focused, excited and learn from the best in the industry.

Sean Samson

Grabbit Stands, https://www.youtube.com/watch?v=Oto9bpYAnAU

Jim Cathcart is a consummate professional, he has been helping people and businesses become their best. He inspires, motivates and focuses on what is important-getting people to put the difficult decision and to-do's first. This book is worth it's weight in gold!!!

Greg Voisen

http://insidepersonalgrowth.com

The only way to move forward is self-motivation. You can't do anything for me, I have to do it myself. You can't bungee jump, or hike the mountains for me. You can't write my book. You can't solve my relationships, and you can't save my money.

You can guide me and inspire me to take action. Thanks Jim, for yet another great road map for success for the journey of life.

Mark Davis

http://www.markdavis.com.au

Jim Cathcart's way of engaging someone in reflecting about their strengths and allowing these to be launching pads for excellence is a well developed art! *The Self-Motivation Handbook* is sure to invite any reader to realize the value of every second of life. It'll get you moving with a clear focus on how to invest time and energy. This book, like all of Jim's creations, is about affirming life! I know this from being mentored by him...He's a treasure.

Melissa Shepherd-Williams

https://1lifeonpurpose.wordpress.com

Since I first heard Jim Cathcart at an NSA Convention in 1990 through to when we developed a professional friendship and I visited him in La Jolla 10 years later he has always created, produced and delivered solid material related to Motivation and the true Value of Self-Motivation.

Robert Alan Black

http://www.cre8ng.com

Jim Cathcart is a wealth of knowledge and inspiration. I once spent fifteen minutes on a bus with him and walked away with a much deeper appreciation for life, family and career. His perspectives added clarity, focus and determination. If he can accomplish this through casual conversation - just imagine what an entire book can do.

Larry Williams

https://www.facebook.com/renodj

I met Jim Cathcart in 1997 at a sales meeting in Boston. He knew just the right words to inspire all of us, give us hope, direction and confidence to pursue our goals with passion. Twenty years later, he's still touching lives and encouraging acorns to grow to oak trees. Thank you Jim!!

Neil Wood

https://www.neilwoodconsulting.com